Deliberative Accountability in Parliamentary Committees

Deliberative Accountability in Parliamentary Committees

CHERYL SCHONHARDT-BAILEY

OXFORD
UNIVERSITY PRESS

OXFORD
UNIVERSITY PRESS

Great Clarendon Street, Oxford, OX2 6DP,
United Kingdom

Oxford University Press is a department of the University of Oxford.
It furthers the University's objective of excellence in research, scholarship,
and education by publishing worldwide. Oxford is a registered trade mark of
Oxford University Press in the UK and in certain other countries

Published in the United States of America by Oxford University Press
198 Madison Avenue, New York, NY 10016, United States of America

British Library Cataloguing in Publication Data
Data available

Library of Congress Control Number: 2021943360

ISBN 978–0–19–284787–4

DOI: 10.1093/oso/9780192847874.001.0001

Printed and bound by
CPI Group (UK) Ltd, Croydon, CR0 4YY

Cover image: smartboy10/Getty Images

To my family, for your love and support.

Preface

This book began as something of an afterthought to my previous book, *Deliberating American Monetary Policy: A Textual Analysis*. I concluded that book by saying that the effectiveness of Congress to hold monetary policymakers to account is limited at best. But, having finished that book, I wondered if perhaps it was simply too much to ask of legislators to have the expertise and the willingness to conduct accountability effectively. After all, they are not economists or experts in central banking, so why should we expect them to ask the right sort of questions of central bankers in monetary policy oversight hearings? Perhaps the inadequacy of monetary policy accountability in legislative hearings is some sort of universal truth, and not unique to the American setting. Out of curiosity, I investigated and analysed accountability hearings in both the US and UK during the time of the financial crisis and found a clear difference in the quality of 'deliberative accountability' between the two country cases. In short, deliberative accountability appeared to be of better quality in the UK setting, particularly in terms of reciprocity (this paper is available separately from this present work). That led to further questions, which centred around potential variations among types of economic policies as well as potential differences in accountability across the two UK parliamentary chambers. In short, these questions and more eventually snowballed into the present work, and after seven years, the answers emerge in the pages to follow.

My debts of gratitude for assistance in researching and writing this work are lengthy. Research funding from the LSE Suntory and Toyota International Centres for Economics and Related Disciplines (STICERD) and the LSE Government Department is gratefully acknowledged. The various chapters have been presented at several conferences over the years, and the content has most definitely benefited greatly from audience feedback. These conferences include: Text as Data, American Political Science Association, European Political Science Association, Political Studies Association, International Studies Association, and European Consortium for Political Research.

A number of individuals have offered advice and assistance well above and beyond what I could have hoped for, and these include Dominic Byatt, Erik Bucy, Thomas Leeper, James Sanders, Albert Weale, Nicole Baerg, Lawrence Broz, Saori Katada, Juliet Johnson and Jacqueline Best. Some anonymous referees were generous with their suggestions and expertise, which certainly pushed me to make the final product better (though, as always, any and all mistakes are mine alone).

Many research assistants have patiently and diligently helped along the way, including Gordon Bannerman, Oliver Besley, Gauri Chandra, Jacob Chapman, Christopher Dann, Richard Glasspool, Pranav Gupta, Alex Hughes, John Li Chi Hon, Barnaby Perkes, James Sanders, and Jack Winterton. I am also grateful to the LSE Behavioural Research Lab personnel for their efficient assistance with the experiment in Chapter 3.

Finally, this book is dedicated to my family—Andrew, Hannah, and Samuel. You have all suffered through long years of my distraction and frustrations in writing this book (sorry, guys!). At every juncture, you each, in your own unique way, have given me the support to do 'just a bit more' in the long road to completion.

Contents

List of Figures

List of Tables

1
Introduction

1.1 Introduction

Accountability is usually thought of as a good thing. As citizens, voters, work-ers, parents, or victims of some accident, we want to know that someone, somewhere, is—or will be—held to account for policies that affect us and for events that may change our lives.

We also tend to applaud and encourage deliberation. Juries and courts de-liberate before deciding the guilt or innocence of the accused; public bodies deliberate before formulating policies; legislatures deliberate when deciding laws; and voters deliberate the merits of candidates before completing their ballots. All these groups of individuals may or may not deliberate well (or in practice, even at all), but the expectation is that the act of deliberating is essential.

This work examines where these two concepts—accountability and deliberation—intersect in a specific parliamentary setting. Beyond the high-profile debates in the chambers of the British House of Commons and House of Lords are specialized 'select' committees whose responsibility it is to hold British government and public life in its broadest sense to account. A key task of these committees is to hold public hearings in which parliamentarians call policymakers—both elected and unelected—to account for decisions made, actions taken or not taken, and policies implemented. Indeed, during the early weeks of the COVID-19 crisis in the United Kingdom, when the Government was implementing unprecedented emergency measures and at the same time, Parliament itself was in recess and the country was in lockdown, select com-mittees were praised for continuing to scrutinize ministers and policymakers through 'highly effective virtual grilling' (2020).[1] While virtual hearings are unusual, the dialogue both in these and the normal face-to-face hearings is expected to be deliberative—namely, reasons are given for decisions taken and outcomes are explained. It is this process which is referred to here as 'deliberative accountability'.

Deliberative Accountability in Parliamentary Committees. Cheryl Schonhardt-Bailey, Oxford University Press.
© Cheryl Schonhardt-Bailey (2022). DOI: 10.1093/oso/9780192847874.003.0001

Why is this important? Why should we care? Historically, neither prime ministers nor governors of the Bank of England were much impressed with providing explanations. Benjamin Disraeli (British Prime Minister in 1868, and from 1874–80) is said to have remarked 'Never complain and never explain' (Morley, 1911, 91)[2] while Montagu Norman's (Governor of the Bank of England from 1921–1944) motto was 'Never explain, never excuse' (Bernanke, 2007).

Yet, modern British politicians take quite a different stance in their expectations that public officials will provide explanations for their actions, as illustrated by Andrew Tyrie, former MP and Chair of the Treasury Select Committee, who commented on Chancellor George Osborne's first budget:

> We made clear as a committee that we were going to look at the distributional impact of the budget in unprecedented detail. As a result, George Osborne responded by giving a lot more detail not only in the budget but also when he came before us. And there were some pretty vigorous and detailed exchanges about the distributional impact of the budget in that hearing. I think everybody gained from that experience. It certainly enabled a wider public to find out exactly what was going on in the budget and the Government was forced to explain its actions.
>
> (UK-Parliament, 2011)

Modern central bankers similarly attest to the importance of the obligation to explain themselves to the public, as Alan Blinder (former vice chairman of the Federal Reserve Board) argues:

> To me, public accountability is a moral corollary of central bank independence. In a democratic society, the central bank's freedom to act implies an obligation to explain itself to the public ... While central banks are not in the public relations business, public education ought to be part of their brief.
>
> (Blinder, 1998, 69)

The contrast between the historical and the modern quotes suggests that times certainly have changed in terms of our expectations of both politicians and central bankers. Accountability has become a central tenet of democratic governance, in which public officials are expected to explain and justify their actions to the publics they serve.

To grasp the extent to which accountability and the reason-giving at its heart have become core principles of democratic governance in the UK, Figures 1.1, 1.2, and 1.3 are illustrative. These figures show the number of references for

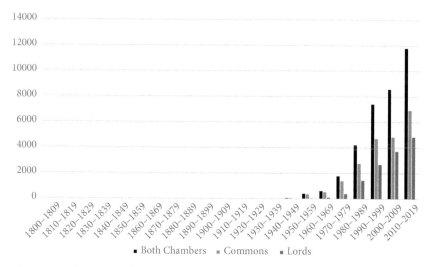

Fig. 1.1 References to 'Accountability' in UK Parliament.

Source: (Compiled by author, using data obtained from https://hansard.parliament.uk/ under Open Parliament License)

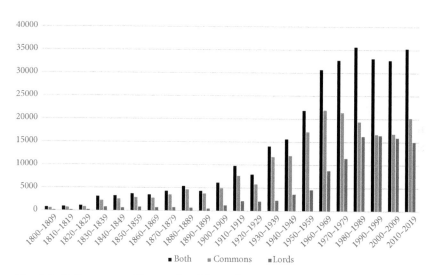

Fig. 1.2 References to 'Reasons' in UK Parliament.

Source: (Compiled by author, using data obtained from https://hansard.parliament.uk/ under Open Parliament License)

the words 'accountability', 'reasons', and 'deliberation' in debates in the House of Commons and the House of Lords from 1800 to 2019. These references were compiled from the Hansard website (https://hansard.parliament.uk/), and grouped into decades. For the whole of the nineteenth century, the word

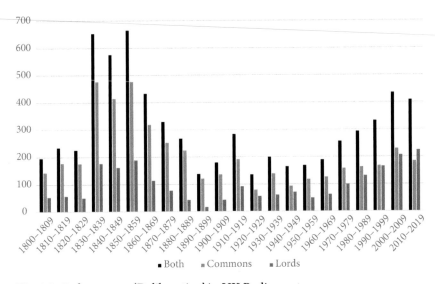

Fig. 1.3 References to 'Deliberation' in UK Parliament.

Source: (Compiled by author, using data obtained from https://hansard.parliament.uk/ under Open Parliament License)

'accountability' never appears more than 14 times in any *decade* of parliamentary debates in either chamber, and so is imperceptible (Figure 1.1). However, starting in the 1940s, the term started gaining traction in the Commons at first, and then escalated in usage in both chambers, particularly from 1970 onwards (and culminating in a usage of nearly 12,000 for the decade 2010–19). If we consider reason-giving to be core to deliberative accountability, we observe a similar trend for the word 'reasons' (Figure 1.2), albeit a trend with a more gradual progression from the nineteenth to the twentieth century, but again displaying extensive usage (with over 35,000 references for the most recent decade). One might attribute much of this escalation in reason-giving to a parallel trend towards greater attention given to deliberation in democratic governance. While a small increase can be detected in the use of the term 'deliberation' (Figure 1.3), references in the decades of the twentieth and twenty-first centuries never sum to more than 435, which is even less than the number found in several decades of the nineteenth century. (Checks on variations of these terms confirm these findings.[3]) Other accountability scholars have found a similar 'sharp and significant upturn' in the use of the word 'accountability', as measured from millions of books published in English over many centuries (Dubnick, 2014, 1) (see also (Mulgan, 2000)). It seems evident that the focus of this work on accountability in select committees is reflected in a much larger, cross-national escalation in the importance of accountability in all aspects of public life. The outcome of this surge in accountability is that we observe a lot of it, and in many guises. More accountability does not, however, equate to better accountability. Indeed, it remains unclear what might constitute the ideal amount of accountability or that, if that ideal were provided, it would be identified as such. *In short, it seems evident that most people appear to want those in positions of power and influence to be held accountable, but would these same people recognize quality or ideal accountability if they saw it?*

The form of accountability examined here is the deliberation in select committee hearings, where officials as witnesses offer explanations and justifications for policy decisions, and these are then challenged and probed by parliamentarians. Holding policymakers to account is clearly the purpose of these hearings, but what is less straightforward is the end goal of these proceedings— e.g., how much accountability is ideal for democratic governance? Also unclear are the metrics by which we might gauge the quality of the explanations and justifications provided. What exactly *is* good accountability—that is, what constitutes high-quality explanations and how might both the institutional setting and the process itself influence this quality? Typically, discussions of accountability focus on quantity rather than quality (Feinstein, 2014). For instance, it is generally agreed that too little accountability weakens the democratic link between the public and their officials, while overly intensive accountability proceedings may destroy trust in public officials (Olsen, 2017, 23, 35–36).

Indeed, in the case of the UK, the so-called 'accountability explosion' is argued to have created a paradox. Whereas the growth in government accountability measures in the late twentieth and early twenty-first centuries should have established greater trust in government, the opposite trend has emerged (OECD, 2013, Edelman, 2019). While the financial crisis and Brexit may account for some of this distrust, Tony Wright (former MP and British academic) suggests an alternative scenario which questions the very purpose of accountability: 'Perhaps what was previously hidden has been brought into public view, and people do not like what they see. Perhaps accountability has been reduced to finding someone to blame. Or perhaps an excess of the wrong kind of accountability crowds out the capacity for good government' (Wright, 2015, 112).

This work does not examine the multifaceted ways in which accountability may operate, nor does it distinguish 'right' or 'wrong' kinds of accountability. It also does not explore *ex ante* controls that legislators might seek to devise for agencies (that is, as in principal–agent theories (Bawn, 1995, Huber and Shipan, 2000, Huber and Shipan, 2002, Strøm, Müller et al., 2003)). Rather, it seeks better to assess the quality of what is arguably the very core of accountability—that is, the process by which government (or its departments and agencies) formally explains itself to Parliament, and during which the latter has the opportunity to challenge these explanations. In contrast to *ex ante* controls, *ex post* accountability is less well understood by political scientists (McGrath, 2013, 349), yet is typical of the Westminster model of accountability, where government explains itself 'after the fact' (Bennister and Larkin, 2018, 144). This explanation-giving aspect of accountability falls squarely into what most deliberative democratic theorists would describe as deliberation. Thus, insofar as this work examines select committee hearings in the UK Parliament, it offers not only an empirical investigation of the quality of accountability, but also an empirical assessment of the quality of deliberation in a legislative setting in which the context varies by policy and parliamentary chamber.

The empirical tools used here are, moreover, varied and rely on multiple methodologies. They include: (1) quantitative text analysis to gauge the verbatim transcripts in legislative committee hearings; (2) qualitative coding combined with experimental methods, which together seek to gauge the extent to which nonverbal communication ('body language') shapes both the process and outcome of these same hearings; and (3) elite interviews with the key actors who participated in the committee hearings (members of Parliament, central bankers, Treasury officials, staff). The selection of these methods is not random. The first technique seeks to measure rigorously the content of 'what' was said, alongside identifying traits of the speaker—that is, who spoke, how often, who emphasized what theme, and what identifying characteristics of speakers were associated with which themes. The second set of techniques examines 'how' the words and arguments were expressed—that is, the delivery adopted by each participant, as well as the tone of the exchange between questioner and witness. The final technique offers a more reflective 'why' component to the analysis by asking participants from these hearings to explain their motivations, their own concerns and their assessments of the deliberative process in these select committee hearings. This merging of the 'what', the 'how', and the 'why' offers a novel template for studying deliberative accountability. To my knowledge, no other study has adopted such a comprehensive methodological approach to examining either accountability or deliberation.

The substantive focus of this work is UK parliamentary committee hearings on economic policy, where scrutiny of the decisions and actions of public officials is conducted. In economic policy, two very different sets of actors are routinely scrutinized by select committees: (1) officials of the Bank of England—who are not elected but appointed—are held accountable by committees in Parliament for their decisions in pursuit of their objectives for monetary policy and financial stability; and (2) elected ministers and officials from the UK Treasury are similarly held accountable for their objectives for fiscal policy by these same parliamentary committees. These hearings entail parliamentarians probing both central bankers and Treasury representatives; reasoned argument is therefore central to the purpose and focus of the hearings—that is, they are intended as a deliberative forum. Accountability in this setting presupposes a reciprocal dialogue and, crucially, necessitates a judgement on the effectiveness and persuasiveness of the policymaker who is being held to account (Bovens, 2010, 951). Thus, the policymakers face questions and the parliamentary committees render judgments. More broadly, it is this obligation to explain decisions taken by policymakers that is central to democratic governance. Accountability hearings legitimate policy decisions and, in the case of the central bank, these hearings legitimate the delegation of authority given to independent policymakers to explain their decisions, which in turn engenders trust in democratic institutions.

To reiterate, the concern here is with the explanations and justifications aspect of accountability, and as such, the focus is on the deliberative component of accountability, rather than the implications or consequences of any judgements (that is, sanctions, penalties, or other consequences of judgements are not explored here). Moreover, the 'judgments' of parliamentary committees are not in the form of votes (at least in respect to these hearings), but rather are continuous and cumulative assessments of ministers and experts. In this way, both the deliberations and the judgements are *dynamic* and inherently *interactional*.

In the British Parliament, both the Treasury Select Committee (TSC) and the House of Lords Economic Affairs Committee (EAC) hold hearings on monetary policy, financial stability, and fiscal policy. This work focuses on the period from 2010 to 2015—that is, the Conservative–Liberal Democrat Coalition Government. This 2010–15 Parliament is especially important for select committee activity, given the much greater prominence of these committees following the fundamental reforms of select committees in 2010. These reforms, among other things, introduced the election of committee members and chairs, thereby stripping the power of the party whips to appoint them and lending the committees greater autonomy in holding the Government to account (Parliament, 2013). The reforms further embedded the expectation that select committees should endeavour to conduct scrutiny in a nonpartisan manner—that is, they 'might exercise their parliamentary, rather than party, muscles by engaging in scrutiny activity geared towards better holding government to account' (Kelso, 2012, 5).

This work's focus on deliberative accountability in UK economic policy is timely, as it follows from the 2007–09 financial crisis, when the Bank of England (BoE) acquired considerably greater statutory powers. With the financial reforms of 2012, the Financial Policy Committee was created, thereby formally giving the Bank the task of ensuring UK financial stability, alongside its previous independence in monetary policymaking (in the Monetary Policy Committee, created in 1997). One product of these new powers is that there is simply more for which the Bank may be held accountable. Another product is the potential for 'interested' parties to feature more prominently in both decision making and accountability. For instance, because financial stability entails regulation at both the macro and micro levels, invariably the effect is to heighten the interests of financial institutions, thereby encouraging more lobbying efforts than in monetary policy. The timeliness of this work's investigation of deliberative accountability is even more evident in the midst of, and the ultimate wake of, the extraordinary and unprecedented actions of both the Bank of England and the UK Treasury in response to the shocks to the economy from the COVID-19 pandemic. In both the short-run and long-run, policymakers will be held accountable for these decisions and actions.

Furthermore, as the BoE (like the Federal Reserve and the European Central Bank) has been given more statutory objectives, this has created trade-offs in broader public policy, such as between housing policy and financial stability policy with respect to mortgage lending. These trade-offs can complicate central bank independence (Fernández-Albertos, 2015: 228).

Against this backdrop, modern UK select committees strive to be nonpartisan in their activities, and particularly in the wake of the 2010 reforms. At the same time, these select committees perceive a more assertive oversight as a means to regain the public trust in Parliament, which has suffered in recent years (e.g., from recent expenses scandals) (Tyrie, 2015: 9–10). Andrew Tyrie, former chairman of the Treasury Select Committee, argued in his 2015 book that '(s)elect (c)ommittees are now much more effective scrutineers and investigators than they were even five years ago' (Tyrie, 2015: 33). It is not self-evident, however, that this 'more effective' oversight translates into better quality deliberation in hearings. Indeed, Tyrie's characterization of select committees as 'effective scrutineers' begs the question as to what *are* the metrics by which we measure effectiveness in a scrutineer? Surely one fundamental metric is that the scrutineer is sufficiently knowledgeable in, say, monetary policy to ask the 'right' questions of central bankers who are, after all, experts in this area. By this simple metric, evidence from the United States Congress strongly suggests that politicians are often not sufficiently knowledgeable (or even properly incentivized to acquire specialist policy knowledge) to effectively challenge central bankers on monetary policy (Schonhardt-Bailey, 2013). We should thus be sceptical of Tyrie's assessment, but even more importantly, we should seek to find an objective, rigorous and systematic means by which to gauge effective scrutiny in the first place. Focusing on the quality of deliberative accountability seems, therefore, a good beginning.

Following a brief contextual description of UK select committees, I set out more fully the analytical framework used in this work to conceptualize deliberative accountability, and then describe the metrics by which deliberative accountability is gauged in the chapters that follow. The sections that follow will unpack more fully both my theoretical and empirical approach to deliberative accountability, but, in brief, there are three themes that underpin my argument. First, deliberative accountability should be seen as a unique term which stands in distinction from either deliberation or accountability. That is, I focus on a specific *adversarial context* in which political tensions influence and shape the quality of the interplay between questioners and witnesses. In this way, deliberation within these accountability hearings is an inherently political exercise. Second, inasmuch as deliberative accountability is situated in an adversarial context, it is essential to gauge its quality according to both the type of economic policy (in particular, the extent to which the policy itself lays bare winners and losers from policy decisions) and whether the parliamentarians who are directing the hearings are elected or appointed to their positions (and thereby, the extent to which the parliamentary committee members are beholden to electoral pressures). Given differences in the partisan political nature of the policy type (here, monetary policy, financial stability, fiscal policy) and in the proximity of parliamentarians to electors (here, elected MPs and unelected peers), we can expect the quality of deliberative accountability to also vary. Third, even as we find variations in the quality of deliberative accountability, it is too simplistic to say that one context (for example, policy type or legislative chamber) is of better or worse quality when viewed in isolation. To properly assess the quality of deliberative accountability we must also widen our lens to observe the broader system of accountability, as it pertains to the relevant policy or set of policymakers under investigation. Ultimately, the framework of analysis and the methodology used in this work seek to offer an answer to the question of *what is quality in accountability* by homing in on the core feature of deliberation in accountability, and seeking to establish metrics by which we can better gauge this not as a fixed or absolute measure, but as one that varies by the adversarial context in which it occurs.

1.2 The Committees

1.2.1 Select Committees in the House of Commons

A first step is to simply introduce and explain the purpose of select committees. Within the larger literature on legislative committees, British select committees have received little attention, and in particular, how parliament 'hold(s) the executive to account is still not widely understood' (Geddes, 2020, 3). Whereas in Congress, committees are purported to enhance the electoral prospects of members (Fenno, 1973, Adler and Lapinski, 1997), enable members to exploit informational advantages (Krehbiel, 1991), and/or pursue partisan objectives (Cox and McCubbins, 1993), the theory and evidence for the motivations of select committee members in Parliament is less advanced.

One explanation for why the larger literature on legislative committees does not always help to inform the motivation of select committee members derives from the relative novelty of the modern select committee system. While select committees may be traced to the nineteenth century, the present departmental system was created in 1979 and was designed to be more comprehensive in its scrutiny of government policy and performance. Indeed, in the view of British politics scholar Philip Norton, this new system 'constituted the most important reform of the latter half of the twentieth century' (Norton, 2013, 126). Whereas scrutiny in the House of Commons Chamber is based on debates and questions, oral evidence in select committee hearings is conducted more forensically and in greater depth (Kelso, 2018). Indeed, the scrutiny purpose behind the creation of the select committee system helps to distinguish it from other legislative committees and makes literature on legislative committees elsewhere less directly applicable. That is, a key feature of British select committees is that, in contrast to many legislative committees elsewhere in the world, they do not also draft legislation. Instead, the normal committee stage of the legislative process is left to temporary and non-specialist 'public bill committees' (Russell and Benton, 2011: 11). Thus select committees do not scrutinize government *legislation* but rather focus on overseeing government *departments*. The independence of these committees from the Executive can be seen in part from the norm that frontbench ministers and opposition shadow ministers are usually not members of select committees. The 2010 reforms of the select committees further solidified this independence of select committees from the executive (Russell and Benton, 2011, Gordon and Street, 2012, Kelso, 2012).

This single purpose feature of select committees—to hold government to account—makes it more challenging to understand the motivations of its members. Why do they serve on these committees and what do they hope to gain from their membership? Whereas members of congressional committees might seek membership to help draft legislation which enhances their electoral prospects (Mayhew, 1974), the representative link to constituents is more remote for parliamentarians and so the motivations of members are less conspicuous. Most definitely select committee members seek to legitimize government by scrutinizing the decisions of policymakers, but if the electoral motive is more remote, what do these members have to gain from membership on select committees? In the view of one parliamentary scholar, parliamentarians who sit on select committees may be seen to be motivated in part by the desire to become policy specialists, to champion their constituencies, or to help pursue partisan objectives (Geddes, 2020, 38); other scholars broadly echo these motivations (Evans, 2019). While these goals are not entirely dissimilar to their congressional counterparts, we must nonetheless recognize that select committees remain at arm's length from the making of legislation itself.

The select committee system covers all government departments, agencies and public bodies, whereby the expenditures, administrative procedures and policy decisions of departments are 'effectively shadowed by a committee of MPs' (Kelso, 2018, 163). As previously noted, select committees are also intended to be nonpartisan. Ostensibly, then, select committees seek to conduct business according to a nonpartisan ethos.

With respect to the partisan composition of select committees, the membership reflects the proportional partisan balance in the House of Commons, so that a government majority will translate into a majority of members on each of the select committees. The committee chairmanships are, moreover, allocated among the main parties (Conservative, Labour, Liberal Democrat—and, since 2015, SNP), in proportion to the partisan balance in the House. From 2010, they have been elected from the whole membership of the House of Commons. In contrast, committee members are elected by their own party cohorts.

To some extent, the widespread regard and respect acquired by these committees since their establishment (Russell and Benton, 2011) is testament to their growing reputation for policy expertise and influence. Quantifiable evidence of the impact of select committees is slim, but is nonetheless indicative of their growing influence (Kelso, 2018, Mellows-Facer, Challender et al., 2019). As a product of their elected status from 2010 (and thus the inability of party whips to deselect chairs if they become too critical of government), committee chairs have acquired greater legitimacy and thus have become emboldened to interrogate ministers and other public officials with greater force and effectiveness. Indeed, appearances before select committees are likened to a survival game, as the author of *How to Survive a Select Committee* illustrates:

> After decades of being relatively unexciting, in recent years select committees have become a terrifying experience for powerful people in our public life. The committee's findings and recommendations may often be ignored, they may even be dismissed—but they are always feared … [S]elect committees are different [from media interviews]. They push you out of your comfort zone. As you take your seat, you are all too aware that there is a camera trained directly on your face, which can expose your nervousness, emphasising any gulps, poor eye contact or fidgety hands. You are then confronted by up to fifteen parliamentarians across party divides who are generally not going to be on your side and are, sometimes, actively hostile. Despite any pre-briefing from the committee's officials, you have little certainty about the questions you are going to be asked.
>
> (Colvin, 2019, xiv–xv)

The 'fear' invoked during select committee appearances has thus provided media outlets with a source of drama. Even prior to the 2010 reforms, the number of articles on select committee hearings acquired the largest share of newspaper coverage on parliamentary affairs (Kubala, 2011: 703, 708). Televised and online coverage of committee hearings has expanded further, and recent historic events in British politics (the 2010–15 coalition government, the 2014 Scottish referendum on independence, the 2016 referendum on Britain's membership of the European Union, the 2017 hung parliament, Brexit and its effect on [as of summer 2021] at least three prime ministers) has heightened awareness and viewing of parliamentary affairs. On one measure of *Parliamentlive.tv*, viewings of select committees grew from 57,000 in 2008 to 1,087,376 in 2016—an astounding eighteen times increase in less than ten years (D'Arcy, 2018, 209).

With this increased media coverage, it is worth returning to assess the motivations of select committee members. One clear career motivation is the potential for an alternative backbench route to parliamentary positions of power (Shephard and Caird, 2018, 189) (Tyrie, 2015, 9), perhaps by acquiring policy expertise or furthering the partisan agenda. Relatedly, media coverage also offers MPs the opportunity to 'grandstand', as noted by a member of the Public Accounts Select Committee: 'MPs know that a sound-bite dressed up as a question gets coverage, whereas detailed probing often does not. The flour-ish usually comes at the expense of the forensic.' And yet, this same MP then goes on to argue that critics of select committees 'are wrong in the lazy asser-tion that all MPs want from these sessions is to grandstand. The incentive for many MPs is to do the job they were elected to do: holding bodies to account on behalf of their constituents' (Barclay, 2013).

Overall, while there is evidence to suggest an increased profile for select committees, measuring their impact on government policy is more difficult to quantify (Bates, Goodwin et al., 2017). There is less doubt, however, that for those who are being held accountable—ministers, representative from gov-ernment departments, central bankers, and so on—appearances before select committees can often be daunting experiences, and in this respect select com-mittees can serve as an important 'brake' or constraint mechanism, or as Geddes describes, they can exercise the power of 'anticipated reactions' (Ged-des, 2020, 11). That is, prior to making decisions, policymakers who regularly appear before select committees may well consider the likely responses (pos-itive or negative) from relevant select committees (Benton and Russell, 2013, 789), and shape their policy decisions accordingly.

1.2.2 Culture and Norms in the Commons and Lords

In both houses of parliament, committee membership is not universal among parliamentarians. Among the 650 MPs in the Commons, 323 held member-ship on at least one (and normally just one) select committee in 2018 (bearing in mind that government ministers and shadow ministers are ineligible for membership). Of the active peers in the House of Lords, just 199 sat on a se-lect committee. Given the high demand for committee membership, only 5 per cent of peers sit on more than one committee (n.a., 2018). Whereas since 2010, members in Commons committees are elected by party groups and chairs are elected in a secret ballot by the whole chamber, members of committees in the Lords are appointed by more traditional means—namely, via the whips.

Committees in the House of Lords operate quite differently from those in the House of Commons. Most importantly, Lords committees do not scrutinize government departments in the way that Commons committees do. Instead, Lords committees are more thematically constructed, focusing on four main areas—economics, Europe, science, and the UK constitution. And, because in-dividuals typically become peers based on years of experience and excellence in their fields, committees in the upper house typically exploit this expertise in the composition of committee memberships. (For instance, a key member of the Economic Affairs Committee in the 2010–15 Parliament was Nigel Lawson, Baron Lawson of Blaby, who served in the Thatcher Cabinet, ultimately as Chancellor of the Exchequer.) Notably, the unelected nature of the Lords means that without electoral constituencies and with life tenure, peers are less concerned with how they appear to outside audiences (Crewe, 2005, 70). Broadly speaking, committees in the Lords have a reputation for investigating issues that are both 'more strategic' and 'more technical'—thereby reflecting the expertise of their members (Russell, 2013: 210).

Comparisons of Commons and Lords committees reveal deep differences in culture and norms. The culture in the Commons is said to be more 'raucous' while that in the Lords is more 'decorous' (Crewe, 2005, 71). The Lords adheres more to courtesy and respect for expertise, as illustrated by a 'typical Lords attitude': 'If there is a difference between the Commons and the Lords, the former is like jungle warfare while the latter is like being parachuted into the desert. In both places, it is war' (Crewe, 2005, 71). MPs and peers are quite critical of the other chamber: MPs regard the Lords as 'sleepy ... dull and stuck in a time warp' (Crewe, 2005, 71), while peers criticize the Commons for being 'infiltrated by a generation of politicians who are not too sure what they believe in or why' (Crewe, 2005, 71). In her comparison of Commons and Lords committees, Russell describes Lords committees as 'less adversarial' in hearings with experts (Russell, 2013: 211). Other commentators have been more blunt, noting that the Lords committees "genuinely cared about getting to the facts" whereas committees in the Commons were "childish" and "focused on showboating"' (Colvin, 2019, 24).

With respect to standards of deliberative accountability, the Lords is rated by commentators more favourably than the Commons, with its 'high-quality and relatively non-partisan deliberation' (Farrington, 2012, 607) and its reliance on independent peers, known as Crossbenchers: 'The Crossbenchers personify in many ways what the Lords is known for: expertise, independence from party and reasoned debate' (Russell and Sciara, 2009, 49). The deliberative capacity of the Lords is also said to be directly linked to its ability to hold government to account by asking better questions:

One of its jobs is to scrutinise the wishes of the government, pointing out difficulties in legislation, scrutinising the actions of ministers and raising issues for public debate. On this count, the House of Lords is sometimes said to be relatively well qualified compared with the Commons—and compared with that other great political estate, the media—because its membership comprises a pool of talented and well-resourced people with expertise, even experience of high office, across a range of domains. This expertise allows them to ask better questions, to spot inconsistencies and elisions better than the layperson.

(Parkinson, 2007, 379)

By most accounts, we could conclude that because the Lords typically have greater expertise (in part, it is this expertise that gains them peerages in the first place), and thereby ask better questions, select committees in the Lords might ultimately generate higher quality deliberation. By the same token, MPs are more noted for their tendency to 'showboat' and to pursue partisan agendas, and thus we might expect lower quality deliberation by MPs in select committees relative to peers. If all we cared about was deliberation, we might award the prize to the Lords and call it a day. But this work is not about deliberation per se; it is about deliberative accountability.

So, what of accountability? By focusing on deliberative accountability, we begin to see a potential trade-off between the pursuit of high quality deliberation and the pursuit of high quality accountability, as deliberative scholars have observed: '... the very features that raise deliberative quality in representative politics—a lack of mass publicity, a lack of party discipline, and the need for consensus-seeking—lower democratic accountability and responsiveness' (Bächtiger and Parkinson, 2019, 11). Whereas (unelected) peers may exhibit greater expertise and less partisanship, (elected) MPs with constituencies are more responsive to electoral and partisan pressures. Conceivably then, the former might achieve higher deliberative ideals while the latter might more aggressively challenge or hold to account policymakers. This more aggressive accountability might be driven by an attempt to be seen to be acting on behalf of constituents, or MPs may be furthering their front bench ambitions by showboating or engaging in partisanship, or more favourably by demonstrating their policy expertise. By one reckoning, then, deliberative accountability may have a fault line across parliamentary chambers, with relatively higher quality deliberation in Lords committee hearings and relatively higher quality accountability in Commons committee hearings. And so, taken together, the chambers might be considered to be delivering fully on deliberative accountability, and in this sense might offer a parliamentary 'system' of deliberative accountability. We will explore this further in the sections that follow.

1.2.3 Parliamentary Select Committees and Policy Committees

The Treasury Select Committee (TSC) is responsible among other things for overseeing the policy responsibilities of both the Treasury (including its ministers) and the Bank of England. Scrutiny of the Treasury is most conspicuous in the form of an inquiry into the Budget statement. Following each spring's Budget statement, the committee gathers evidence from witnesses (including the chancellor of the Exchequer) on the government's proposals, and then publishes its recommendations and conclusions. In turn, the government responds to the committee's findings, often incorporating information from the Office for Budget Responsibility.

Like other independent central banks, the Bank of England is subject to formal legislative oversight. The objective of UK monetary policy is laid down in the 1998 Bank of England Act, where the stated priority is price stability and 'subject to that', the legislation mandates the Bank to support the government's policies for growth and employment. The Bank pursues an inflation target (currently 2 per cent) which is set by the government. The Bank is independent with respect to the instruments chosen (usually a short-term interest rate, but also quantitative easing via asset purchases) to achieve the objective of low inflation, without interference from political actors. The Bank's Monetary Policy Committee (MPC) is tasked with formulating monetary policy decisions. With respect to financial stability, financial services reforms of 2012 created the Bank's Financial Policy Committee (FPC), which has statutory responsibility for financial stability by lessening the scope for systemic risks and preventing the likelihood of future financial crises (or reducing their impact).

To be clear, these committees within the Bank are a separate subject of academic study. As policy committees, the MPC and FPC are the focus of the literature on decision making by monetary policy committees (Chappell, McGregor et al., 2005, Chappell, McGregor et al., 2012, Gardner and Woolley, 2016, Baerg, 2020, Moschella and Diodati, 2020). Previously, I examined both the decision making within a monetary policy committee as well as its oversight before legislative committees (Schonhardt-Bailey, 2013); however, the focus of this present work is exclusively on the parliamentary committees before which economic policy experts must appear to explain their policy decisions.

The Treasury Select Committee conducts hearings with representatives from the Bank's MPC[4] and FPC on their policy decisions. In contrast to fiscal policy, the Treasury committee does not produce a subsequent report following these monetary policy and financial stability oversight hearings.

The Economic Affairs Committee is responsible for reviewing economic affairs—which, broadly defined, may range from tax avoidance to the economic ramifications of shale gas. The EAC conducts occasional hearings, some of which contribute to formal reports and others are meant as information gathering exercises. Of significance is that the EAC is a relatively new committee, growing from ad hoc status in 1998 to permanency in 2001, in part, to monitor the newly created MPC.[5] When in 2002 the committee created a sub-committee to scrutinize the government's budget (that is, the Finance Bill), concerns were expressed by government that the committee was encroaching on the primacy of the Commons over financial matters (Russell, 2013: 216). While the division of responsibility between the TSC and the EAC is not always clear, the official role of the former is said to nonetheless cover policy while the latter focuses on 'technical issues of administration, clarification and simplification' (Russell, 2013: 216–17). So, while the TSC retains the formal responsibility for economic policy oversight, it is less clear where, exactly, the EAC contributes to the broader rubric of holding the government to account for economic policy. In terms of the content of the hearings, we might expect the TSC to focus more on policy and the EAC to focus more on administrative and technical issues, but even this division of labour is not always conspicuous.

1.3 Deliberative Accountability in Parliament: Contributions to Deliberation, Accountability, and Central Bank Communications Literatures

The merits of deliberation are not unambiguous, although on balance most analysts consider it to be a desirable, if not ideal, component of democratic governance. As such, the literature on deliberative democracy generally assumes that deliberation among citizens, representatives and public officials has beneficial outcomes, such as enhancing political legitimacy and stability. As Mutz summarizes,

> (C)ertain kinds of outcomes are consensually valued by theorists and empiricists alike. These include, but are not limited to, more public-spirited attitudes; more informed citizens; greater understanding of the sources of, or rationales behind, public disagreements; a stronger sense of political efficacy; willingness to compromise; greater interest in political participation; and, for

some theorists, a binding consensus decision. The perceived legitimacy of the decision is also argued to be enhanced through deliberation ...

(Mutz, 2008: 523)

As an extension to these benefits, deliberation is said to improve the quality of public policy, partly through reducing the likelihood of errors of analysis and judgement but also by increasing public spirit attitudes among public officials (Lascher, 1996: 504, Bächtiger, Spörndli et al., 2005: 153)—the latter by forcing them to characterize their intentions in terms of a public rather than private good.

Empirical studies of deliberation offer a foundation for studying deliberative discourse (Bächtiger and Hangartner, 2010a, Bächtiger, Niemeyer et al., 2010b), with its focus on reasoned argument. Such studies of deliberation in legislatures have sought to analyse both floor debates and committee sessions (Steiner, Bächtiger et al., 2004, Quirk, 2005, Mucciaroni and Quirk, 2006, Bächtiger and Hangartner, 2010a), and some have focused on the dissenting behaviour of backbench members of Parliament against their party leaders (Proksch and Slapin, 2014). One finding from these studies is that deliberation is of higher quality in second chambers as opposed to first chambers (Steiner, Bächtiger et al., 2004, Mucciaroni and Quirk, 2006), which accords with the more subjective appraisals of the Lords versus the Commons, as discussed in Section 1.2.2. Another finding is that, inasmuch as legislative committees are less public arenas than floor debates, they may exhibit higher quality deliberation as they are less exposed to external influences; additionally, the smaller face-to-face arenas in committees may better enable legislators to reflect on issues (Steiner, Bächtiger et al., 2004). (This may well hold, but the comparison with floor debates extends beyond the focus of this work on select committee hearings.) A third finding is that deliberation is of higher quality on issues where legislators are less polarized (Steiner, Bächtiger et al., 2004), and by extension, this may similarly apply to issues on which legislators are less divided by partisan ideology. We will return to the issue of partisanship in Section 1.5.2.

Studies have also sought to gain traction on the empirics of deliberation by isolating and then measuring one or two critical dimensions (e.g., 'information' (Mucciaroni and Quirk, 2006); or 'open-mindedness' (Barabas, 2004)). This focus on a small number of key metrics for studying deliberation empirically is adopted here, as it allows better traction on both theory and measurement. In a later section, I outline three core dimensions for measuring the quality of deliberative accountability in committee hearings: respect, non-(or minimal) partisanship, and reciprocal dialogue.

Not only does the present study offer an extension to the empirical literature on deliberation—by focusing specifically on deliberation within accountability—but it also moves beyond the use of quantitative methods to include invaluable insights from the participants themselves through in-depth interviews, as recommended by recent deliberative scholars (Bächtiger and Parkinson, 2019, 75). This addresses a broader criticism of *quantitative* (as opposed to qualitative) approaches to empirically measuring deliberation, which maintains that while they gauge deliberative content (and possibly also quality), this is done from the perspective of researchers who exist outside the deliberative context and as such, their assessments arguably lack the understanding of nuances and subtleties which may have been easily appreciated by the deliberative participants themselves (Bächtiger, 2018).

This work is distinctive in several respects, relative to previous empirical work on deliberation in legislatures. First, I am able to capture quite distinct sets of participants engaging in deliberative accountability—e.g., elected MPs and elected ministers; elected MPs and unelected central bankers; unelected peers and elected ministers; and most unusually, *un*elected peers and *un*elected central bankers. Second, unlike studies of parliamentary debates, the purpose of the select committee hearings under investigation here is to hold both the Bank of England and the Treasury to account, thereby constituting a form of legislative deliberation which is motivated by the specific goal of accountability. Third, the approach taken here is explicitly multi-method, in that deliberation is examined not only as what participants say, but also how they say it, and then—crucially, in the *qualitative* interpretations of the participants themselves—why they say it. As such, this study addresses the limitation of some studies which rely only on the perspective of researchers without also drawing upon the understandings of participants themselves. Thus, overall, this study fuses together both quantitative and qualitative dimensions of deliberation into a single comprehensive analytical framework.

Aside from these specific features, this work also offers accountability scholars a unique empirical investigation into the *process* of accountability (Patil, Vieider et al., 2014), by examining this process in terms of what is said, how it is said, and why it is said. It also contributes to accountability studies a novel insight into the role of nonverbal communication in shaping the views of those who are holding policymakers to account. To my knowledge, aside from investigations into visual media such as pictures and graphs (Davison, 2014), scholars have not previously investigated how nonverbal communication might impact accountability. More broadly, the accountability literature is often focused on typologies, case studies and definitions (Brandsma, 2014, 1), or in some cases on the normative aspects of delegated power (Tucker, 2018). In contrast, this work offers accountability scholars an empirical study into a particular *deliberative* form of accountability, which some have alluded to as 'meaningful accountability' (Bovens and Schillemans, 2014). These scholars argue that '(t)he focus on deliberation in accountability is relevant because standards for what constitutes accountable behaviour are not written in stone' but rather are adapting to the contextual circumstances, as well as the relevant interest at stake (Bovens and Schillemans, 2014, 7). Thus, by varying both the policy type and the electoral sensitivity of the accountability setting, the analysis of this work helps us to understand how deliberative accountability can be 'domain-specific' (Bovens, Schillemans et al., 2014, 8).

Finally, a related literature on accountability is specifically focused on central banks and how they communicate their actions and decisions to wider audiences. This literature on central bank communication has sought to understand the motives and means of communication by central banks such as the Bank of England, the Federal Reserve, the European Central Bank and in a somewhat different context, the International Monetary Fund. Typically, scholars have sought to explore cross-national differences in communications strategies and accountability of central banks (Moschella and Pinto, 2018, Högenauer and Howarth, 2019, McPhilemy and Moschella, 2019), but they have not focused on *deliberation* within the accountability framework. Moreover, while many of these studies have employed quantitative text analysis to gauge various forms of communication (minutes, speeches, press releases) (Johnson, Arel-Bundock et al., 2019, Baerg, 2020), including in some cases parliamentary hearings (Fraccaroli, Giovannini et al., 2020, Lisi, 2020), none have as yet explored the importance of *nonverbal communication* in accountability. In sum, both the focus here on deliberation in accountability and the mixed methods approach adopted in this work (including measuring nonverbal communication) offer a distinct contribution to the study of central bank communications and accountability.

1.4 Deliberative Accountability: Theoretical Underpinnings

Both accountability and deliberation are broad topics, each with its own rich theoretical literature. The intent of this section is to narrow our focus to a very specific application of the term 'deliberative accountability'. From this narrower conceptual framework, we can then begin to extract meaningful indicators to measure the quality of deliberative accountability in parliamentary select committees.

It should be noted that the term *deliberative accountability* is not novel e.g., (Mansbridge, 2009, Staszewski, 2009, Borowiak, 2011 [Chapter 4], Kreiczer-Levy, 2012, Vibert, 2014, Montanaro, 2019), although most previous studies have taken a theoretical rather than an empirical approach. That is, while the term has been used in the literature, as yet there has not been an empirical translation or systematic application of the concept. The usage of the term in this work follows the broad agreement that, at its core, accountability 'involves an obligation to explain and justify one's past conduct' (Brandsma and Schillemans, 2012, 955), wherein there is a discussion phase in which questions may be raised and policymakers are given the opportunity to provide reasons for their decisions and policy actions. Even where accountability scholars embark upon quantitative assessments of accountability, they do not generally focus on this discussion stage (Brandsma and Schillemans, 2012, 957).

To begin from a slightly different angle, the term *political* accountability is a familiar one to most people. That is, voters are understood to hold their elected representatives to account through elections. Voters have the right to select candidates for a fixed term in public office, and these representatives then hold their positions by virtue of the support of voters. Elections are the vehicle through which representatives are held accountable: those politicians who enact poor policies or conduct themselves unfavourably are removed from office and replaced with more promising candidates. Often, political accountability is equated to democratic accountability, with the presumption that legitimacy is conferred upon a government of elected representatives through the mechanism of the ballot box. This is sometimes referred to as the 'dominance of the political accountability paradigm' (Staszewski, 2009, 1256).

An alternative means to democratic legitimacy is through *deliberative* accountability, where legitimacy is contingent upon the explanations given by policymakers (elected or unelected) for their policy decisions (Staszewski, 2009, 1255). These explanations should be reasoned and should be public regarding. Moreover, the explanations given should be reasonably compelling to citizens who hold potentially opposing views (Karpowitz and Mendelberg, 2018). Both political accountability and deliberative accountability are essential to democracy, but the former is an inherently blunt instrument which is limited to the frequency of elections, and also condenses all policy issues into a limited choice set. In contrast, deliberative accountability provides a more explicit link between the specific policy choices of policymakers (*both* elected and unelected) and the voting public (Staszewski, 2009). The reason-giving component of deliberative accountability thus forces policymakers to provide justifications for their decisions, and at the same time it offers citizens the opportunity to discuss and question specific government actions. Reason-giving can also potentially deter policymakers from behaving (more narrowly) as delegates of interested groups or factions within society and instead encourage them to behave as trustees, whose actions seek to benefit society (or the nation) more broadly.[6]

Aside from the merits of deliberative accountability as an avenue for democratic legitimacy, deliberation itself offers its own unique benefits to a democratic public, as noted in the literature on deliberative democracy. These scholars are largely in agreement that reason-giving is central to the deliberative process (Page, 1996, Elster, 1998, Fishkin and Laslett, 2003, Pettit, 2003, Barabas, 2004, Gutmann and Thompson, 2004, Quirk, 2005, Austen-Smith and Feddersen, 2006, Crowley, Watson et al., 2008, Thompson, 2008), so that public officials are expected to engage in reasoned argument on the merits of public policy.

Arguably, this reason-giving may include not only intellectual reasoning but also the use of emotional appeals, rhetoric and personal experiences or narratives (Thompson, 2008). Recent deliberative scholars have rightly emphasized that interaction and reciprocity are core to deliberation: 'reason-giving alone is usually not considered a sufficient marker of deliberative activity: it needs to be combined with listening, interactivity, or engagement, a reciprocal, mutual duty' so that even if participants do not agree and cannot find common ground, they at least engage with one another's arguments and do not ignore them (Bächtiger and Parkinson, 2019, 21–24). Whereas 'respect' may be implied in the willingness to engage with one another's arguments, recent depictions of deliberation have argued that too much weight by deliberative scholars upon the requirement of respect may in fact deny voice to a wider variety of participants (who may not faithfully adhere to polite discourse), and thereby may lessen societal inclusiveness (Goodin, 2018, 888).

Setting aside for a moment the role for 'respect', we can accept that reason-giving is central, but it needs to be made clear just why we deem it to be essential to deliberative accountability, particularly in the context of select committee hearings on public policy. One clear answer is that having policymakers give reasons for their decisions in turn compels them to explain how and why their decisions are good for public policy and in particular, how their policies seek to enhance a *public* good rather than a *private* good—that is, their reasons must not be self-serving; they must serve the broader public. In terms of content, the reasons should exhibit at least two features—information and arguments. Information may include empirical evidence, like facts, figures, scientific findings, and economic modelling. It may also extend to analyses of past, present and/or future policies and their consequences (Bessette, 1994: 49). Arguments aim 'to connect mere facts with desirable goals' (Bessette, 1994: 52), and as such, offer the potential for actors to employ ideas and ideology as roadmaps (Goldstein, 1993, Goldstein and Keohane, 1993) or as a means to present a particular interest as one that is beneficial to society in general (Schonhardt-Bailey, 2001, Schonhardt-Bailey, 2006).

A corollary to reason-giving is that participants must be willing to learn from one another—that is, they must be willing to be *persuaded* by the merits of reasoned argument. They must at least be willing to change their minds. A change of one's mind may be incremental or even quite marginal. Persuasion need not entail a complete reversal of position, but rather may simply mean that a previously ambiguous understanding of an issue sharpens into a clear policy position:

> When legislators develop reasoned judgments on legislative matters about which they originally had no opinion or only broad preferences, they are as much 'persuaded' by the information and arguments brought to their attention as when they change their mind from a previously affirmed position.
>
> (Bessette, 1994: 55)

Importantly, persuasion in select committees may also (or even predominantly) be directed at audiences outside the committee rooms—that is, voters, the media, markets, or government ministers.

Persuasion has typically been ignored by scholars concerned with preferences of political actors, and particularly the aggregation of these preferences within a rational choice framework (Hinich and Munger, 1997, Shepsle and Bonchek, 1997). And yet, as this work maintains, reason-based deliberation is a fundamentally important means by which these preferences can possibly change.

Bächtiger and Parkinson note that beyond 'reason-giving, listening, and open-mindedness, almost all deliberative scholars consider *equality of participation and non-domination* as important aspects of high-quality deliberative exchanges' (Bächtiger and Parkinson, 2019, 22) (italics added). This emphasis on equality of participation and non-domination is where deliberative theory appears to depart from accountability, since it is the very political representation that parliamentarians seek to deliver when they hold policymakers to

account that gives them power over these policymakers. In public accountability, an inherent power differential exists between those who are holding
policymakers to account, and the policymakers themselves. It is here where,
as some have observed, deliberative theory is lacking: '… since deliberative
theory has been overly occupied with inalienable democratic principles of
equality, justice, and inclusion, uneasiness with the implications of political
representation writ large prevails within the theory' (Rinne, 2016, 31).

In short, democratic legitimacy implies that political representatives hold
the government and its agencies accountable, but to do so means that policymakers from government departments and agencies must defer to, and be
willing to be held accountable by, political representatives. This in turn means
that deliberation in an accountability setting comprises two sets of unequal
actors: (1) those who are tasked with holding policymakers to account, and
(2) those who are being held to account. Between these two sets of actors is
an adversarial relationship, where one holds power over the other. The two
sets of actors do not participate on equal footing and one set (the political
representatives) holds authority over the other (the policymakers). This is a
clear departure from what deliberative scholars would normally expect in a
'high quality deliberative exchange'. We thus begin with an acceptance that
the deliberative setting under investigation in this work has already foregone
the 'equality of participation and non-domination' expectation because at its
heart is the goal of accountability. And it is this goal of accountability for which
elected politicians in turn are held to account by their constituents, in what
is, more broadly, a chain of accountability where voters delegate public policy decision making to politicians and politicians in turn delegate the drafting
and implementation of policy to government departments or agencies, and at
each link, the principal holds the agent to account (Bovens, Schillemans et al.,
2014, 14).

Before moving to our empirical measures, there is one final component
of deliberative theory which helps to underpin the chapters that follow, and
this pertains to the overall interconnectedness of deliberative accountability.
Deliberative scholars are not entirely in agreement on whether a deliberative
democracy requires all component (and individually distinct) interactions
within a democratic system to be deliberative or whether the system should
instead be judged as a whole, with interdependent parts acting together to produce a deliberative system (Mansbridge, Bohman et al., 2012, Owen and Smith,
2015, Bächtiger and Parkinson, 2019). For our purposes here, the question
is, do we judge deliberative accountability in both the Commons committee (where parliamentarians are elected representatives) by the same standard

as deliberative accountability in the Lords committee (where parliamentarians are not subject to election)? And, similarly, do we judge deliberative accountability in areas of public policy (like monetary policy)—where the policymakers themselves are not elected but appointed, and are also deemed to be independent—by the same standard as other areas of public policy (like fiscal policy)—where policymakers are elected representatives and are thereby not only subject to deliberative accountability but also to political accountability (that is, they are also directly accountable to voters)? The very simple answer which is developed in subsequent chapters is that deliberative accountability should not be seen as constant across different contexts, but rather its quality should be judged to be contingent on the goals pursued within each context as well as the constraints imposed by the nature of the policy in question. For my argument, I draw on the deliberative systems approach to deliberative democracy (Parkinson, 2006, Goodin, 2008, Mansbridge, Bohman et al., 2012, Bächtiger and Parkinson, 2019), and particularly on the importance of context, where deliberation is seen as contingent upon the goals of the actors and the setting in which the deliberation under investigation occurs.

By focusing on three key empirical measures for deliberative accountability, and then employing a mixed methodological approach to gauge deliberative accountability in contexts that vary, I seek to flesh out a better understanding of how deliberative accountability can deliver on aspects of *both* deliberation *and* accountability. For instance, in the Commons committee, deliberation may suffer from the representative and partisan goals of the elected parliamentarians who sit on that committee, and in the Lords committee, deliberation may be enhanced by the expertise of peers and by the very fact that they are not subject to the constraints of electoral pressures. At the same time, MPs in the Commons committee are highly sensitive to the chain of accountability, and so are better situated to behave as political representatives who are subject to accountability pressures from their constituents and party. On balance, MPs may veer more towards accountability, and Lords may veer more towards deliberation, but together the chambers compensate for the other's weakness as pertains to deliberative accountability. And, as we will see in Section 1.5.2, highly partisan rhetoric in one area of policy—which lessens the quality of deliberative accountability on that policy in committee—may similarly be compensated by *political* accountability at the ballot box. In brief, the core argument of this work is that it is only when deliberative accountability is viewed as a whole, across contexts and partly as a broader system, that we can properly assess its contribution to democratic legitimacy. This is not to say that one should not examine the component parts of deliberation (within a chamber or with a view to a specific policy)—and indeed, this work examines those parts in detail. But rather, having examined the individual components, one must then stand back and assess the individual components against one another, as an interconnected whole.

1.5 Empirical Measures for Deliberative Accountability

Having set out the framework for understanding deliberative accountability, we can better comprehend why it is valued and why it is essential in modern democracies. We are not, however, any closer to ascertaining the quality of deliberative accountability in any particular context. We can appreciate that public officials are expected to provide explanations and reasoned arguments which citizens can accept. We can also recognize that these arguments should appeal to rationality, and the arguments should demonstrate that goals were achieved and statutory obligations were met (Olsen, 2017, 74). That is, the questions asked by select committee members in accountability hearings should focus on the statutory obligations of policymakers and the answers should provide reasons for how and why these obligations were met, or if they were not met, why not.

And yet we are still left in a quandary as to what might constitute a systematic means to gauging not only the quality of the questions but also the quality of the proffered responses. Are the questions asked of policymakers appropriate to gleaning quality responses from them? Are the arguments of the witnesses credible? Is anyone persuaded by the arguments? In the context of questions asked and answers given, how would we go about *systematically* gauging the quality of deliberative accountability?

One way to address this task is simply to offer a template of questions. For instance, Olsen maintains that there is a 'clear, consistent, stable, and agreed-upon' template for accountability questioning: 'What happened? Is what happened good or bad? Why did it happen and could it have been avoided? Who made it happen? Who authorized, supported, or opposed it? Who is responsible and who is to blame or be praised for what? Who can be called to account and possible sanctioned? What can be done or has to be done?' (Olsen, 2017, 75). Nonetheless, he also recognizes that certainty as to the success or failure of policy decisions is often impossible, since 'purposes, mandates, intentions, roles, and rules are not clear' and even more, interpretations can be uncertain and accurate depictions of the relevant events may be absent (Olsen, 2017, 75). Even this 'agreed-upon' template fails to offer a systematic measurement of the *process* of deliberative accountability. Apart from whether a particular policy decision is deemed a success or failure, how do we go about deciding whether the *means* for judging its success is 'good'? What, indeed, is a 'good' *process* of democratic accountability? What would it look like? In Sections 1.5.1 to 1.5.3 I outline three basic, but in my view essential, attributes of high quality deliberative accountability.

1.5.1 Respect

A fundamental premise which underpins the analysis here is that deliberative accountability is a dynamic exercise. At its heart is the give-and-take between the committee questioner and the public official witness. Questions and responses are not units to be isolated and examined separately. One approach to gauging deliberation empirically is the 'Discourse Quality Index' or DQI (Steiner, Bächtiger et al., 2004), within which *respect towards others* is a critical factor. Extensions to this measure have sought to include interactive communication processes (Bachtiger, Pedrini et al., 2010), and these have been employed by subsequent scholars to gauge a form of reciprocity in deliberation—namely between privileged and minority groups (Pedrini, Bächtiger et al., 2013). Reciprocity as a separate measure is discussed in Section 1.5.3. However, it should be noted at this point that the DQI is not employed as an empirical measure in this study, since, as described in its codebook,[7] the coding is selective and does not include all participants in the discussion. The quantitative text analysis used in Chapter 2 of this work, on the other hand, analyses the transcripts of the meetings verbatim, excluding nothing.

In any case, the DQI's focus on *respect towards others* is important and is adopted here. That is, the way in which committee members and policymakers relate to one another during hearings might be considered a first principle of deliberative accountability. If actors fail to respect one another, the entire legitimacy of the process is undermined, as it brings into question why anyone should take the process seriously.

Drawing upon the seminal work of Habermas (Habermas, 1996), Steiner and co-authors create categories for respect which focus on the content of each speech act, and thus gauge the extent to which this content is respectful towards other groups and respectful of the arguments of others (Steiner, Bächtiger et al., 2004). Yet respect and disrespect can be expressed not just in the words themselves but also in the body language which accompanies them, through smiling, smirking, use of posture, tone of voice, and so on. Oddly, deliberative scholars pay scant attention to the role of nonverbal communication and the way that this can lend insight into whether participants respect one another or not. Respect is also subject to perceptions and interpretations, and so the more subjective judgements of the participants themselves (about their own behaviour and that of others) matter for gauging the degree of respect observed in exchanges between questioners and witnesses in select committee hearings. In short, *respect* in deliberative accountability is not just about what is said but is also captured by how it is said and why it is said. In this work, both the subsequent chapters on nonverbal communication in select committee hearings and on the insights from the participants of the hearings themselves—in the interviews chapter—offer unique methods for gauging respect.

As described in the discussion of the adversarial relationship inherent to accountability, the actors in the exchange are not on equal footing. Questioners are seeking answers while witnesses are expected to respond to their questions: 'it implies *rights of authority*, in that those calling for an account are asserting rights of superior authority over those who are accountable, including the rights to demand answers and to impose sanctions' (Mulgan, 2000, 555). This feature of deliberative accountability means that the adversarial relationship between actors is of fundamental importance: 'The dialogue of accountability occurs between parties in an authority relationship and can only be understood in the context of that relationship. This relationship is crucially different from that presupposed by democratic debate which takes place in a public space between citizens conceived of as equals' (Mulgan, 2000, 570). Deliberative accountability in select committee hearings is thus of a hierarchical nature. That is, policymakers—whether they be senior ministers like the chancellor of the exchequer or the governor of the Bank of England—are in a subordinate role when questioned by select committee members, and so, one aspect of the respect metric is whether both sets of actors understand and behave according to their positions (dominant or subordinate) in the accountability hierarchy. It should be noted, however, that with respect to deliberative accountability in fiscal policy, this hierarchy is the reverse of the standard parliamentary hierarchy, where frontbench MPs outrank their backbench counterparts. As select committee membership is reserved for backbench MPs, the hierarchical relationship is turned on its head as these (backbench) MPs hold (frontbench) Treasury ministers to account.

In short, as a first measure of quality in deliberative accountability, committee members and policymakers who are being held to account should behave respectfully towards one another. They should implicitly recognize the unique hierarchical nature of deliberative accountability. By this, respect is gauged in terms of what is said (are the words and arguments of one party taking on board those of the other party in the exchange?—which is effectively the measure of reciprocity discussed in Section 1.5.3), how it is said (does the body language of actors indicate respect, or is there blatant hostility, anger or contempt by one actor towards another?), and why it is said (do the actors themselves perceive others as having respected both their views but also their position within the accountability hierarchy?).

1.5.2 Partisanship/Electoral Incentives

Should partisanship play a role in deliberative accountability? There are several considerations which do not all conflate into a single clear stance. Viewed negatively with respect to deliberation, political parties may elevate ideological/partisan objectives and thus exacerbate conflict. Political parties are also adept at framing conflicts in a way that enhances their own legislative agenda (Slothuus and Vreese, 2010, Stewart, Eubanks et al., 2019), and so may lessen the scope for deliberation to be public-regarding. Simply put, by virtue of appealing to their partisan base, political parties are incentivized to 'distort deliberation' (Quirk, Bendix et al., 2018, 277).

At the same time that partisan rhetoric can diminish core ideals of deliberation—such as open-mindedness, reason-giving and respect—arguably it may deliver other ideals, such as inclusivity (Mansbridge, Bohman et al., 2012, 2–3). More broadly, partisanship within a deliberative setting might fall into what is termed 'ritual deliberation', or a form of performance in which the participants adhere to 'socially prescribed' roles which, although deliberation is the perceived intent, in actuality other purposes are served. As the concept of ritual deliberation sheds light on both partisanship and reciprocity (our next empirical measure), it is worth fleshing out what is meant by the term. Tanasoca and Sass explain that,

> (I)n political deliberation actors routinely talk past one another. They offer arguments as a way of scoring points or rationalizing existing beliefs. They fail to reflect on the reasons offered by others and, in consequence, seldom learn from their interactions or update their view of the world. From the perspective of democratic theory, such discursive exchanges are pointless: they consume time, energy, and other resources, but do not achieve any standard deliberative ends. Despite this, political actors routinely engage in these practices … and political theorists need to find some way of accounting for that fact.
>
> (Tanasoca and Sass, 2019, 139)

Inasmuch as ritual deliberation serves a number of purposes, like enabling participants to demonstrate their commitment to a shared group identity and values, a key feature in the context of deliberative accountability is that the ritual allows parliamentarians to serve their role as political representatives in holding the government to account: '(p)olitical actors exchange arguments because that behaviour is socially seen as *appropriate* in the legislative setting and in their *role* as representatives' (Tanasoca and Sass, 2019, 146). Moreover, partisan rhetoric in deliberative accountability helps to structure disagreement, by clarifying 'partisan positions for the audience, making it easier for people across the political community at least to agree what it is that they are disagreeing about' (Tanasoca and Sass, 2019, 157).

This notion of ritual deliberation accords with what some have argued for in terms of the need to '*repoliticize* deliberation' by moving away from contexts where the conditions may be deemed as ideal, and instead examine deliberation in more realistic settings of 'mass democracy, a communicative environment characterized by intense competition and communicative abundance, created by agents acting purposively, set in a sometimes collaborative but often competitive political context' (Bächtiger and Parkinson, 2019, 152–153). These authors note that 'deliberativeness under the public eye of good democratic accountability may require that actors use narratives to make positions intelligible to the electorate as well as emotional language to create awareness effects' (Bächtiger and Parkinson, 2019, 73). In the context of evidence hearings in select committees, the pursuit of political representation may compromise deliberative ideals, but may well deliver on other ideals, like holding policymakers to account as a form of validating MPs' credentials as political representatives to their constituents.

It is thus worth emphasizing that while partisan rhetoric may wreak havoc with deliberative ideals, its purpose may instead allow parliamentarians to behave as political representatives, whose job it is in select committees to hold the government to account. The danger, however, is that with the growing importance of select committees in the UK Parliament, partisanship may also become more pronounced, and thereby risk the apolitical deliberations to which these committees aspire. As Tyrie notes, as the stakes become higher, partisanship may also increase, and thereby undermine the very effectiveness which select committees seek (Tyrie, 2015, 67). There are, therefore, limits to just how much partisan rhetoric can be reconciled within a setting of deliberative accountability.

This work seeks to measure empirically deliberative accountability within a very specific setting (select committee hearings) and by focusing on economic policy—namely, fiscal policy, monetary policy, and financial stability. Whereas all three seek to deliver a stable, and growing national economy with a stable financial system, their statutory remits, tools, and institutional frameworks are quite different, and these differences have implications for partisan politics.

Fiscal policy deals with tax and spending decisions, and so there are typically clear winners and losers from any given fiscal policy decision. In the UK, fiscal policy is formulated primarily by the chancellor of the exchequer, together with the Treasury. As such, it lies at the heart of partisan politics, with each political party maintaining its own priorities and concerns with respect to national budgetary decisions. The operation of monetary policy is delegated to the Monetary Policy Committee of the Bank of England, as it pursues an inflation target which is set by the government. Importantly, it is intended to do so *independent* of partisan politics. The rationale for independence in central banking comprises a large literature, and is not explored here.[8] However, we can recognize that monetary policy, as decided by an independent central bank, is intended to operate at a distance from party political pressures. In part, this is because the idea of the neutrality of money maintains that a central bank's monetary policy does not affect the real economy, since in the long run, prices and wages adapt. In other words, conventionally monetary policy does not itself influence the long-run rate of growth of the economy; rather, low, and stable inflation is a necessary condition to allow other economic policies to affect the long-run growth rate. Those other economic policies are typically in the direct control of government and politicians—for example, fiscal policy, welfare, and structural economic policies. Nonetheless, monetary policy can have a short-run impact on particular sectors of the economy as a necessary condition for achieving and maintaining low inflation and stable growth.

Like monetary policy, financial stability is intended to function at a distance from party politics, with responsibility for its policy delegated to the Bank of England's Financial Policy Committee. However, relative to monetary policy, financial stability has a greater potential to directly affect the economic interests of financial institutions and individuals (say, by setting capital requirements for banks), and so winners and losers can be more conspicuous and immediate than in monetary policy. Don Kohn, former vice chair of the US Federal Open Market Committee and member of the Bank's Financial Policy Committee, characterizes monetary policy and financial stability as each requiring a different toolkit but also a different focus on risks, with financial stability focusing on markets and institutions which pose less likely but potentially severe risks:

Protecting financial stability efficiently and effectively requires a different focus and set of tools than does monetary policy. Attention is most often centered on tail risks, rather than on the most likely outcomes that are often at the heart of monetary policy decisions. It's those tail risks—the unlikely event not fully priced into the market—that can have the most severe implications for financial stability. Macroprudential policy action is called for when those tail events are expected to have externalities—ramifications for the whole economy and not just for the parties involved in the transactions. Those ramifications often play out through the response of highly leveraged lenders or borrowers to the unexpected event—or the actions of the counterparties to these lenders or borrowers, as they fear for the safety of the lending or funding they have supplied.

(Kohn, 2016, 6–7)

In other words, particular issues within markets and institutions can have a highly significant negative impact on the entire financial system, and so financial stability is focused more on identifying those vulnerabilities and taking policy action to alleviate the systemic risk. These actions, or the potential for these actions, can foster efforts at lobbying which are absent from monetary policy. And it is this lobbying which invites partisan leanings to shape the priorities of parliamentarians, as they consider whether the Bank's Financial Policy Committee has met its statutory obligations.

In any case, both monetary policy and financial stability are highly technical policy activities, and so the delegation to unelected central bankers is meant to rely on their expertise, but also their commitment to delivering policies which serve the broader public interest (in stable economic growth and financial stability). Some scholars strongly argue that central bankers are indeed neutral technocrats whose own professionalism dictates constraint and predictability in policymaking (Miller and Whitford, 2016), and where they benefit personally, it is in their concern for sustaining and enhancing their own (and their institution's) reputation for competence (Busuioc and Lodge, 2016, 249). Other scholars maintain that central bankers are driven more by power-seeking and personal career motivations (Adolph, 2013, Jacobs and King, 2016). From a different perspective, others maintain that as central banks have acquired more powers and statutory obligations, these in turn have created more, potentially political, trade-offs for central bankers, which politicians may, in turn, be tempted to influence (Fernández-Albertos, 2015, 228). Indeed, since the financial crisis, considerable research has focused on central bank decision making, and one key strand examines central bank communications, as discussed in Section 1.3. Much of this empirical analysis seeks to gauge outputs such as policy meeting transcripts and minutes, central bank news conferences and reports, and so on. Less attention has been devoted to gauging empirically how central bankers communicate directly to legislators in accountability hearings.

Because the focus of this work is not on the policy decisions themselves, but rather on the explanations given by policymakers to politicians who would hold them to account, the more targeted question here is, how much partisanship is acceptable and appropriate in the questioning by these politicians? Are the politicians who serve on select committees overstepping their accountability remit by infusing in their questions some element of self-serving partisan point-scoring or by pandering to constituents? If we accept that political representation almost invariably means that politicians will infuse partisan rhetoric into accountability hearings, just how much of this rhetoric can be deemed acceptable within a framework of deliberative accountability?

To be clear, modern parliamentary select committees do strive to be non-partisan (particularly after the reforms of 2010 (Wright, 2015, 106)), and so one might (naively) assume that partisanship is absent from select committee hearings. We may indeed find little in the way of partisanship in these hearings, but there is reason for caution as we observe elsewhere that elected representatives in oversight hearings are inherently susceptible to partisan and electoral concerns. In a previous book, I found clear evidence of partisanship and electoral concerns driving deliberative processes in the US Congress, when both the Senate and House committees hold the chair of the Federal Reserve to account for monetary policy (Schonhardt-Bailey, 2013). In interviews with former members of the Federal Open Market Committee (the monetary policy committee of the Federal Reserve), the prevailing view is that members of Congress who conduct hearings on US monetary policy are simply not that interested in, or knowledgeable about, monetary policy. For instance, according to former vice chair of the FOMC, Alan Blinder, members of Congress are more concerned with their appearances before the cameras than with the deliberation on monetary policy:

> **Blinder**: There is a legitimate role for oversight, a necessary role for oversight, so I'm completely on board about that. The problem is that … if the chairman of the Fed is in the witness seat, it is always high-profile, [and the hearings] are media circuses, and all the members are doing is preening for the cameras. You don't exercise oversight by doing that. Oversight is boring. [Having] any

meeting of the minds or real intellectual interchange ... would be nice but that's not, from the point of view of the members, that's not what they are there for. They may want their opportunity to excoriate the chairman of the Fed in public, so that they can show [to constituents that], 'he is causing all this unemployment and I'm fighting him' or they may want his endorsement ... for their pet policy but they are not really trying to do oversight of monetary policy ... [And] some Fed chairs go there willingly like Greenspan did, and some Fed chairs like Bernanke go there kicking and screaming, 'I don't want to endorse this or that policy' but that's what they want, so they are looking for the sound-bite that says 'Chairman Greenspan agreed with me that ...'

(Schonhardt-Bailey, 2013, 382–383)

Another former FOMC member, Jerry Jordan, characterizes the questioning as dysfunctional, where personalities dominate:

Jordan: [It depended on] what kind of game was being played out in those oversight hearings, and the styles of the chairmen ... Arthur Burn's style was basically to threaten, belittle and ridicule any congressman or senator that said something stupid, so they mostly wanted to get through the hearings without being totally embarrassed. Whereas Greenspan played the rope-a-dope approach of just lull them into incoherent babble and they would work hard at trying to get him to utter anything coherent. He was very, very good at avoiding saying anything coherent in most of those hearings ... When you had Barney Frank versus Ron Paul, even when Frank was the ranking minority member, before he became chairman, you knew going in that one of them would start it off and the other one was going to come back and it was really a by-play between two flamboyant personalities on the committee attacking the central bank from a different vantage point. But it was really the two congressmen trying to out-play each other on their side and [for] the chairman of the Fed ... [it] was simply an opportunity for these guys to go at each other ...and neutralize each other. It was kind of fun to watch but whether it was all productive to any purpose I have no idea.

(Schonhardt-Bailey, 2013, 384)

And, other former FOMC members (Al Broaddus, Alice Rivlin) highlight the explicit partisan political motivations of members of Congress, namely, to score points with their constituents:

Broaddus: Most of these people ... are not professional economists, they are politicians. Many of them have backgrounds in law or business, and so they are not only not conversant they are really not entirely interested in policy, except in terms of its immediate impact. They often have a political motive in the questions, you know their questions are all scripted and most of them by their staff and so they are using this as an opportunity to indirectly communicate with their constituents, their voters ... Playing to the cameras is a good brief ... I think it's mainly just there is nothing that they can benefit from in terms of talking about monetary policy per se that is going to help them get a vote in the next election.

(Schonhardt-Bailey, 2013, 384)

Rivlin: Various members of the committee ... may actually be trying to make points for themselves, and to say, you know, 'I come from a farm district in Iowa and we think interest rates are too high here and it is bad for farmers, what do you think about that Mr. Chairman?' He doesn't care what the chairman thinks, he wants to make [his point that] he is speaking to the folks back home ... Most of them don't have a very keen grasp of monetary policy. They think it is something sort of mysterious and they don't want to sound stupid so they don't take it on ...

(Schonhardt-Bailey, 2013, 385)

Evidence from the US thus suggests that partisanship and electoral concerns have a deleterious effect on deliberation in monetary policy oversight hearings. Observers and participants find that partisan and electoral concerns encourage committee members to refocus the discussion away from monetary policy, and towards their own self-serving political motives. In contrast to the deliberative ideal where individuals are challenged 'to listen to others who do not share their beliefs, values or interests, to engage in constructive dialogue, to gain knowledge, and perhaps be persuaded about the merits of views that differ from their predispositions,' (Esterling, Fung et al., 2015, 529) monetary policy oversight hearings in the US can frequently be a forum for members of Congress to 'grandstand'.

More broadly, it may simply be too much to expect legislators to be sufficiently knowledgeable about technical subjects like monetary policy and financial stability to effectively challenge policy experts, so that the legislators revert to partisanship and electioneering should come as no surprise. And so, the motivation for partisan and electoral point-scoring in monetary policy and financial stability hearings maybe one of *avoiding* the technicalities of the subject matter. And yet, in other research, I found that distinct differences in deliberative quality are apparent between accountability hearings on monetary policy in the US versus those in the UK (Schonhardt-Bailey, 2021). Quantitative text analysis of the monetary policy accountability hearing transcripts for both countries revealed virtually no partisan rhetoric in the UK Treasury Select Committee, relative to a larger component of this rhetoric in the two US congressional committees. It is thus worth exploring the unique finding in the UK more fully, by examining accountability hearings for other types of economic policy and by expanding the analysis to both parliamentary chambers, as is done in this work.

The motivation for partisanship in *fiscal* policy is quite different from that in monetary policy, given its conspicuous redistributive implications and the ease with which this maps onto ideological understandings of haves and have-nots in society. Some degree of partisanship may be simply unavoidable in fiscal policy hearings. We may thus conclude that the more values-based the policy area, the greater the scope for partisan conflict and the less scope for deliberative quality. Indeed, deliberative theorists make pretty much the same argument:

> [T]he more the discussion takes up questions of truth and fact, and the less it deals with values, the more isolated it becomes from the social pressures that deliberative theory would regard with alarm, and the more rational and argument-driven it becomes, as deliberative theory would like. On matters of value, opportunities for deliberation are likely to turn anti-deliberative. And even if they manage to turn argument-centered, they are unlikely to change minds. Advocates of deliberation would do well to promote deliberation on issues of fact but to advance alternatives to deliberation on issues of value … Less obvious but equally important is the implication for severe conflict. When deliberation deals with an issue that has long generated deep conflict, it is unlikely that many novel arguments will be aired. And if novel and valid arguments are aired, they are not likely to persuade many people.
>
> (Mendelberg, 2002, 160–161)

We thus begin to question whether quality deliberation is at all possible in areas of public policy where political parties are highly divided on the societal values that underpin spending and taxing decisions. It may well be that because the traditional values and brand-name reputation of political parties constrain their reasoning on fiscal policy, to insist on standards of deliberation in the context of accountability is to ignore the value that political parties bring to democracy through *political accountability* (Walter, 2017). Voters decide their governments based on partisan reputations, and in this way, political accountability delivers legitimacy to fiscal policy. In short, it may be unrealistic to judge deliberative accountability in fiscal policy by the same standard as that in monetary policy or financial stability policy. This important point brings us back to one aspect of our core argument, that is, that in order to properly assess deliberative accountability, we must consider the context in which this is occurring. Moreover, we must also note that democratic legitimacy relies on deliberative accountability but also, as noted earlier, on political accountability. And so, if fiscal policy hearings are lacking in the quality of deliberative accountability, the fact that fiscal policymakers (in the UK, the chancellor and more broadly the government in power) are also subject to political accountability suggests that as a system, accountability in fiscal policy should be judged by the two in tandem.

One conclusion from this section is that select committee hearings on fiscal policy are likely to contain more partisanship (which may harm deliberative accountability) than hearings on monetary policy or financial stability (although it may nonetheless remain a tempting line of questioning). Overall, we might expect partisanship to be a metric for quality in deliberative accountability which varies by policy type. With more partisan conflict, we may anticipate lower quality deliberative accountability in fiscal policy hearings than in monetary policy or financial stability policy hearings.

1.5.3 Reciprocity

The third and final metric for high quality deliberative accountability is, for our purposes, the most important—namely, reciprocity. The concept of reciprocity is not only fundamental to deliberative democracy; it lies at the root of human ethics. For game theorists and cognitive scientists (Ostrom and Walker, 2005), as well as scholars of conflict studies (Diekmann, 2004), anthropology (MacCormack, 1976), and computational neuroscience (Mahmoodi, Bahrami et al., 2018), reciprocity has implications for trust between individuals and groups of individuals. In psychology, it is known as the 'rule for reciprocation,' whereby 'we should try to repay, in kind, what another person has provided us' and in so doing, this creates a sense of obligation which is said to be pervasive in human culture, where 'there is no human society that does not subscribe to the rule' (Cialdini, 2007, 17–18). With echoes of the biblical golden rule (do unto others ...), reciprocity means that a favour is meant to be met with a counter-favour; an action towards another is entitled a *reciprocal* action (Cialdini, 2007, 37). While the concept of reciprocity has received attention by deliberative theorists mostly at a theoretical level (e.g., (Goodin, 2000, Gutmann and

Thompson, 2004)), there have also been studies that have sought to explore its empirical implications (e.g., (Weale, Bicquelet et al., 2012, Pedrini, Bächtiger et al., 2013)). As noted earlier, Pedrini and colleagues have explored deliberative reciprocity between privileged and minority groups (Pedrini, Bächtiger et al., 2013). However, as far as I know, reciprocity has not been explored in the context of deliberative accountability.

Reciprocity in deliberation is both conceptual and empirical. Conceptually, reciprocity means that 'citizens owe one another justifications for the mutually binding laws and public policies they collectively enact' (Gutmann and Thompson, 2004, 98–99). These citizens should, moreover, ratify or acknowledge the arguments of others. As Goodin notes: '(t)here must … be uptake and engagement—other people must hear or read, internalize and respond—for that public-sphere activity to count as remotely deliberative' (Goodin, 2000: 92). This internalization, in turn, requires a degree of shared meaning:

> In real conversations between real people, there is a constant cross-checking and renegotiation of meanings. That facilitates interlocutors' understanding of one another. People who are merely overhearing a conversation sometimes find it hard to understand what is going on, precisely because they cannot interject into the conversation to cross-check their own understandings of what others mean to be saying … In real conversations, a code of dyadically shared meanings emerges.
>
> (Goodin, 2000: 101)

Goodin contrasts this form of communication as one in which people are essentially *talking to one another* with other practices, such as posting material on the internet or pontificating from a soapbox, where people are essentially 'posting notices for all to read'—notices which may or may not be read or internalized. The latter, in his view, does not constitute deliberation for the simple reason that it is not reciprocal (Goodin, 2000: 91–92). And finally, reciprocity in deliberation assumes that in conversing, 'people characteristically talk more or less 'loosely'. They make more or less cryptic allusions to more full-blown arguments' (Goodin, 2000: 93) In essence, the full-blown arguments are not generally articulated as such, but rather exist in the form of *conceptual clouds*. Others then acknowledge the implied meaning as a form of 'catching one's drift'—for example, by completing the syllogism and applying the reasoning to some more specific instance. To this, we can add that reciprocity in deliberation entails 'both interactivity and respect. It involves an effort to listen to and engage with people with whom we disagree …'

(Pedrini, Bächtiger et al., 2013). Reciprocity therefore requires participants to 'engage with one another' so that 'they do not only give reasons *but listen and take up the reasons of other participants*' (italics added) (Pedrini, Bächtiger et al., 2013: 488).

But why is reciprocity essential to economic policy deliberative accountability? The simple answer is that without reciprocity, without evidence that participants are talking *to* rather than *past* one another, we have no evidence that the explanations for decisions taken by the central bank and Treasury are being conveyed to legislators sufficiently to enable them to hold representatives from these institutions to account. In other words, a reciprocal exchange entails not only offering up arguments, but also an 'effective listening' to those arguments—that is, citizens must '*hear* the reasons offered by others' (Morrell, 2018, 238).

Quality in deliberative accountability is thus inextricably linked to the degree to which participants talk to rather than past one another, thereby 'listening' to the reasoning of others, and presumably being in a better position to appreciate their positions and judge the extent to which policymakers have met their statutory obligations. In parliamentary select committee hearings, evidence of reciprocity would be that individuals talk in conceptually coherent ways ('conceptual clouds') which others may share (by agreeing, disagreeing, or pursuing in some way). This implies, for instance, that any empirical investigation of text emanating from such hearings should be able to capture these shared concepts, or themes—and should, moreover, also be able to gauge the extent to which individual members participate in these shared themes.[9] *In short, the empirical task is not simply one of capturing the content of the hearings as a form of notice-posting, but rather as a reciprocal and interactive form of communication, and this should appear across all relevant themes.*

1.6 Persuasion

There is one remaining aspect to deliberative accountability that requires further attention. Earlier, I noted that an anticipated product of deliberation is persuasion—that is, participants in deliberation must be willing to learn from, and be persuaded by the reasoned arguments of other participants. Although this is not the view of the present work, admittedly some scholars would dispute that persuasion is even a product of deliberation, instead arguing that persuasive dialogues are inherently adversarial while deliberative dialogues are meant to be cooperative (Atkinson, Bench-Capon et al., 2013).

More in line with the approach taken here, other scholars rightly note that persuasion is often 'latent, indirect, delayed, or disguised' (Mackie, 2006, 295) and consequently is difficult to identify, let alone measure.

We should thus be cautious about how we approach any empirical investigation of deliberation that may entail persuasion as an outcome. There are a number of features of persuasion that we should note before moving forward with an empirical study of deliberative accountability. First, similar to reciprocity, persuasion is interactional: '(p)ersuasion is not something one person does *to* another but something he or she does *with* another' (Reardon, 1991, 3). This suggests that, once again, our methods should seek to somehow gauge the dynamic between individuals as they deliberate, and so it is crucial to examine the *how* of deliberation—the *means* by which words and arguments are conveyed in a back-and-forth dynamic. We may or may not find any evidence of persuasion, but it is pointless looking for it without recognizing its relational dynamic.

Second, communications scholars also note that persuasion has its limits. When participants are so divided (perhaps for reasons of rigid partisanship or even institutional differences) that they do not share common understandings, persuasion is not possible: '(p)eople 'talk past each other' when they do not share similar constructions of their environments. It is simply not possible to persuade someone whose construction of the world is so foreign to our own that we cannot comprehend it' (Reardon, 1991, 18). And so, when we find that people talk past one another, that they do not share in 'conceptual clouds', not only does this suggest an absence of reciprocity, it may also suggest the impossibility of persuasion occurring. Yet, in the adversarial context of accountability hearings, particularly in those where partisanship is likely to play a fundamental role in the goal of political representatives messaging their constituents, we should also bear in mind that persuasion within the committee rooms themselves may be far less relevant than persuasion targeted at audiences *outside* the committee rooms.

Third, persuasion relies not only on reasoned argument but also on emotional appeal, as well as the demonstrated credibility and sincerity or truthfulness of the actor (Reardon, 1991, 108–09, Borg, 2013). In some cases, reason may even serve as a superficial cover for underlying emotional preferences, thereby aiming to disguise emotions in a persuasive appeal to logic. As Mendelberg explains: '(n)ot only may emotion be at least as effective as reason in a discussion, reason can serve as an excuse for emotion. Reasonable discourse can serve as a means of justifying pre-existing, emotionally charged preferences' (Mendelberg, 2002, 168). Moreover, Mendelberg notes that persuasion may be incorrectly attributed to the reasoned arguments (the content) of the speaker, where in fact, it is the delivery, the nonverbal communication that changed minds: 'people easily misattribute their affective states … For example, citizens are likely to misattribute the enthusiasm they feel for a speaker to the content of the speech rather than the speaker's happy facial expressions even when it is actually the latter that affects them more' (Mendelberg, 2002, 169).

Persuasion is clearly multifaceted and its place in deliberative discourse is difficult to pin down. At the very least, then, to capture empirically the potential for sincerity/truthfulness, credibility and emotions to influence both deliberation as well as persuasion, our methods should seek to include ways in which these expressions become manifest—for example, in the words expressed (content), in the ways they are expressed (nonverbal behaviour such as facial expressions, gestures, tone of voice), and in the interpretations and judgements given by the participants themselves.

1.7 Conclusion

This chapter has covered a fair bit of territory, and so it might be useful to boil the argument down to four key points. First, the focus of this work is on deliberative accountability—not deliberation and not accountability but rather the intersection of these two concepts in a form of accountability where policymakers are expected to explain their policy decisions to parliamentarians, whose presumed goal is to hold these policymakers to account. Second, in contrast to an ideal deliberative setting in which the participants are seen to be equal, the select committee accountability hearings under investigation here are comprised of two quite unequal sets of actors. In accountability hearings, an implicit hierarchical relationship exists between parliamentarians and policymakers, with the former having the authority to demand answers and explanations and the latter expected to provide these. It is this hierarchical relationship which makes the setting an adversarial one, since explanations may sometimes be judged as inadequate and moreover, the subservient policymaker may not always recognize or respect the authority of the parliamentary committee to demand explanations. And so, this adversarial context makes deliberative accountability in select committee hearings a distinct and somewhat unique setting in which to examine the dynamics of deliberative discourse.

Third, a critical reader might dismiss accountability hearings as something of an outlier within the deliberation literature, perhaps something of limited interest. But we need only remind ourselves of what has been described in this chapter as the 'accountability explosion'—and as Figures 1.1 and 1.2 clearly show, accountability and reason-giving have become the bread and butter of modern democratic governance. Just as in all areas of public life, those in positions of influence and power are expected to be held accountable to the broader public. This notion of accountability has become so ubiquitous that it risks losing any real meaning, since, as in the earlier quote from Tony Wright, it can become nothing more than an exercise in 'finding someone to blame'. In a world where voters, citizens, the media, politicians, and policymakers themselves all seek more accountability, it has become curiously difficult to find any agreement or clear empirical measures for what, exactly, constitutes accountability. Would people recognize the desired quality or quantity of accountability, if indeed this was obtained? In this work, the focus on the deliberative aspect of accountability allows us to home in on what is arguably the very core of public accountability, namely the obligation to explain policy decisions to the larger public affected by these decisions.

Fourth, by focusing specifically on deliberative accountability, this work sets out empirical measures to gauge this across different types of economic policy and across parliamentary chambers. We anticipate variations across these dimensions, and not surprisingly we do indeed find variations. These variations are not only significant in their own right, but they provide us with the building blocks which comprise a larger system of accountability. That is, by taking into account the political and institutional context in which the deliberative accountability occurs and by widening our lens to observe the broader system of accountability as it pertains to the relevant policy or set of policymakers under investigation, we begin to grasp the potential trade-offs that may occur in the simultaneous pursuit of high-quality deliberation and high-quality accountability.

The chapters that follow seek to unpack the three metrics of quality in deliberative accountability—respect, minimal partisanship and reciprocity—and at the same time allow for contextual factors which may influence the *process* of deliberative accountability to yield the potential *outcome* of persuasion. At the heart of the analysis is the focus on what constitutes high-quality deliberative accountability and how do the metrics of respect, partisanship and reciprocity affect this?

Returning to the earlier paradox—why we find so little trust in governing officials alongside an explosion in accountability—I argue that trust suffers where (1) there is little respect among actors (e.g., where actors on both sides of the table are aggressive and confrontational), (2) reason-giving is replaced with partisan point-scoring (e.g., questioners seek to publicly 'bash' policymakers, or policymakers—typically as politicians—seek to whitewash their decisions), and (3) reciprocity in deliberation is absent (e.g., answers are diversionary or seek to obfuscate, or questions themselves are inappropriate or unanswerable). By all three metrics, we can gauge the quality of deliberative accountability, and this work finds that quality to be better when holding independent agencies like central banks to account than when holding elected politicians to account. In the latter case (here, exemplified in fiscal policy), quality is deemed to be poor. In these cases, I argue that trust in government may be better served through political accountability (the ballot box) than through deliberative accountability.

Looking forward, Chapter 2 analyses the content of select committee hearings on monetary policy, financial stability, and fiscal policy, focusing on the verbatim transcripts for these hearings and using quantitative text analysis. This chapter examines the two UK committees in the Commons and the Lords during the 2010–2015 Parliament, thus allowing us to systematically analyse *what* was said, who focused on what arguments or themes, and identify patterns of deliberation across three policy areas, and two parliamentary chambers.

Chapter 3 studies the *how* of deliberative accountability by gauging the extent to which nonverbal communication—in the form of facial expressions, vocal cues, and gestures—influences deliberation in the two parliamentary select committee hearings. Comparisons are made between the three policy areas which lend insights into latent aspects of respect between and among treasury ministers, central bankers, and parliamentarians. This chapter has two parts. The first part systematically examines facial expressions, vocal cues and gestures, based upon a qualitative coding of a sample of the full set of hearings during the 2010–2015 Parliament. The second part of the chapter analyses findings from a laboratory experiment which sought to gauge the effect of nonverbal behaviour on perceptions of credibility, competence, and persuasiveness.

Chapter 4 examines the *why* of deliberation by directly asking the participants of the hearings—parliamentarians, treasury officials, central bankers, committee staff—for their views. Using about two dozen in-depth interviews, this chapter explores several dimensions of deliberative accountability, including the motivations of the actors themselves, and their perceptions as to the value of deliberation within the hearings. The interviews also serve as a check on the findings from Chapters 2 and 3, by asking the participants themselves whether the findings from these chapters accorded with their own experiences in the hearings.

In the concluding chapter of this work, I bring together the three-pronged methodological approach to studying deliberative accountability and offer an assessment of the three policy areas and two parliamentary committees, based on the metrics of respect, partisanship and reciprocity.

Notes

1. Notably, when the UK was in lockdown owing to Covid-19 and Parliament was in its 2020 Easter recess (25 March—21 April), the committee of primary investigation in this work—the Treasury Select Committee—held three virtual hearings.
2. The context for this quote derives from a dinner party at which Lord Chancellor Lyndhurst had provided advice to both Gladstone and Disraeli. Gladstone recounted the advice at length, as 'Never defend yourself before a popular assemblage, except with and by retorting the attack; the hearers, in the pleasure which the assault gives them, will forget the previous charge'. Disraeli's recollection of Lyndhurst's advice was far more succinct (Morley, 1911, 91).
3. Distributions were also obtained for the words 'accountable' and 'deliberate' and while the number of references for both were much smaller, the trends were exactly parallel to those for 'accountability' and 'deliberation'. The one exception for the word 'accountable' appears in June 1894, where 77 references emerge in respect to a Finance Bill, where MPs were considering whether the executer would be accountable for duty on estate taxes.
4. A rotation of members of the Monetary Policy Committee testify on the Inflation Report. The MPC consists of both internal and external members, with the former comprised of the governor, three deputy governors, and the chief economist. There are four external members who hold no other position at the BoE. MPC members rotate before the TSC, but the delegation almost always includes the governor.
5. The Blair-Brown Labour Government made the Bank operationally independent with respect to monetary policy in 1997, coming into effect in 1998.
6. The distinction between delegates and trustees is traced to Edmund Burke (Burke, 1774 (1906)), but is widely used in contemporary research in legislative studies and elsewhere (Hill, 1929, Eulau, 1962, Burke, 1996, Uslaner, 1999).
7. See the online supplementary materials to (Pedrini, Bächtiger et al., 2013), at https://www.cambridge.org/core/journals/european-political-science-review/article /deliberative-inclusion-of-minorities-patterns-of-reciprocity-among-linguistic- groups-in-switzerland/464A6D7BCE2B66D1CB374C1E3E3AD8F8#fndtn- supplementary-materials.
8. For a longer discussion, see (Schonhardt-Bailey, 2013). Succinctly, the idea that an independent central bank responsible for monetary policy is the best institutional structure around which countries can achieve lasting low inflation and stable economic growth became widespread in the late twentieth century. The academic literature on independent central banks has been prolific (Cukierman, 1992, Bernhard, 1998, Blinder, 1998). Its premise is that when politicians formulate monetary policy, they are

compromised by their electoral incentives. Mistakes were made from a belief among politicians that it was possible to raise the level of output and employment permanently by accepting a higher rate of inflation—that is, there was an assumed long-run trade-off between unemployment and inflation. As politicians attempted to exploit this trade-off for electoral advantage (by boosting demand through higher government spending or seeking lower interest rates) permanently higher inflation generally resulted. The presumed trade-off therefore did not exist, at least not in the long-run. Politicians seeking re-election nevertheless remained tempted to exploit any presumed short-run trade-off between unemployment and inflation, and thus were found repeatedly to prefer more inflationary monetary policies—which Kydland and Prescott termed the problem of 'time inconsistency' (Kydland and Prescott, 1977).

9. (Weale, Bicquelet et al., 2012) provide a good example of the empirical application of deliberative reciprocity in parliamentary discourse.

Reference

(2020). Bagehot-Back to Normal: The Virtual Parliament Brings a Welcome Return to Scrutiny. *The Economist*. **April 25**: 25.

Adler, E. S. and J. S. Lapinski (1997). "Demand-Side Theory and Congressional Committee Composition: A Constituency Characteristics Approach." *American Journal of Political Science* **41**(3): 895–918.

Adolph, C. (2013). *Bankers, Bureaucrats, and Central Bank Politics: The Myth of Neutrality*. Cambridge, Cambridge University Press.

Atkinson, K., et al. (2013). "Distinctive Features of Persuasion and Deliberation Dialogues." *Argument and Computation* **4**(2): 105–127.

Austen-Smith, D. and T. J. Feddersen (2006). "Deliberation, Preference Uncertainty, and Voting Rules." *American Political Science Review* **100**(2): 209–218.

Bächtiger, A. et al. (2010). Process Analysis of Political Decisions: Deliberative Standards, Discourse Types and Sequencing. *Yearbook for Action and Decision Theory*. J. Behnke, T. Bräuninger and S. Shikano. Wiesbaden, VS Publishing House for Social Sciences: 193–226.

Bächtiger, A. et al. (2005). "The Deliberative Dimensions of Legislatures." *Acta Politica* **40**: 225–238.

Bächtiger, A., et al. (2010b). "Symposium: Toward More Realistic Models of Deliberative Democracy, Disentangling Diversity in Deliberative Democracy: Competing Theories, Their Blind Spots and Complementarities." *Journal of Political Philosophy* **18**(1): 32–63.

Bächtiger, A. (2018). A Preface to Studying Deliberation Empirically. *The Oxford Handbook of Deliberative Democracy*. A. Bächtiger, J. S. Dryzek, J. Mansbridge and M. E. Warren. Oxford, Oxford University Press: 657–662.

Bächtiger, A. and D. Hangartner (2010a). "When Deliberative Theory Meets Empirical Political Science: Theoretical and Methodological Challenges in Political Deliberation." *Political Studies* **58**: 609–629.

Bächtiger, A. and J. Parkinson (2019). *Mapping and Measuring Deliberation: Towards a New Deliberative Quality*. Oxford, Oxford University Press.

Baerg, N. R. (2020). *Crafting Consensus: Why Central Bankers Change their Speech and How Speech Changes the Economy*. Oxford, Oxford University Press.

Barabas, J. (2004). "How Deliberation Affects Policy Opinions." *American Political Science Review* **98**(4): 687–701.

Barclay, S. (2013). Are Parliament's Select Committees Working?—I Say No. *Spectator Coffeehouse Blog*

Bates, S., et al. (2017). "Do UK MPs Engage More with Select Committees Since the Wright Reforms? An Interrupted Time Series Analysis, 1979–2016." *Parliamentary Affairs* **70**: 780–800.

Bawn, K. (1995). "Political Control versus Expertise: Congressional Choices about Administrative Procedures." *American Political Science Review* **89**(1): 62–73.

Bennister, M. and P. Larkin (2018). Accountability in Parliament. *Exploring Parliament*. C. Leston-Bandeira and L. Thompson. Oxford, Oxford University Press: 143–151.

Benton, M. and M. Russell (2013). "Assessing the Impact of Parliamentary Oversight Committees: The Select Committees in the British House of Commons." *Parliamentary Affairs* **66**: 772–797.

Bernanke, B. S. (2007). *Federal Reserve Communications*. Cato Institute 25th Annual Monetary Conference, Washington, D.C.

Bernhard, W. T. (1998). "A Political Explanation of Variations in Central Bank Independence." *American Political Science Review* **92**(2): 311–328.

Bessette, J. M. (1994). *The Mild Voice of Reason: Deliberative Democracy and American National Government*. Chicago, University of Chicago Press.

Blinder, A. (1998). *Central Banking in Theory and Practice*. Cambridge, MA, MIT Press.

Borg, J. (2013). *Persuasion: The Art of Influencing People*. London, Pearson.

Borowiak, C. T. (2011). *Accountability and Democracy: The Pitfalls and Promise of Popular Control*. Oxford, Oxford University Press.

Bovens, M. (2010). "Two Concepts of Accountability: Accountability as a Virtue and as a Mechanism." *West European Politics* **33**(5): 946–967.

Bovens, M., et al. (2014). Public Accountability. *Oxford Handbook of Public Accountability*. M. Bovens, R. E. Goodin and T. Schillemans. Oxford, Oxford University Press. https://www.oxfordhandbooks.com/view/10.1093/oxfordhb/9780199641253.001.0001 /oxfordhb-9780199641253-e-012.

Bovens, M. and T. Schillemans (2014). Meaningful Accountability. *Oxford Handbook of Public Accountability*. M. Bovens, R. E. Goodin and T. Schillemans. Oxford, Oxford University Press. https://www.oxfordhandbooks.com/view/10.1093/oxfordhb /9780199641253.001.0001/oxfordhb-9780199641253-e-038: 1–11.

Brandsma, G. J. (2014). Quantitative Analysis. *Oxford Handbook of Public Accountability*. M. Bovens, R. E. Goodin and T. Schillemans. https://www.oxfordhandbooks.com/view /10.1093/oxfordhb/9780199641253.001.0001/oxfordhb-9780199641253-e-041, Oxford University Press: 1–26.

Brandsma, G. J. and T. Schillemans (2012). "The Accountability Cube: Measuring Accountability." *Journal of Public Administration Research and Theory* (https://www.researchgate.net/publication/274999940_The_Accountability_Cube_ Measuring_Accountability) **23**(4): 953–975.

Burke, E. (1774 (1906)). Speech to the Electors of Bristol. *The Works of the Right Honorable Edmund Burke*, vol. II. New York, Oxford University Press.

Burke, E. (1996). Mr Edmund Burke's Speech to Bristol Voters, November 3, 1774. *The Writings and Speeches of Edmund Burke, Vol. III Party, Parliament, and the American War 1774–1780*. W. M. Elofson and J. A. Woods. Oxford, Clarendon Press: 64–70.

Busuioc, E. M. and M. Lodge (2016). "The Reputational Basis of Public Accountability." *Governance: An International Journal of Policy, Administration, and Institutions* **29**(2): 247–263.

Chappell, H. W., et al. (2005). *Committee Decisions on Monetary Policy: Evidence from Historical Records of the Federal Open Market Committee*. Cambridge, MA, MIT Press.

Chappell, H. W. et al. (2012). "Deliberation and Learning in Monetary Policy Committees." *Economic Inquiry* **50** (July): 839–847.

Cialdini, R. B. (2007). *Influence: The Psychology of Persuasion*. New York, HarperCollins Publishers.

Colvin, S. (2019). *How to Survive a Select Committee*. London, Biteback Publishing Ltd.

Cox, G. and M. McCubbins (1993). *Legislative Leviathan: Party Government in the House*. Berkeley, University of California Press.

Crewe, E. (2005). *Lords of Parliament*. Manchester, Manchester University Press.

Crowley, J. E. et al. (2008). "Understanding "Power Talk": Language, Public Policy, and Democracy." *Perspectives on Politics* **6**(1): 71–88.

Cukierman, A. (1992). *Central Bank Strategy, Credibility, and Independence*. Cambridge, MIT Press.

D'Arcy, M. (2018). Media Scrutiny of Parliament. *Exploring Parliament*. C. Leston-Bandeira and L. Thompson. Oxford, Oxford University Press: 207–217.

Davison, J. (2014). Visual Accountability. *Oxford Handbook of Public Accountability*. M. Bovens, R. E. Goodin and T. Schillemans. Oxford, Oxford University Press. https://www.oxfordhandbooks.com/view/10.1093/oxfordhb/9780199641253.001.0001/oxfordhb-9780199641253-e-044: **1–17 (accessed 11 Dec 2019)**.

Diekmann, A. (2004). "The Power of Reciprocity: Fairness, Reciprocity, and Stakes in Variants of the Dictator Game." *Journal of Conflict Resolution* **48**(4): 487–505.

Dubnick, M. J. (2014). Accountability as a Cultural Keyword. *Oxford Handbook of Public Accountability*. M. Bovens, R. E. Goodin and T. Schillemans. Oxford, Oxford University Press. https://www.oxfordhandbooks.com/view/10.1093/oxfordhb/9780199641253.001.0001/oxfordhb-9780199641253-e-017: 1–20.

Edelman (2019). Edelman Trust Barometer: Annual Global Study (https://www.edelman.com/sites/g/files/aatuss191/files/2019-02/2019_Edelman_Trust_Barometer_Executive_Summary.pdf).

Elster, J. (1998). *Deliberative Democracy*. Cambridge, Cambridge University Press.

Esterling, K., et al. (2015). "How Much Disagreement is Good for Democratic Deliberation?" *Political Communication* **32**: 529–551.

Evans, P. (2019). "Conclusion: So, What Is Good Scrutiny Good For?" *Parliamentary Affairs* **72**: 987–995.

Farrington, C. (2012). "Does It Matter If the House of Lords isn't Reformed? Perspectives from a Symposium at Trinity Hall, Cambridge." *Political Quarterly* **83**(3): 599–608.

Feinstein, B. D. (2014). Congressional Control of Administrative Agencies. Harvard Law School Working Paper, http://dx.doi.org/10.2139/ssrn.2304497.

Fenno, R. (1973). *Congressmen in Committees*. Boston, Little, Brown and Company.

Fernández-Albertos, J. (2015). "The Politics of Central Bank Independence." *Annual Review of Political Science* **18**: 217–237.

Fishkin, J. S. and P. Laslett, eds. (2003). *Debating Deliberative Democracy*. Oxford, Blackwell Publishing.

Fraccaroli, N., et al. (2020). Central Banks in Parliaments: A Text Analysis of the Parliamentary Hearings of the Bank of England, the European Central Bank and the Federal Reserve (No 2442, Working Paper Series), European Central Bank.

Gardner, J. and J. T. Woolley (2016). "Measuring Deliberative Conditions: An Analysis of Participant Freedom and Equality in Federal Open Market Committee Deliberation". *Political Research Quarterly* **69**(3): 594–605.

Geddes, M. (2020). *Dramas at Westminster: Select Committees and the Quest for Accountability*. Manchester, Manchester University Press.

Goldstein, J. (1993). *Ideas, Interests, and American Trade Policy*. Ithaca, Cornell University Press.

Goldstein, J. and R. O. Keohane, eds. (1993). *Ideas and Foreign Policy: Beliefs, Institutions, and Political Change*. Ithaca, Cornell University Press.

Goodin, R. (2008). *Innovating Democracy*. Oxford, Oxford University Press.

Goodin, R. E. (2000). "Democratic Deliberation Within." *Philosophy and Public Affairs* **29**(1): 81–109.

Goodin, R. E. (2018). If Deliberation is Everything, Maybe It's Nothing. *The Oxford Handbook of Deliberative Democracy*. A. Bächtiger, J. S. Dryzek, J. Mansbridge and M. E. Warren. Oxford, Oxford University Press: 883–899.

Gordon, R. and A. Street (2012). *Select Committees and Coercive Powers*. London, The Constitution Society.

Gutmann, A. and D. Thompson (2004). *Why Deliberative Democracy?* Princeton, Princeton University Press.

Habermas, J. (1996). *Between Facts and Norms: Contributions to a Discourse Theory of Law and Democracy*. Cambridge, MA, MIT Press.

Hill, R. L. (1929). *Toryism and the People, 1832–1846*. London, Constable and Co., Ltd.

Hinich, M. J. and M. C. Munger (1997). *Analytical Politics*. Cambridge, Cambridge University Press.

Högenauer, A.-L. and D. Howarth (2019). "The Parliamentary Scrutiny of Euro Area National Central Banks." *Public Administration* **97**: 576–589.

Huber, J. D. and C. R. Shipan (2000). "The Costs of Control: Legislators, Agencies, and Transaction Costs." *Legislative Studies Quarterly* **25**(1): 25–52.

Huber, J. D. and C. R. Shipan (2002). *Deliberate Discretion? The Institutional Foundations of Bureaucratic Autonomy*. Cambridge, Cambridge University Press.

Jacobs, L. and D. King (2016). *Fed Power: How Finance Wins*. Oxford, Oxford University Press.

Johnson, J. et al. (2019). "Adding Rooms onto a House We Love: Central Banking After the Global Financial Crisis." *Public Administration* 97: 546–560.

Karpowitz, C. F. and T. Mendelberg (2018). The Political Psychology of Deliberation. *The Oxford Handbook of Deliberative Democracy*. A. Bächtiger, J. S. Dryzek, J. Mansbridge and M. E. Warren. Oxford, Oxford University Press: 535–555.

Kelso, A. (2012). Development and Reform in the UK House of Commons Departmental Select Committee System: The Leadership Role of Chairs and the Impact of Government/Opposition Status. *ECPR Standing Group on Parliaments General Conference*. Dublin: 51.

Kelso, A. (2018). Select Committees. *Exploring Parliament*. C. Leston-Bandeira and L. Thompson. Oxford, Oxford University Press: 163–173.

Kohn, D. (2016). Monetary Policy and Financial Stability (Speech Given at Tsinghua University, Beijing), Bank of England (https://www.bankofengland.co.uk/speech/2016/monetary-policy-and-financial-stability).

Krehbiel, K. (1991). *Information and Legislative Organization*. Ann Arbor, University of Michigan.

Kreiczer-Levy, S. (2012). "Deliberative Accountability Rules in Inheritance Law: Promoting Accountable Estate Planning." *University of Michigan Journal of Law Reform* 45(4): 937–964.

Kubala, M. (2011). "Select Committees in the House of Commons and the Media." *Parliamentary Affairs (Hansard Society)* 64(4): 694–713.

Kydland, F. E. and E. C. Prescott (1977). "Rules Rather Than Discretion: The Inconsistency of Optimal Plans." *Journal of Political Economy* 85(3): 473–492.

Lascher, E. L. (1996). "Assessing Legislative Deliberation: A Preface to Empirical Analysis." *Legislative Studies Quarterly* 21(4): 501–519.

Lisi, G. (2020). Essays on Central Bank Transparency, Accountability and Reputation. Department of Government. London, London School of Economics and Political Science. **PhD**.

MacCormack, G. (1976). "Reciprocity." *Man (New Series)* 11(1): 89–103.

Mackie, G. (2006). "Does Democratic Deliberation Change Minds?" *Politics, Philosophy and Economics* 5(3): 279–303.

Mahmoodi, A., et al.(2018). "Reciprocity of Social Influence." *Nature Communications* 9(1): doi: 10.1038/s41467-41018-04925-y.

Mansbridge, J. (2009). "A 'Selection Model' of Political Representation." *Journal of Political Philosophy* 17(4): 369–398.

Mansbridge, J., et al. (2012). A Systemic Approach to Deliberative Democracy. *Deliberative Systems*. J. Parkinson and J. Mansbridge. Cambridge, Cambridge University Press: 1–26.

Mayhew, D. R. (1974). *Congress, The Electoral Connection*. New Haven, Yale University Press.

McGrath, R. J. (2013). "Congressional Oversight Hearings and Policy Control." *Legislative Studies Quarterly* 38(3): 349–376.

McPhilemy, S. and M. Moschella (2019). "Central Banks Under Stress: Reputation, Accountability and Regulatory Coherences." *Public Administration* **97**: 489–498.

Mellows-Facer, A., et al. (2019). "Select Committees: Agents of Change." *Parliamentary Affairs* **72**: 903–922.

Mendelberg, T. (2002). The Deliberative Citizen: Theory and Evidence. *Political Decision Making, Deliberation and Participation, vol. 6.* M. X. D. Carpini, L. Huddy and R. Y. Shapiro. Greenwhich, CT, JAI Press: 151–193.

Miller, G. J. and A. B. Whitford (2016). *Above Politics: Bureaucratic Discretion and Credible Commitment.* New York, Cambridge University Press.

Montanaro, L. (2019). "Discursive Exit." *American Journal of Political Science* **63**(4): 875–887.

Morley, J. (1911). *The Life of William Ewart Gladstone, vol. 1.* London, Macmillan and Co., Ltd.

Morrell, M. E. (2018). Listening and Deliberation. *The Oxford Handbook of Deliberative Democracy.* A. Bächtiger, J. S. Dryzek, J. Mansbridge and M. E. Warren. Oxford, Oxford University Press: 237–250.

Moschella, M. and N. M. Diodati (2020). "Does Politics Drive Conflict in Central Banks' Committees? Lifting the Veil on the European Central Bank Consensus." *European Union Politics* **21**(2): 183–203.

Moschella, M. and L. Pinto (2018). "Central Banks' Communication as Reputation Management: How the Fed Talks Under Uncertainty." *Public Administration* https://doi.org/10.1111/padm.12543.

Mucciaroni, G. and P. J. Quirk (2006). *Deliberative Choices: Debating Public Policy in Congress.* Chicago, University of Chicago Press.

Mulgan, R. (2000). "'Accountability': An Ever-Expanding Concept?" *Public Administration* **78**(3): 555–573.

Mutz, D. C. (2008). "Is Deliberative Democracy a Falsifiable Theory?" *Annual Review of Political Science* **11**: 521–538.

n.a. (2018). Parliamentary Monitor 2018 (https://www.instituteforgovernment.org.uk/publication/parliamentary-monitor-2018/select-committees). London, Institute for Government.

Norton, P. (2013). *Parliament in British Politics, 2nd ed.* Basingstoke, Palgrave Macmillan.

OECD (2013). Trust in government, policy effectiveness and the governance agenda. *Government at a Glance 2013* (https://doi.org/10.1787/gov_glance-2013-en). Paris, OECD Publishing.

Olsen, J. P. (2017). *Democratic Accountability, Political Order, and Change.* Oxford, Oxford University Press.

Ostrom, E. and J. Walker, eds (2005). *Trust and Reciprocity: Interdisciplinary Lessons from Experimental Research.* New York, Russell Sage.

Owen, D. and G. Smith (2015). "Survey Article: Deliberation, Democracy, and the Systemic Turn." *Journal of Political Philosophy* **23**(2): 213–234.

Page, B. I. (1996). *Who Deliberates? Mass Media in Modern Democracy.* Chicago, Chicago University Press.

Parkinson, J. (2006). *Deliberating in the Real World*. Oxford, Oxford University Press.

Parkinson, J. (2007). "The House of Lords: A Deliberative Democratic Defence." *The Political Quarterly* **78**(3): 374–381.

Parliament, H. o. C. (2013). Revisiting Rebuilding the House: The Impact of the Wright Reforms, Third Report of Session 2013–14 (Political and Constitutional Reform Committee). London, The Stational Office Ltd. **1**.

Patil, S. V., et al. (2014). Process Versus Outcome Accountability. *Oxford Handbook of Public Accountability*. M. Bovens, R. E. Goodin and T. Schillemans. Oxford, Oxford University Press. https://www.oxfordhandbooks.com/view/10.1093/oxfordhb/9780199641253.001.0001/oxfordhb-9780199641253-e-002: **1–25 (accessed 11 Dec 2019)**.

Pedrini, S., et al. (2013). "Deliberative Inclusion of Minorities: Patterns of Reciprocity Among Linguistic Groups in Switzerland." *European Political Science Review* **5**(3): 483–512.

Pettit, P. (2003). Deliberative Democracy, the Discursive Dilemma, and Republican Theory. *Debating Deliberative Democracy*. J. S. Fishkin and P. Laslett. Oxford, Blackwell Publishing: 138–159.

Proksch, S.-O. and J. B. Slapin (2014). *The Politics of Parliamentary Debate: Parties, Rebels and Representation*. Cambridge, Cambridge University Press.

Quirk, P. J. (2005). Deliberation and Decision Making. *The Legislative Branch*. P. J. Quirk and S. A. Binder. Oxford and New York, Oxford University Press: 314–348.

Quirk, P. J., et al. (2018). Institutional Deliberation. *The Oxford Handbook of Deliberative Democracy*. A. Bächtiger, J. S. Dryzek, J. Mansbridge and M. E. Warren. Oxford, Oxford University Press: 273–299.

Reardon, K. K. (1991). *Persuasion in Practice*. London, Sage Publications.

Rinne, J. M. (2016). "How Not to Talk Past Each Other: The Convergence of Political Representation and Deliberation." *Representation* **52**(1): 29–41.

Russell, M. (2013). *The Contemporary House of Lords: Westminster Bicameralism Revived*. Oxford, Oxford University Press.

Russell, M. and M. Benton (2011). Selective Influence: The Policy Impact of House of Commons Select Committees. London, The Constitution Unit, University College London: 103 pages.

Russell, M. and M. Sciara (2009). "Independent Parliamentarians En Masse: The Changing Nature and Role of the 'Crossbenchers' in the House of Lords." *Parliamentary Affairs* **62**(1): 32–52.

Schonhardt-Bailey, C. (2001). The Strategic Use of Ideas: Nationalizing the Interest in the Nineteenth Century. *International Trade and Political Institutions: Instituting Trade in the Long Nineteenth Century*. F. McGillivray, I. McLean, R. Pahre and C. Schonhardt-Bailey. Cheltenham, UK, Edward Elgar Publishing Ltd: 146–197.

Schonhardt-Bailey, C. (2006). *From the Corn Laws to Free Trade: Interests, Ideas and Institutions in Historical Perspective*. Cambridge, MA, MIT Press.

Schonhardt-Bailey, C. (2013). *Deliberating American Monetary Policy: A Textual Analysis*. Cambridge, MA,, MIT Press.

Schonhardt-Bailey, C., et al. (2021). 'The Accountability Gap: Deliberation on Monetary Policy in Britain and American During the Financial Crisis,' London School of Economics and Political Science Working Paper.

Shephard, M. and J. S. Caird (2018). The Role of a Backbench MP. *Exploring Parliament*. C. Leston-Bandeira and L. Thompson. Oxford, Oxford University Press: 187–195.

Shepsle, K. A. and M. S. Bonchek (1997). *Analyzing Politics: Rationality, Behavior, and Institutions*. New York, W.W. Norton & Co.

Slothuus, R. and C. H. d. Vreese (2010). "Political Parties, Motivated Reasoning, and Issue Framing Effects." *Journal of Politics* **72**(3): 630–645.

Staszewski, G. (2009). "Reason-Giving and Accountability." *Minnesota Law Review* **93**(4): 1253–1326.

Steiner, J., et al. (2004). *Deliberative Politics in Action: Analysing Parliamentary Discourse*. Cambridge, Cambridge University Press.

Stewart, P. A., et al. (2019). "Visual Priming and Framing of the 2016 GOP and Democratic Party Presidential Primary Debates." *Politics and the Life Sciences* **38**(1): 14–31.

Strøm, K., et al., eds (2003). *Delegation and Accountability in Parliamentary Democracies*. Oxford, Oxford University Press.

Tanasoca, A. and J. Sass (2019). "Ritual Deliberation." *Journal of Political Philosophy* **27**(2): 139–165.

Thompson, D. F. (2008). "Deliberative Democratic Theory and Empirical Political Science." *Annual Review of Political Science* **11**: 497–520.

Tucker, P. (2018). *Unelected Power: The Quest for Legitimacy in Central Banking and the Regulatory State*. Princeton, Princeton University Press.

Tyrie, A. (2015). *The Poodle Bites Back: Select Committee and the Revival of Parliament*. Surrey, Centre for Policy Studies.

UK-Parliament (2011). Select Committees in the House of Commons (http://www.parliament.uk/about/podcasts/theworkofparliament/select-committees-in-the-house-of-commons/).

Uslaner, E. M. (1999). *The Movers and the Shirkers: Representatives and Ideologues in the Senate*. Ann Arbor, University of Michigan Press.

Vibert, F. (2014). The Need for a Systemic Approach. *Oxford Handbook of Public Accountability*. M. Bovens, R. E. Goodin and T. Schillemans. Oxford, Oxford University Press: 10.1093/oxfordhb/9780199641253.9780199641013.9780199640001: 1–6.

Wahlke, J.C., et.al., eds. (1962). *The Legislative System*. New York, John Wiley.

Walter, R. (2017). "Rhetoric or Deliberation? The Case for Rhetorical Political Analysis." *Political Studies* **65**(2): 300–315.

Weale, A., et al. (2012). "Debating Abortion, Deliberative Reciprocity and Parliamentary Advocacy." *Political Studies* **60**: 643–667.

Wright, T. (2015). The Politics of Accountability. *The Cambridge Companion to Public Law*. M. Ellio and D. Feldman. Cambridge, Cambridge University Press: 96–115.

2

Deliberation as Words, Arguments, and Themes

2.1 Introduction

One objective of this work is to examine the content and mood of hearings in committees of the UK Parliament in order to understand whether there are systematic differences depending on the area of public policy (specifically whether it is pursued by an operationally independent agency or not), and the different chambers of Parliament. At issue here is the quality of deliberative accountability for the decisions made by policymakers, and to what extent this relates to attributes of the hearings (respect, partisanship, reciprocity) or the policymaking process itself (in fiscal policy, monetary policy, and financial stability).

In this chapter, I focus on the content of hearings by analysing systematically the words and arguments of parliamentarians, central bankers, and Treasury ministers as they deliberate on monetary policy, financial stability, and fiscal policy. Comparisons in the quality of deliberative accountability during legislative hearings are made between (1) parliamentary chambers (Commons versus Lords), and (2) type of economic policy (monetary policy, financial stability, and fiscal policy).

In Chapter 1, I set out three metrics for gauging deliberation, namely, evidence of respectful exchanges between questioners and witnesses, limited recourse to partisan/electoral point-scoring, and a clear indication that dialogue is reciprocal. As the methodological approach of this chapter is to study the verbatim content of the hearings, the metrics of concern here are measures of reciprocity and partisanship. The respect metric is not addressed directly in this chapter for the simple reason that parliamentarians and policymakers are likely to *appear* to be respectful of one another on these occasions. Hearings in parliamentary committees are conducted formally and according to rules of protocol, and thus it is unlikely that the content of these hearings would exhibit overt disrespect. Instead, such disrespect (should it exist) is more likely

Deliberative Accountability in Parliamentary Committees. Cheryl Schonhardt-Bailey, Oxford University Press.
© Cheryl Schonhardt-Bailey (2022). DOI: 10.1093/oso/9780192847874.003.0002

to be more evident in less conspicuous ways—like smiling, smirking, use of posture, tone of voice, and so on—and is also likely to be discerned more subjectively by others, particularly based upon multiple appearances before these committees. Hence, the 'respect' metric is examined in Chapter 3 within a framework of nonverbal communication, and in the context of the interpretations of the participants themselves, as conveyed in interviews with these participants (Chapter 4).

To recap, evidence of reciprocal dialogue would be that participants engage with one another on key themes, that participants on both sides of the table listen to each other, and that they talk *to* rather than *past* one another. Broadly speaking, quality in deliberative accountability would mean that committee members ask policy-relevant questions, and witnesses provide answers to these same questions (that is, their responses are not diversionary). Underpinning this is the notion that in legislative hearings, individuals talk in conceptually coherent ways ('conceptual clouds') which others may share (by agreeing, disagreeing, or pursuing in some way). This implies, therefore, that any empirical investigation of text emanating from such hearings should be able to capture these shared concepts, or themes—and should, moreover, also be able to gauge the extent to which individual members participate in these shared themes.[1] *In short, the empirical task is not simply one of capturing text as a form of notice-posting, but rather as a reciprocal and shared form of communication.* The greater the reciprocity, the stronger the evidence that explanations for decisions taken are being conveyed to legislators, and as a result, the better able these legislators are to hold policymakers to account.

A second metric for deliberative accountability is that the exchanges between committee members and witnesses should relate to policy processes and outcomes, rather than exhibit overt partisanship or political point-scoring. The partisan metric is, however, subject to the extent to which a given policy is conspicuous in its redistributive implications, and the extent to which these implications have bearing on broader ideological frameworks. Inasmuch as the redistributive implications of fiscal policy and its inherent ideological underpinnings are quite prominent, it is reasonable to anticipate that fiscal policy will exhibit more partisanship than monetary policy or financial stability, despite the fact that select committees strive to be nonpartisan. As a result, arguably deliberative accountability may be found to be of lower quality in fiscal policy hearings. And yet, inasmuch as fiscal policy is decided by elected representatives (in contrast to monetary policy and financial stability, which are both delegated to unelected experts), these politicians may also be replaced at elections (again, in contrast to unelected central bankers, who are appointed for specific terms). Thus, even though fiscal policy may be compromised in terms of deliberative accountability, the parallel facility for political accountability (elections), may potentially compensate for this shortfall.

This chapter uses quantitative text analysis to gauge deliberative accountability in select committees in both the House of Commons and House of Lords, focusing on the Treasury Select Committee and the Economic Affairs Committee. The verbatim transcripts for all the hearings on monetary policy, financial stability, and fiscal policy during the 2010–15 Conservative-Liberal Democrat Coalition Government are analysed.

As the details from this analysis are extensive, some readers may find a 'pre-summary' helpful. To that end, the findings of the quantitative text analysis reveal that deliberative accountability is of highest quality (that is, focused and relevant questions and responses, and little or no partisanship) in monetary policy hearings and of lowest quality in fiscal policy hearings, with financial stability hearings falling somewhere in between. However, because fiscal policy is also subject to political accountability, it is reasonable to discount the relatively poorer level of deliberative reciprocity between parliamentarians and Treasury ministers. Yet, for monetary policy and financial stability, where policymakers are independent and not directly subject to political accountability, it is reasonable to set the threshold higher for quality in deliberative accountability, since this is the only formal setting for accountability. We find that monetary policy does indeed appear to achieve a higher quality, but less so for financial stability. Reciprocity in financial stability hearings appears to be compromised both by deficiencies in technical expertise by parliamentarians, and the parallel lure of financial scandals, for which political and media awareness offers greater rewards to politicians.

Across parliamentary chambers, we find that in monetary policy, MPs tend to be more adept than peers at juggling multiple themes. From a different perspective, this same finding might also be interpreted that peers are better able to focus in depth on a specific theme. In either case, both committees exhibit clear evidence of deliberative reciprocity in monetary policy hearings, although arguably this is greater in the Commons.

2.2 Methodological Approach

Quantitative text analysis has grown rapidly both in its usage by political scientists and in the plethora of applications and software. Surveys, overviews, and critical analyses of quantitative text analysis are not difficult to find (for example, (Grimmer and Stewart, 2013, Illia, Sonpar et al., 2014, Slapin and

Proksch, 2014, Bholat, Hansen et al., 2015, Lemercier and Zalc, 2019, Benoit, 2020).[2] For the purposes of this work, the discourse of both legislators and policymakers in committee hearings is seen as a form of deliberation, leading (potentially) to persuasion. Whereas others have sought to scale policy positions of political parties along an ideological continuum (Laver, Benoit et al., 2003, Slapin and Proksch, 2008) or perhaps have envisaged the purpose of legislative speech first and foremost as a partisan act, which sets out a policy position and communicates this to constituents (Proksch and Slapin, 2014), the approach taken here aims to capture deliberative discourse within its contextual setting.

I adopt a 'thematic' approach which assumes that speakers of textual data convey meaning in a distinctly thematic fashion, so that it is not just the words that help to classify content but also the context in which the words appear. Elsewhere this approach is referred to as keyword-in-context, or KWIC (Illia, Sonpar et al., 2014)). Applications of thematic approaches may be found across the social sciences, including political science (Weale, Bicquelet et al., 2012, Klüver and Mahoney, 2015, Klüver, Mahoney et al., 2015, Anstead, 2018). Thematic approaches to textual data are particularly effective in settings in which the form of argumentation or deliberation is of interest, as it allows one to capture the sequencing, reciprocal and interactive nature of the argumentative structure. In the pre-processing stage, words are reduced to their lemmas and aspects of the text such as punctuation are retained to identify how words appear together in a section of text. Software using this approach employs co-occurrence analysis to examine the bivariate associations between words and phrases in order to map out concept clouds (specifically, the existence of words and phrases that tend to co-occur), and the relationships between concept clouds within a single corpus. A common feature of these approaches is to cluster textual units according to their semantic similarity. Such classifications are normally achieved by finding a partition of classes that maximizes variation in the vocabulary across the different groupings. The interpretation of the clusters obtained proceeds by analysing the occurrences of terms in any given class. Besides this, thematic approaches also rely upon multiple spatial representations of the associations (correspondence analysis, dendrograms [or distance trees]) to capture relationships between themes in the corpus and independent variables which identify unique characteristics of the authors of the text (names, party affiliation, role, and so on) and the setting (speech, hearing, date, place).

As recent analytical critiques and overviews of quantitative text analysis will attest, there is no single all-purpose approach to analysing textual data

(Grimmer, Roberts et al., 2018, Lemercier and Zalc, 2019, Benoit, 2020). The position taken here is that a thematic approach is, prima facie, the preferred methodology for a study of deliberation. A thematic approach allows the researcher to capture and measure the sequencing of arguments and moreover how others respond to the arguments made. Because deliberation requires reasoned argument, any approach that fails to capture how arguments develop and the extent to which others respond (or not) to a form of argumentation, is inherently missing the key component of deliberation. Moreover, a thematic approach is particularly useful in settings where the corpus under investigation exhibits an internal cohesion—such as a focus on monetary policy—and where the investigation is concerned not simply with whether or not speakers talk about, say, the central bank or monetary policy but how they relate that to other parts of the world. For instance, 'monetary policy' could be used in a sentence or paragraph that is mostly comprised of pleasantries but linking monetary policy to a word like 'risk' could indicate that the speaker is talking about how he or she is thinking about the risk around central bank policies. And, moreover, knowing that this occurs in the context of, say, managing risk in terms of inflation expectations as opposed to risk in terms of risk to the solvency of commercial banks matters a great deal to interpreting the reasons offered by central bank officials for their policy decisions. Hence, the methodology adopted here allows us to capture the context and meaning of themes in a deliberative context. Here the assumption is that speakers convey meaning in a more thematic fashion, and so it is not just the words that help to classify content, but also the *context* in which the words appear.

This is not to say, however, that an alternative approach like topic modelling (Blei and Lafferty, 2006, Blei and Lafferty, 2009, Grimmer, 2010, Quinn, Monroe et al., 2010, Grimmer, Roberts et al., 2018) is inappropriate for studying deliberation, and indeed more recent applications of word embeddings hold much promise for future explorations of deliberative text (Bronner, 2018, Benoit, 2020, Chatsiou and Mikhaylov, 2020). Topic models enable one to capture the underlying content of the deliberation, which can be of fundamental importance. Knowing the content of the deliberation is a precursor to understanding how the arguments implicit within that content develop as a sequence over time and how others respond to the reasons given in these arguments. Elsewhere (Sanders, Lisi et al., 2018) I explore the same UK data from this chapter using *both* thematic and a Structural Topic Model (STM) (Roberts, Stewart et al., 2014), in order to lend new insights into the understanding of the content of the discourse and how that content varies over a set of covariates. Importantly, the findings from *both* approaches are consistent, with the thematic approach offering a visualization of the reciprocity aspect of deliberation, and the STM approach offering further precision in the partisan metric, by providing point estimates for topic proportions across different topics.

Simply put, a key task in examining the hearings is to ascertain the extent to which witnesses are effectively held to account. Do they answer the questions asked? Is the dialogue reciprocal or diversionary? Are parliamentarians more interested in making partisan jabs than in uncovering and understanding the reasons for decisions made and actions taken?

2.2.1   Alceste

The primary quantitative textual analysis software used here is referred to as 'Alceste', and has been used widely in the social sciences (Yager and Schonhardt-Bailey, 2007, Schonhardt-Bailey, 2008, Weale, Bicquelet et al., 2012, Schonhardt-Bailey, 2013, Illia, Sonpar et al., 2014, Vallès, 2015), in central banking (Bholat, Hansen et al., 2015), and in the field of medical education (Osman, Schonhardt-Bailey et al., 2014, Ostapenko, Schonhardt-Bailey et al., 2018). Alceste is a thematic analysis software, meaning it considers co-occurrences across lexical units (key words) to form stable classes that are representative of the text. The methodology proceeds by identifying a set of 'gauged sentences' (or Elementary Context Units, ECUs), from a preexisting division of the text specified by the user. This constitutes the sampling unit of the analysis. In our case, the sampling unit is represented by single interventions in committee hearings.

Using the occurrence of words in each ECU, Alceste builds the classification using an iterative descending hierarchical classification algorithm which decomposes the classes until a predetermined number of iterations fails to result in further significant divisions (Reinert, 1998). Alceste requires the researcher to apply semantic meaning to a list of characteristic lemmas and Elementary Context Units (ECUs), ordered by their ϕ and χ^2 values. This involves first looking at the list of the most representative words for each semantic class and, second, analysing the ECUs most strongly associated with each class. The labelling process is repeated for each class, until the user has assigned a label to all lists, after which, more complex analyses (that is, dendrograms, correspondence analysis and so on) can begin. Further details of its processes are given in Lahlou, 1995b, Schonhardt-Bailey and Yager, 2012 and Sanders, Lisi et al., 2018.

2.3 Data

The Treasury Select Committee holds regular hearings with MPC members on the Bank of England's Quarterly Inflation Report [3] and with FPC members of the Bank on the Financial Stability Report,[4] and with the chancellor of the Exchequer on the government's budget. In contrast, the hearings of the Economic Affairs Committee are less frequent for both monetary and fiscal policy, and during 2010–15 Conservative-Liberal Democratic Government it held no hearings on the Financial Stability Report.[5] Appendix 1 lists the hearings included for each committee: in total, thirty for the TSC (sixteen on monetary policy, seven on financial stability, and seven on fiscal policy), and seven for the EAC (four for monetary and three for fiscal policy). Appendix 2 provides further details of the committee memberships and partisan affiliations. Because the contingent of MPC members varies across the hearings, Appendix 3 provides a full list of those MPC members who gave oral evidence in each committee hearing (both for the Treasury Select Committee and the Economic Affairs Committee), along with the committee members appearing for each hearing. Key terms in the hearings (such as 'VAT', 'interest rate', and so on) are identified and controlled through the lemmatization process, in order to improve the robustness of the results. Appendix 4 details the specific list of terms that required lemmatization supervision prior to analysis.

The data are structured into five text files, comprised of the above hearings for each committee—that is, each committee's hearings on economic policy are separated into those covering monetary policy, financial stability and fiscal policy. The text files are structured so that each speech or remark constitutes a 'case', and each is identified (or 'tagged') with identifying characteristics—the name of the speaker, his or her party affiliation (including 'crossbenchers' for the Lords and 'no party' for central bank officials and Treasury witnesses), the speaker's role (committee chair, committee member, MPC internal member, MPC external member, chancellor, Treasury staff), and the date of the hearing. All the hearing transcripts are analysed in their entirety.

2.4 Analysis of 2010–15 TSC and EAC Hearings

2.4.1 Identifying the Themes

Tables 2.1 and 2.2 provide summaries of the basic statistics from Alceste for each of the five sets of hearings. The sizes[6] of TSC hearings are considerably

Table 2.1 Basic Statistics for Treasury Select Committee Hearings on Monetary Policy, Financial Stability and Fiscal Policy, 2010–15.

	Monetary Policy	Financial Stability	Fiscal Policy
Total Word Count	275,792	138,466	160,369
(Minimum χ^2 for word selection) Unique Words Analyzed (freq>3)	(20) 103,475	(11.5) 49,040	(10.6) 60,659
Passive Variables (Tagged Indicators)	70	57	51
I.C.U.s (= number of speeches / comments)	4119	2273	2535
Classified E.C.U.s	81% (= 7047)	72% (= 3458)	59% (= 3193)
Stable Classes	5	4	5
Distribution of Classes (%)	**1 (18)** *Bank of England Lending Facilities* **2 (24)** *Real Economy, Productivity & Competitiveness* **3 (33)** *Monetary Policy Decisions & Decision Making Process* **4 (17)** *Inflation Forecast & Outlook for Inflation* **5 (8)** *Forward Guidance & Outlook for Monetary Policy*	**1 (28)** *Bank Capital, Leverage, & Lending Capacity* **2 (26)** *Housing & Household Indebtedness* **3 (26)** *Governance of the Bank of England* **4 (20)** *Barclays and LIBOR*	**1 (30)** *Tax and Benefit* **2 (11)** *Budget Process and Role of Ministers* **3 (34)** *Budget Leaks* **4 (15)** *Economic Effects of Budget* **5 (10)** *Public Deficit and Debt*

larger than the EAC hearings—as we would expect, given the explicit oversight responsibility of the TSC versus the more selective investigative nature of the EAC. A more interesting feature is that for both committees, monetary policy hearings taken together exhibit a larger word count than that in financial stability hearings and fiscal policy hearings. Monetary policy hearings occur relatively frequently, as they are contingent on quarterly reports of the Bank. For financial stability, fewer hearings occurred during this period since they only began in 2012, with the creation of the FPC. Fiscal policy hearings are less frequent, as these hearings with the chancellor are focused on the annual budget.

Table 2.2 Basic Statistics for Lords Economic Affairs Committee Hearings on Monetary and Fiscal Policy, 2010-15.

	Monetary Policy	Fiscal Policy
Total Word Count	59,328	37,248
(Minimum χ^2 for word selection) Unique Words Analyzed (freq>3)	(2.6) 23,357	(2.6) 13,917
Passive Variables (Tagged Indicators)	48	33
I.C.U.s (= number of speeches / comments)	407	282
Classified E.C.U.s	65% (= 1073)	46% (= 483)
Stable Classes	6	4
Distribution of Classes (%)	1 (9) *Pensions, Savings & Annuities* 2 (40) *Real Economy & Economic Forecast* 3 (15) *Financial Stability & Macro Prudential Policy* 4 (17) *Banking & Bank Regulation* 5 (10) *Too Big to Fail & Bank Resolution* 6 (9) *Stress Testing Banks & Bank Lending*	1 (15) *Energy, Energy Prices, Gas & Shale Oil* 2 (38) *Real Economy & Bank Lending* 3 (33) *Financial Services & Regulation* 4 (14) *Scotland & Regions*

The passive variables[7] (or tags) define the characteristics of each speech or 'case', and these include the speaker's name, role, and so on. Each speech within each corpus constitutes a sampling unit and is designated as an Initial Context Unit (ICU) by the software. As a measure of goodness-of-fit, we observe that both the monetary policy and financial stability hearings in the TSC obtain higher classification rates than the equivalent hearings in the EAC. Moreover, in both committees, monetary policy obtains higher classification rates than fiscal policy. Inasmuch as the classification rate is one measure of the internal cohesion of the discourse, there are two explanations for the array of classification rates—one is related to the nature of each policy and the second is an institutional feature. First, in both committees, monetary policy constitutes a more cohesive dialogue than fiscal policy (simply put, monetary policy has a number of core concepts around which discussion can be focused—for example, growth in the economy, labour markets, inflation expectations—whereas the array of potential topics relating to fiscal policy is much broader). It is worth bearing in mind this inherent cohesion when evaluating deliberative accountability—that is, it may be easier for questioners and witnesses to focus on accountability when the conceptual framework surrounding the policy under discussion contains well-established and agreed-upon concepts.

Second, an explanation for the higher classification rates in the TSC relative to the EAC may be that peers have fewer opportunities to pose questions to central bank and Treasury officials, and thus appear to exploit these fewer occasions with a 'stockpile' of topics (for example, for monetary policy, the EAC had no other opportunity to query the new institutional arrangement for prudential regulation [the Prudential Regulation Authority], and for fiscal policy, the committee exploited the opportunity to explore issues of the Scottish Referendum on independence). And, as noted earlier, the division of responsibility between the TSC and EAC—perhaps with the latter more focused on technical and administrative issues—may help to account for what appears to be the more diverse array of topics. Again, with respect to deliberative accountability, it is unclear whether the more cohesive discourse in the TSC or the less-focused, more diverse approach to questioning in the EAC offers a higher quality of deliberative accountability. This is a question that will be explored further in subsequent chapters.

The bottom two rows indicate the number of classes identified and the size of each class (as measured by the percentage of the total ECUs classified within each). While the assigned class labels may seem straightforward, it is important to clarify that these are not automatically given by the software. The output provides the researcher with several different tools for conceptualizing the content of classes. Two of these tools are particularly useful—characteristic words and characteristic ECUs. The most characteristic function words for each class (ranked in order by phi [ϕ] and chi square [χ^2] statistical significance,[8] with the minimum χ^2 of 20, 11.5 and 10.6 for each of the TSC corpora, with one df[9]) provide an indication of the theme or frame of argument that unifies a class. As an example, the top ten characteristics words for Class 1 from the TSC monetary policy hearings are: *lend, small, bank, size, enterprise, sheet, fund, money, reserve,* and *bond.* Furthermore, the top representative phrase (ECU) provides the context surrounding the characteristic words (in bold):

David Miles (MPC External): That was the **order** of 1 **billion pounds.**
The **corporate bond scheme** is still **open** still **functioning** and the credit guarantee scheme **paper** was **guaranteed by** the **government.**(χ^2 = 60; ϕ = 0.02)

The lists of characteristic words and phrases for each class provide an understanding of the thematic content for each class. For this class, the label *Bank of England Lending Facilities* is assigned; the remaining class labels are similarly assigned.[10]

The TSC hearings on monetary policy and financial stability obtain the highest classification rates (81 per cent and 72 per cent, respectively). Thus, we are confident that the five classes for monetary policy (*BoE Lending Facilities, Real Economy, Monetary Policy Decision Making Process, Inflation,* and *Forward Guidance*) and the four classes for financial stability (*Bank Capital and Lending Capacity, Housing and Household Indebtedness, BoE Governance,* and *Barclays/LIBOR*) capture the substance of these hearings reasonably well. The two fiscal policy hearings obtain lower classification rates—59 per cent for the TSC and just 46 per cent for the EAC. While the five classes identified for the TSC (*Tax and Benefit, Budget Process [and the Role of Ministers in this Process], Budget Leaks, Economic Effects of the Budget,* and *Public Deficit and Debt*), and the four for the EAC (*Energy/Energy Prices, Real Economy and Bank Lending, Financial Services and Regulation,* and *Scotland and Regions*) are informative, further analysis is warranted. The software allows one to extract the set of ECUs for each corpus that was not successfully classified in the initial analysis and subject these ECUs to a new analysis. (These residual ECUs then comprise a new corpus, albeit one lacking the original verbatim flow of the original.)

For the TSC fiscal policy hearings, an analysis of the unclassified ECUs (41 per cent of the original corpus) produces three further classes with an 80 per cent classification rate: *Housing and Fiscal Policy, the Economic Outlook for Debt and Deficit,* and *Capital Expenditure/Long-term Spending.* The equivalent analysis of the initially unclassified ECUs for the Lords' fiscal policy hearings obtains a lower classification rate (46 pr cent) and five classes (*Britain and the EU, Financial Stability/Banks, Shale Oil and Gas, Government Debt/Deficit,* and *EU Membership/Currency Unions*). These subsequent classes are less focused in their content, and in some cases (Shale Oil) have some overlapping content with the initial analysis.

One point is clear from this thematic classification: monetary policy hearings exhibit more thematically focused discourse, which is more readily classifiable into discrete themes, whereas fiscal policy hearings (and to a lesser extent, financial stability) tend to be less focused, as the discourse ranges across a more varied set of topics and consequently has less internal coherency.

The themes identified for each of the hearings do confirm some of what the informed observer might have anticipated. For instance, the TSC focuses not only on the core components of monetary policy (real economy, inflation, outlook for monetary policy) but also on the monetary policy decision making process. It is an interesting conjecture whether an informed observer would estimate that in these TSC hearings, about *one-third* of the discourse focuses on the monetary policy decision-making process. Thus, for the TSC, it is not only the outcomes of monetary policy that are held to account, but also substantial consideration is given to the institutional *process* by which the Bank reaches those policy outcomes. The informed observer may also have predicted that the Lords' hearings on monetary policy tend to cover areas not addressed in depth by the TSC (for example, pensions, savings, annuities), but may not have concluded that the EAC also tends to conflate financial stability issues into these hearings. The weights given to each of the thematic classes are revealing in depicting the overall extent of discourse given to the various themes over the course of the 2010–15 Parliament: for instance, the TSC devoted about as much discourse to discussions challenging the Bank of England's governance practices as it did to discussions concerning both bank capital and housing.

We will now delve deeper into the characteristics of individuals speaking to each of these themes.

2.4.2 Partisanship (First Cut)

Tables 2.3 and 2.4 provide a first cut into the role of partisanship affiliations in the hearings on monetary policy, financial stability, and fiscal policy in both the Commons and Lords committees. Using the *Tri-Croisé* or Cross-Data analysis[11] in Alceste, we cross a variable—in this case, party affiliation—with the entire corpus, thereby obtaining statistical associations between that variable and other words and phrases in the text. (Simply put, this holds constant the specified tag or term, allowing all else to vary.) The resulting words and phrases for each value—here, each party affiliation—are given, but as these do not form a particularly distinct set of thematic classes, they are not reported here.

Instead, the percentage weights for each party affiliation are given, thereby allowing insight into differences both across the policy areas and between the Commons and Lords. Notably, the Bank of England's MPC and FPC members are assigned as *no* party affiliation. Similarly, government ministers are assigned their own category in the fiscal policy hearings, although of course former Chancellor George Osborne is Conservative and the former Chief Secretary to the Treasury, Danny Alexander, is Liberal Democrat. While these Treasury witnesses could have been assigned their actual partisan affiliation,

Table 2.3 Partisan Weights of Committee Discourse for Treasury Select Committee. (Conservative N = 6; Labour N = 5)

MONETARY POLICY HEARINGS	FINANCIAL STABILITY HEARINGS	FISCAL POLICY HEARINGS
Conservative (23%)	Conservative (24%)	Conservative (18%)
Labour (10%)	Labour (9%)	Labour (18%)
Liberal Democrat (2%)	Liberal Democrat (2%)	Liberal Democrat (2%)
Scottish National Party (2%)	Scottish National Party (2%)	Scottish National Party (2%)
None (BoE MPC) (63%)	None (BoE FPC) (63%)	(Government Ministers) (60%)

Table 2.4 Partisan Weights of Committee Discourse for Economic Affairs Committee. (Conservative N = 4 [3 in 2012]; Labour N = 4 [5 in 2012])

MONETARY POLICY HEARINGS	FISCAL POLICY HEARINGS
Conservative (16%)	Conservative (28%)
Labour (7%)	Labour (3%)
Liberal Democrat (1%)	Liberal Democrat (2%)
Crossbencher (3%)	Crossbencher (3%)
None (BoE MPC) (73%)	(Government Ministers) (64%)

this would have the effect of overestimating (and thereby distorting) the percentages for Conservative and Liberal Democrat parliamentary committee members.

From Table 2.3 we can see that the TSC hearings exhibit roughly the same proportion of discourse by each party affiliation for both the monetary policy and financial stability hearings. The percentage breakdown is: 23 per cent or 24 percent for Conservatives, 9 per cent or 10 per cent for Labour, 2 per cent each for Liberal Democrat and for Scottish National Party, and 63 per cent for the Bank of England witnesses. For fiscal policy, however, the share of discourse by Labour members increases to 18 per cent while that of Conservative members falls to 18 per cent. Overall, this seems to suggest that although select committees seek to be entirely nonpartisan, there is nonetheless some tendency by Labour committee members to 'have a greater say' when confronting a Conservative chancellor on fiscal policy than when questioning officials from the Bank of England. While it is not self-evident that this increased discourse translates into partisan point-scoring, it does suggest that the TSC is not quite as blind to partisan divides in fiscal policy as it is in monetary policy or financial stability.

Table 2.4 provides a partisan breakdown for the Economic Affairs Committee, with the addition of the crossbenchers and the absence of the SNP. Noting that the balance of Conservative/Labour membership of each committee is quite similar (roughly 6/5 for the TSC and 4/4 for the EAC), it is striking that in the Lords, a considerably larger share of the discourse is given to the Bank's MPC members (73 per cent in the Lords, compared to 63 per cent in the Commons). This suggests that peers allow (perhaps even encourage) MPC members to be more discursive, whereas MPs tend to constrain this. Interestingly, however, peers are not quite so generous when it comes to fiscal policy, where the share of discourse by government ministers (64 per cent) is closer to their share in the TSC hearings (60 per cent). Again, these findings are suggestive rather than definitive on the question of partisanship. The greater allowance given by peers to the Bank's MPC members to respond to the questions (relative to that given by backbench MPs in the TSC) does, however, suggest that peers are more willing to 'listen' to Bank of England officials, which is one factor contributing to better deliberative quality. This greater facility to 'listen' is not, however, as applicable to fiscal policy.

2.4.3 Correspondence Analysis and Partisanship (Second Cut)

The analysis thus far has not considered the spatial relationships between the thematic classes identified in each of the hearings. Our approach facilitates this by cross-tabulating classes and words in their root form in order to create a matrix that can then be subjected to factor correspondence analysis.[12] In this way, we obtain a spatial representation of the relations between the classes. The positions of the points is contingent on correlations rather than coordinates (Reinert, 1998: 45), where distance reflects the degree of co-occurrence.[13] With respect to the axes, correspondence analysis aims to account for a maximum amount of association[14] along the first (horizontal) axis. The second (vertical) axis seeks to account for a maximum of the remaining association, and so on. Hence, the total association is divided into components along principal axes. The resulting map provides a means for transforming numerical information into pictorial form. It provides a framework for the user to formulate her own interpretations, rather than providing clear-cut conclusions.[15]

Figures 2.1 through 2.4 are maps of the correspondence analysis of the classes as well as the tags (name, role, date) for each of the hearings, where distance between a class and a tag (or between two classes) reflects the degree of association. Given its low classification rate, the correspondence graph of the fiscal policy hearings in the EAC is not shown here.

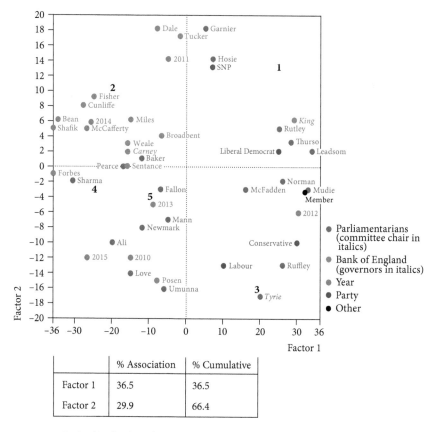

	% Association	% Cumulative
Factor 1	36.5	36.5
Factor 2	29.9	66.4

1 Bank of England Lending Facilities
2 Real Economy, Productivity and Competitiveness
3 Monetary Policy Decisions and Decision Making Process
4 Inflation Forecast and Outlook for Inflation
5 Outlook for Monetary Policy and Forward Guidance

Fig. 2.1 Correspondence Analysis of Treasury Select Committee Hearings on Monetary Policy, 2010–15.

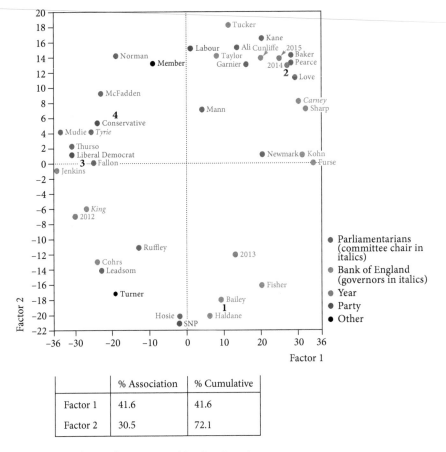

	% Association	% Cumulative
Factor 1	41.6	41.6
Factor 2	30.5	72.1

1 Bank Capital, Leverage, and Lending Capacity
2 Housing and Household Indebtedness
3 Governance of the Bank of England
4 Barclays, and Libor

Fig. 2.2 Correspondence Analysis of Treasury Select Committee Hearings on Financial Stability, 2012–15.

Beneath the correspondence maps are the percentage associations for each factor, along with the cumulative for the two. Hence, in Figure 2.1, a two-dimensional correspondence space accounts for 66.4 per cent of the total variation in the TSC hearings on monetary policy. Variation in the other sets of hearings is similarly captured in a two-dimensional space.[16] Importantly, however, dimensionality in this context requires careful dissection and analysis before a coherent picture may be obtained.

While much could be said about the relationship between thematic classes from these graphs, interpretation will focus predominantly on the question

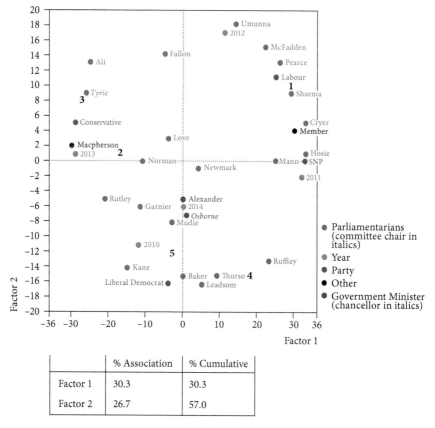

	% Association	% Cumulative
Factor 1	30.3	30.3
Factor 2	26.7	57.0

1 Tax and Benefit
2 Budget Process and Role of Ministers
3 Budget Leaks
4 Economic Effects of Budget
5 Public Deficit and Debt

Fig. 2.3 Correspondence Analysis of Treasury Select Committee Hearings on Fiscal Policy, 2010–15.

of reciprocity. It is one thing to understand reciprocal dialogue as a sharing of conceptual clouds, where parliamentarians and witnesses participate in shared themes. But it is another thing to know what reciprocal might 'look like' in a two-dimensional correspondence graph. Once we establish how a correspondence graph helps to uncover the degree of reciprocal dialogue, we can then ascertain specifically whether committee members and witnesses (elected or unelected) engage in reciprocal dialogue across all the thematic classes.

In a previous quantitative text analysis of US congressional hearings on monetary policy oversight in both the House Financial Services Committee

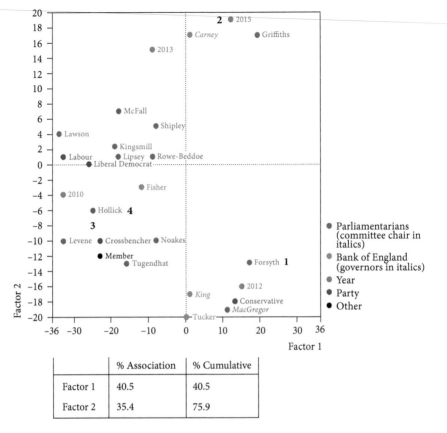

	% Association	% Cumulative
Factor 1	40.5	40.5
Factor 2	35.4	75.9

1 Pensions, Savings and Annuities
2 Real Economy and Economic Forecast
3 Financial Stability and Macroprudential Policy
4 Banking and Bank Regulation
5*Too Big to Fail and Bank Resolution
6*Stress Testing Banks and Bank Lending
   *These classes are not shown on the graph, but are discussed in the text.

Fig. 2.4 Correspondence Analysis of Lords Economic Affairs Committee Hearings on Monetary Policy, 2010–15.

and the Senate Banking Committee, I found a lack of reciprocal dialogue between members of Congress and the Chairman of the Federal Reserve (Schonhardt-Bailey, 2013). Specifically, I found that the discourse of committee members diverged from key fundamentals of monetary policy (for example, real economy, monetary aggregates, inflation), and towards other more politically partisan themes (for example, fiscal policy, US labour market, US competitiveness). Conversely, the discourse of the Chairman of the Federal Reserve focused on the key fundamentals of monetary policy and much less on political partisan themes. In correspondence graphs of congressional hearings on monetary policy from 1976 to 2008, this was depicted in a spatial divide between themes statistically associated with Congress and those associated with the Fed Chairman (Schonhardt-Bailey, 2013, 206–207). That is, members of Congress appeared on one side of the correspondence graph and the Fed Chairman on the other side. Moreover, in another work, where US and UK legislative oversight hearings on monetary policy during the period of the financial crisis (2006–09) were compared, the same 'discourse divide' between Congress and the Federal Reserve was observed, but was entirely absent in the UK setting (Schonhardt-Bailey, Dann et al., 2021).

In the present analysis, we again do not find a discourse divide between legislators and central bankers in the UK select committee hearings. Turning to Figures 2.1 through 2.4, we can evaluate this reciprocity by coding the names of the speakers according to their role (committee member, committee chair, MPC member, and so on).

In Figure 2.1, we observe a close proximity[17] of *both* MPC and TSC members for four of the five classes—namely for *BoE Lending Facilities* (Class 1), *Real Economy* (Class 2), *Inflation Forecast* (Class 4) and *Forward Guidance* (Class 5). The one exception is Class 3—*Monetary Policy Decision Making*—where Chairman Andrew Tyrie is predominantly associated with this theme. Moreover, the close proximity of both the Conservative and Labour party tags to the focal point for this class suggests a cross-party (or nonpartisan) consensus on the importance of challenging the BoE on its institutional decision-making process and governance. In short, except for this class, the TSC's monetary policy hearings exhibit a reciprocal dialogue between legislators and witnesses—that is, for each thematic class, both MPs and MPC members appear in the quadrant in which the class appears. Unlike the finding for US congressional hearings, we do *not* see parliamentarians and central bankers spatially divided into different quadrants of the correspondence graph.

Figure 2.1 also suggests a clustering of themes. That is, the primary horizontal axis (which accounts for 36.5 per cent of the total association) appears to bifurcate two cuts into accountability. In the left quadrants, the real economy, inflation forecast, and forward guidance all pertain to economic policy outcomes, whereas in the right quadrant, the Bank's lending facilities and its decision-making process both capture questions pertaining to the financial market operations of, and institutional organization within the Bank itself. This two-pronged approach to accountability sets the stage for a clash between the TSC chairman, Andrew Tyrie, and Bank of England governor,

Mervyn King. As we will see from the interviews with both these individuals (Chapter 4), Tyrie interpreted the remit of the TSC to include challenging the organization and governance internal to the Bank of England, while Mervyn King maintained that the Bank should be held accountable for its policy decisions, not its internal governance.

Finally, Figure 2.1 illustrates a spatial gap between the two governors—Mervyn King (whose term included years 2010, 2011 and 2012) and Mark Carney (whose term began in mid-2013)—with King nearer to Class 1 and Carney closer to Classes 2, 4 and 5. This aptly captures the timeline of Bank's activities in the wake of the financial crisis—moving from a focus on the Funding for Lending Scheme to an era of low inflation.

In the financial stability hearings (Figure 2.2) we see conspicuously less reciprocity, as measured by parliamentarians and central bankers speaking to the same themes (and as judged by their appearance in the same quadrant of the correspondence graph). Whereas housing/household indebtedness (Class 2) and Bank of England governance (Class 3) exhibit a clustering of both FPC and TSC members around these themes, the discourse on bank capital and lending capacity (Class 1) is predominantly the remit of BoE internal FPC members (Bailey, Haldane and Fisher), and the discourse on the Libor-fixing scandal—involving Barclays, leading to the resignation of its CEO, Bob Diamond—falls in the upper left quadrant (Class 4), in close proximity to Chairman Andrew Tyrie and other TSC members. In short, there appears to be little sharing of discourse for Classes 1 and 4. An interpretation may be that in some areas like bank leverage ratios and lending capacity, the technical expertise of the policymakers exceeds that of TSC members, and so the latter are simply less prepared to engage with the experts on these issues. At the same time, in other areas of intense media interest—a financial scandal leading to the resignation of a high-profile CEO—TSC members exhibit far greater interest and thereby have more to say in committee. Overall, this finding suggests that deliberative reciprocity in financial stability is less than it is in monetary policy. This is likely from parliamentarians' limited technical expertise in financial stability relative to that of FPC members, and the greater scope for financial scandals to emerge and distract from financial stability policymaking. In short, in financial stability, central bankers tended to speak more to their areas of technical expertise whereas MPs gravitated to discussing the politicization of financial scandals.

In Figure 2.2 we again observe a dimensional divide on the horizontal axis between the King and Carney governorships—that is, questions of BoE governance and the Libor scandal fell in the King era (Classes 3 and 4), while by the time Carney became governor, the focus had moved to issues of bank capital ratios and UK housing (Classes 1 and 2).

For fiscal policy (Figure 2.3), a two-dimensional correspondence graph is instructive, but more limited in providing traction on the question of deliberative reciprocity. To begin, the cumulative association captured in a two-dimensional graph is just 57 per cent (compared to 66.4 per cent and 72.1 per cent for monetary policy and financial stability [Figures 2.1 and 2.2]), and thus we are missing the spatial representation of the two higher dimensions. However, in a more substantive vein, the very fact that fiscal policy oversight entails a 'one versus many' scenario (that is, the chancellor or other minister standing alone, or with a Treasury staff official) rather than multiple MPC or FPC members vis-à-vis the parliamentary committee, means that the opportunity for the fiscal policy witnesses to be situated in proximity to multiple classes is impossible. (In other words, each name tag has just one centre point in a correspondence graph; multiple MPC/FPC members allow more name tags to be clustered around multiple thematic classes.) What we see is a positioning of Osborne and Alexander roughly in the centre of the spatial graph, though nearer to the theme of public debt/deficit. In terms of the positions of the party tags, we observe a clear partisan divide across the horizontal dimension, with (a) the Conservatives (led by Chairman Tyrie) focusing on the role of ministers and the leaking of the budget (and here, Permanent Secretary Macpherson is held directly accountable), (b) the Liberal Democrats falling midway between the two major parties, and in close proximity to the public debt/deficit theme, and (c) Labour situated very near the theme of tax/benefit. Whereas partisanship appeared virtually non-existent in the monetary policy hearings, in fiscal policy, the discourse divide between the parties is readily apparent.

For the Lords committee (Figure 2.4),[18] the correspondence graph again suffers a limitation: the close overlap in word co-occurrence between bank resolution and the stress testing of banks (Classes 5 and 6) means that the focal points for these classes could not be statistically confirmed in the correspondence space and therefore are not plotted by the software. Moreover, in practice, deliberative reciprocity is constrained by the committee's tendency to sometimes limit the number of MPC members testifying to just the governor (see Appendix 3). However, even given this constraint, there is evidence of reciprocity for the *Real Economy* (Class 2) with both Governor Carney and Lord Griffiths converging around this theme. Reciprocity is also in evidence for *Financial Stability* and *Banking* (Classes 3 and 4), with Fisher from the

Bank, along with several peers, in proximity. For *Pensions and Savings* (Class 1) King and Tucker from the Bank are joined with Lords Forsyth and MacGregor, who all fall roughly in the same quadrant.

In contrast with monetary policy hearings in the TSC, there appears to be a partisan divide between the Conservatives and Labour. However, this result may be largely driven by (Conservative) Chairman MacGregor's predominant focus on the theme of pensions (Class 1). A final observation for Figure 2.4 is the apparent horizontal dimensional divide between the macroeconomic themes (Classes 1 and 2) and those focused on financial stability (Classes 3 and 4), but with the absence of the focal points for Classes 5 and 6, this is not explored further.

The correspondence graphs help us to visualize the spatial relationships between themes, committee members, and other identifiers. They also help to gauge deliberative reciprocity across the different sets of hearings, and as such, it is apparent that of the three policy areas, monetary policy exhibits the greatest reciprocity in discourse between witnesses from the Bank of England and parliamentarians. This is not to say that deliberative reciprocity exists in every hearing, but rather that across the 2010–15 Parliament, monetary policy hearings tend to exhibit the greatest reciprocal discourse in each of the themes identified. That is, the tendency in monetary policy is for parliamentarians and central bankers to speak to common themes—in other words, to share the same conceptual clouds.

2.4.4 Committee Members: Significance at the Micro Level

Figures 2.5 through 2.9 present the final visualizations of discourse across the five select committee hearings. These figures sum the individual or partisan phi coefficients, as estimated for each of the thematic classes, and display these in bar chart format. Because ϕ is standardized, it is possible to sum the coefficients across the classes, and thereby make comparisons across the sets of hearings. So, for instance, Figure 2.5 groups the internal MPC member on the left, followed by external MPC members, TSC committee members and finally the partisan identifiers. Each bar is colour coded, as indicated by the class legend. Larger ϕ coefficients suggest that a particular individual or party is more statistically significant for a given thematic class, relative to all other classes. Moreover, these graphs provide further ways to measure *reciprocity* in deliberation—that is, if we find that *both* the members of the parliamentary

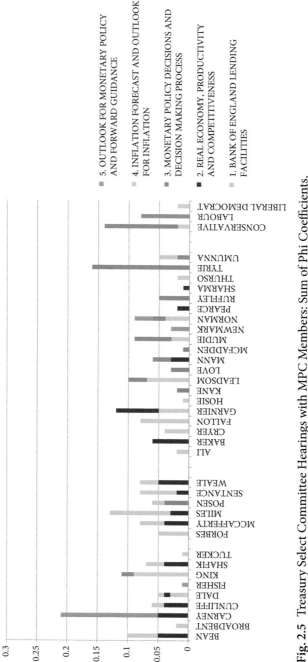

Fig. 2.5 Treasury Select Committee Hearings with MPC Members: Sum of Phi Coefficients.

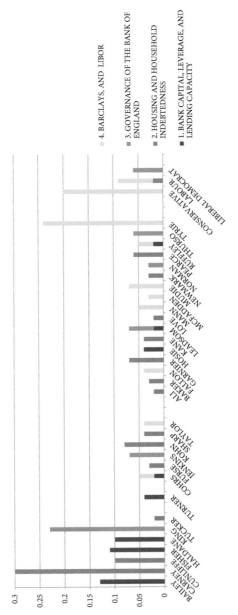

Fig. 2.6 Treasury Select Committee Hearings with FPC Members: Sum of Phi Coefficients.

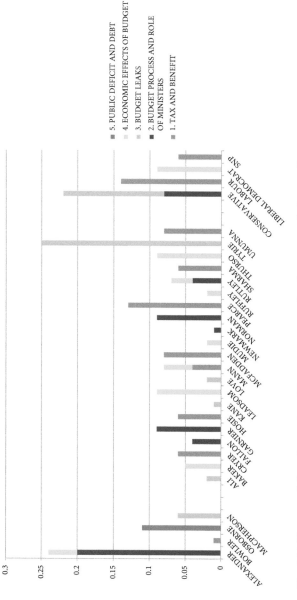

Fig. 2.7 Treasury Select Committee Hearings on Fiscal Policy: Sum of Phi Coefficients.

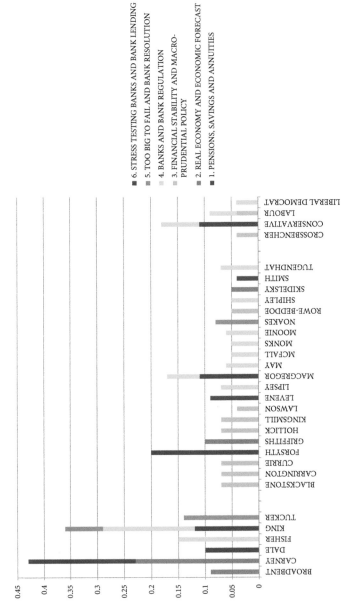

Fig. 2.8 Economic Affairs Committee Hearings with MPC Members: Sum of Phi Coefficients.

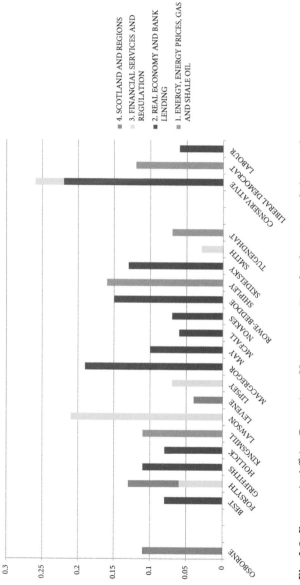

Fig. 2.9 Economic Affairs Committee Hearings on Fiscal Policy: Sum of Phi Coefficients.

committee *and* the representatives from either the BoE or Treasury are significant for a given thematic class, this suggests a degree of reciprocity. If one or the other set of actors dominates a particular thematic class, reciprocity is more suspect. In terms of the colour bar charts of the phi coefficients, the greater the equivalence in colours between parliamentary committee members and witnesses, the stronger is the evidence that all relevant themes are shared across the two sets of actors. At the same time, multicolour bars for an individual or party indicate that the discourse of the individual or party is spread across multiple themes.

In Figure 2.5, one feature stands out. With the conspicuous exception of Chairman Andrew Tyrie, most of the BoE officials and TSC members with larger φ coefficients tend to obtain significance for multiple themes. Both governors, for instance, obtain significance for two themes: King, for the Bank's lending facilities and monetary policy decision-making; Carney, for forward guidance and the real economy. Given Carney's relatively fewer appearances before the committee in this time period than those by King,[19] his large φ for forward guidance (Class 5) is striking and reveals his commitment to making a case for the fundamental shift in monetary policy decision making as he embarked upon his governorship. For King, the period from 2010 to mid 2013 was largely one of being held to account for the Bank's execution of the Funding for Lending Scheme.

With respect to TSC members (excluding Tyrie), many appear to carry out their questioning across several topics: of those with φ coefficients summing to 0.05 or more, six obtain significance for two or more themes, whereas four focus on just one theme. In the latter category, Tyrie is most conspicuous. His singular focus on the Bank's institutional monetary policy decision making corresponds well with his own comments. In his book, Tyrie discusses at length his (and the committee's) efforts to push the Bank into reforming its policy committees (for example, allowing greater transparency, and giving more of a role to external members) and to make itself more accountable. For the subsequent changes made to the practices of the Bank of England, he credits the 'recommendations and subsequent pressure' of the TSC (Tyrie, 2015: 28):

In December 2014 the Bank of England announced its acceptance of many of the proposals initially made by the Treasury Committee in 2011 ... (T)o have influence a [Select] Committee needs to invest a good deal of time in taking evidence on, and then thinking through, what needs to be done. Force of argument counts for a lot.

(Tyrie, 2015)

In short, Figure 2.5 suggests a degree of reciprocity in monetary policy over-sight, with members of both committees largely speaking to a variety of dif-ferent themes, though with the committee chairman more singularly focused on reforming institutional decision-making practices of the Bank. In terms of accountability, it thus appears that Chairman Tyrie (perhaps consciously) created something of a division of labour between himself and committee members in questioning the MPC: Tyrie himself focused predominantly on the decision-making process of the MPC and the governance of the Bank of England, while committee members challenged the MPC on policy outcomes (for example, forward guidance, inflation forecast, lending facilities).

Turning to Figures 2.6 and 2.7, the story is quite different. For financial sta-bility (Figure 2.6), none of the internal members of the FPC are statistically significant for more than one theme, and except for just one person (Cohrs), the same is true of the external FPC members. Each person tends to speak to just one theme. The same holds for TSC members, where only Leadsom and Ruffley speak to more than one theme. However, if we examine both the FPC and TSC members collectively as committees rather than at the indi-vidual level, one could make the case that some reciprocity exists across the two committees. For example, *both* King and Jenkins on the FPC *and* Lead-som, Norman and Thurso on the TSC address Bank of England governance (Class 3). And, as we saw in the correspondence graph for these hearings, TSC members—and particularly Chairman Tyrie—devote a great deal of time to discussing this during the hearings, particularly relative to FPC members. The phi coefficients reveal that while none of the internal FPC members exhibit any significance for this theme, two of the external members (Cohrs and Taylor) do engage with the TSC on this theme of governance. For the remaining themes of bank capital/lending capacity and household indebtedness (Classes 1 and 2), there does appear to be some sharing of conceptual clouds, but with greater subject specialization in financial stability policy than we saw in monetary pol-icy. For instance, some members of the FPC (Carney, Cunliffe, Tucker, Furse, Kohn, Sharp) along with others in the TSC (Ali, Baker, Garnier, Kane, Love, Newmark, Pearce) are significant for just one theme—housing and household indebtedness. Other FPC members (Bailey, Fisher, Haldane, Turner) are sig-nificant solely for bank capital/leverage, and this is matched with just one TSC member who is singularly focused on this theme (Hosie).

What does this tell us about reciprocity in financial stability hearings? Certainly, at the individual level, this analysis suggests that specialization of expertise by central bankers combined with a conspicuous focus on financial scandal by parliamentarians are both factors that limit reciprocal deliberation.

As for the reasons why this is the case (and as we will see more clearly from the explanations given in the interviews in Chapter 4), financial stability as an academic and policy subject matter is less well understood than is monetary policy. Consequently, the central bank experts in this area are challenged less by MPs, since the knowledge gap in the technicalities of such topics as bank capital requirements and leverage ratios is far wider, and the policy 'target' is more difficult to gauge than in monetary policy. So, on the one hand, while at the committee level, TSC and FPC members manage to share conceptual clouds, this sharing appears to be more constrained by subject specialization than in monetary policy. At the same time, TSC members gravitate more towards politically charged topics, like financial scandals, while central bankers tend to (for the most part) avoid being drawn into these themes. Overall, then, while there is some scope for reciprocal dialogue in financial stability, it is more limited than in monetary policy.

Fiscal policy hearings (Figure 2.7) resemble the thematic specialization evident for financial stability, with witnesses from the Treasury and TSC members both tending to obtain statistical significance for just one theme. The distinct feature for fiscal policy is that there is something of a 'talking across one another' phenomenon that occurs between Chancellor George Osborne and select committee members. That is, Osborne's discourse is significant for one class—public deficit/debt (Class 5)—which is conspicuously absent for all the TSC members. Instead, the TSC members acquire statistical significance for the remaining classes (tax/benefit; role of ministers in the budget process; budget leaks and economic effects of the budget), but not for Osborne's public deficit and debt. Chairman Tyrie is particularly focused on the problem of the leaking of details of the budget prior to its formal announcement (where the Permanent Secretary to the Treasury, Nicholas Macpherson, is held accountable for the management of the department). These fiscal policy hearings in the TSC illustrate what might be deemed a poor level of reciprocity, particularly with the key witness—the Chancellor of the Exchequer (Osborne)—entirely focused on the one theme which members of the committee appear least willing to discuss.

Figures 2.8 and 2.9 present equivalent results for the two EAC hearings. Relative to monetary policy oversight in the TSC, hearings with the MPC members in the Lords committee appear to gravitate to more specialization among members. Indeed, *only* the two governors and the committee chairman (MacGregor) obtain significance for more than one theme, while the remaining MPC members and EAC committee members focus on discrete topics. One interesting finding in these hearings is that while peers tend to focus on a broader aspect of financial stability (macroprudential policy, Class 3), MPC members tend to speak to more specific themes, like stress testing banks (Class 6) and the 'too big to fail' problem (Class 5). Somewhat unexpectedly, some partisan differences in discourse appear between Conservative and Labour peers, with Conservatives more likely to focus on pensions and savings (Class 1), while Labour peers were more likely to discuss financial stability (Class 3). Nonetheless, all three major parties were significant for the theme of banks and bank regulation (Class 4).

For fiscal policy (Figure 2.9), we again see thematic specialization, though here Chancellor Osborne devotes his discourse to the issue of Scottish independence and fails to obtain any significance for three remaining themes. Notably, inasmuch as the EAC held just three hearings with Osborne on fiscal policy during the 2010–15 Parliament (compared to seven in the Commons committee), these results should be viewed with some caution. Nonetheless, they do seem to confirm the findings on fiscal policy in the TSC, and that is that the chancellor appears to be singularly focused on a particular theme in his appearances before the parliamentary committees, and this theme does not appear to be the one(s) that either the MPs or Lords on the committees wish to explore.

2.5 Conclusion

This chapter has examined the content (or the 'what') of deliberative account-ability by focusing on two measures, namely the degree of reciprocity and the degree of partisanship. At issue is whether reciprocity and partisanship, as measures of deliberative accountability, are found to vary systematically by the context (that is, the type of policy and the parliamentary chamber).

To simplify our findings thus far, Table 2.5 reduces the two measures of deliberative accountability into three basic categories—low, medium, and high—and presents these for each of the contextual settings. From this one il-lustration, we can observe quite starkly the differences in quality of deliberative accountability both across different economic policy types (monetary policy, financial stability, fiscal policy) and across the two parliamentary chambers. Chapters 3 and 4 will add further columns to this table, to enable a broad overview of the more detailed empirical findings in this work.

One point that is implicit in these summary findings is that, of course, there is another variation of witness type within the economic policies, namely monetary policy and financial stability witnesses who are unelected officials from the Bank of England; and fiscal policy witnesses who are predominantly

Table 2.5 Summary Findings for Deliberative Accountability in the Content of Parliamentary Hearings.

Contextual Setting	Reciprocity between Parliamentarians and Witnesses, across Themes	Non-Partisanship exhibited in Discourse of Parliamentarians
Economic Policy Type		
Monetary Policy	**High**	**High**
Financial Stability	**Medium**	**High**
Fiscal Policy	**Low**	**Medium**
Legislative Chamber (by Policy Type)		
Monetary Policy		
TSC (Commons)	**High**	**High**
EAC (Lords)	**Medium**	**Medium**
Fiscal Policy		
TSC (Commons)	**Low**	**Low**
EAC (Lords)	**Low**	**Medium**

elected representatives (the chancellor and the chief secretary to the Treasury, Danny Alexander). So, with respect to the variation in deliberative accountability across the economic policies (with monetary policy gauged as of highest quality, financial stability medium quality, and fiscal policy low), this also suggests that when unelected officials are witnesses deliberative accountability tends to be better than when elected officials are witnesses. The key difference is that hearings with BoE officials tend to exhibit greater reciprocity in deliberation, whereas those on fiscal policy exhibit more of a 'talking across' one another phenomenon. In monetary policy, both MPs and peers tend to converge with MPC members on each theme (except for the theme of monetary policy decision making, where Chairman Tyrie was more singularly focused). In these hearings, many members on both sides of the table acquire significance for multiple themes—in short, individual members appear to be able and willing to speak to multiple themes.

In fiscal policy, there is less reciprocity, as the chancellor tends to speak to one theme, whereas committee members focus on other themes, and there is less of a multiple focus at the individual level. As for non-partisanship, in monetary policy hearings, there is virtually no cleavage between the two main parties, whereas in fiscal policy in the TSC, MPs of the minority party (Labour) tend to have a greater say in questioning the Conservative chancellor. Deliberation in financial stability hearings exhibits more of a committee-level reciprocity—that is, FPC members and MPs speak to the same set of themes, but there is more topic specialization than in monetary policy. As in monetary policy, however, there is little evidence of partisan discourse in financial stability hearings, with only some small amount of partisanship discerned in the greater tendency of Labour members to speak to the housing issue.[20]

In the comparison between chambers, in monetary policy, deliberative reciprocity is evident for both sets of committee hearings; however, in the TSC, members tended to speak to multiple themes, whereas in the EAC peers tended to focus on one theme, and so on balance reciprocity can only be said to apply at the committee level rather than the individual level. Moreover, as some partisan differences were observed in the discourse of Conservative and Labour peers, the overall score for non-partisanship is given as 'medium'.

Comparing across chambers for fiscal policy, it is clear that deliberative accountability is low for both MPs and peers, though with less overt partisanship in the EAC, as Figure 2.9 indicates at least some shared focus for Conservatives and Labour peers on the theme of the real economy and bank lending (Class 2).

A final note concerns the unique assertiveness of the TSC chairman, Andrew Tyrie. As one of the parliamentarians leading the push for greater select committee scrutiny of government departments, he stands out in each of the policy areas with a pronounced and singular focus on a particular theme. For monetary policy, Tyrie sought to push the Bank of England to reform its institutional governance in monetary policy decision making. This is clear from his high level of significance for this class in Figure 2.5. In financial stability, he was singularly focused on challenging FPC members on the Bank's practices with respect to the Libor scandal (Figure 2.6). And, finally, in fiscal policy, he again displayed a singular focus on reigning in the tendency to 'leak' the budget to journalists in advance of its formal announcement (Figure 2.7).

Notes

1. (Weale, Bicquelet et al., 2012) provide a good example of the empirical application of deliberative reciprocity in parliamentary discourse.
2. The methodological explanation draws from (Sanders, Lisi et al., 2018).
3. The Bank of England publishes the Inflation Report quarterly (February, May, August and November), although in 2019 this was renamed the Monetary Policy Report. The Treasury Select Committee does not necessarily hold hearings on each of the reports (for example, in 2006 and 2007, hearings were held on three of the four Reports).

4. The Bank of England publishes the Financial Stability Report semi-annually (July, December). This study includes the hearings on these reports from their statutory origin in 2013.

5. Financial Stability hearings began in the TSC with the 'interim FPC' in 2012. Following the passage of financial services legislation in 2013, the Financial Stability Committee formally came into existence.

6. Plurals and conjugation endings are reduced to a single form and nonce words are eliminated from the analysis. This leaves a smaller word count which is analysed by the program.

7. These are deemed 'passive' as they do not contribute to either the calculation of the word classes or the factors in the correspondence analysis.

8. Phi derives from chi square and both are measures of association. However, χ^2 depends on the sample size and therefore is not comparable across different corpora, whereas φ eliminates sample size by dividing χ^2 by the sample size (n) and taking the square root. Phi varies between -1 (strong negative association) and 1 (strong positive association). Importantly for this study, φ can therefore be summed across different corpora, as discussed later in this paper, and following the example of Vallès (Vallès, 2015). Chi square values rely on a standard table of statistical significance. Specifically,

Statistical Significance (df = 1)	χ^2 value
N.S.	< 2.71
10%	< 3.84
5% (*)	< 6.63
1% (**)	< 10.80
< 1% (***)	$\geq$ 10.80

Very high values (e.g., over 50) are, on the other hand, highly robust. Interpretation does not adhere rigidly to the specific intervals of these values (e.g., 200 as exactly ten times the significance of 20), but rather to a more relative standard in levels of categories, and particularly the designation of highly robust values (e.g., $\chi^2 \geq 50$).

9. This minimum value for word selection within Alceste varies from about 2 to 20, with smaller text files tending toward the lower threshold and larger ones toward the high threshold (thus, the value for selection for each of the EAC corpora is 2.64). The basic rule of thumb with Alceste is (as with any statistical analysis)—the more data, the easier it is to attain statistical significance (hence larger text files have to attain a higher threshold to be statistically significant).

10. The complete lists of words and phrases may be obtained from the author.

11. For a good example of this technique applied to parliamentary debates see (Bicquelet, 2009).

12. (Greenacre and Hastie, 1987: 437–447) (Greenacre, 1993). While correspondence analysis is well-established in the French literature (see (Benzecri, 1973), and the journal *Cahiers de l'Analyse des Donnees*) its use has spread with the publication of English applications (Greenacre and Underhill, 1982, Greenacre, 1984, Weller and Romney, 1990) and is occasionally used by political scientists (Blasius and Thiessen, 2001).

13. For this, correspondence analysis uses the 'chi-squared distance', which resembles the Euclidean distance between points in physical space. (Here, chi-squared distance—which is distinct from the chi-squared statistic used to measure the significance of the words and tags—can be observed in Euclidean space by transforming the profiles before constructing the plots.) In correspondence analysis, each squared difference between coordinates is divided by the corresponding element of the average profile (where the profile is a set of frequencies divided by their total). The justification for using the chi-squared concept is that it allows one to transform the frequencies by dividing the square roots of the expected frequencies, thereby equalizing the variances. This can be compared to factor analysis, where data on different scales are standardized. For more detailed discussion and further geometric reasons for using the chi-squared distance in correspondence analysis, see (Greenacre, 1993: 34–36).

14. Correspondence analysis usually refers to the 'inertia' of a table, which can also be called 'association' (Weller and Romney, 1990). A corresponding chi-squared value can be obtained by multiplying the association value by the total n of the table.

15. The association and chi-squared statistic may be interpreted geometrically as the degree of dispersion of the set of rows and columns (or, profile points) around their average, where the points are weighted.

16. In total, four factors are identified in the correspondence analysis for the TSC monetary policy hearings (with the remaining factors obtaining a percentage association of 18.9 and 14.7). For Figure 2.2, three factors are identified, and the remaining percentage association is 28; for Figure 2.3, there are four factors, with the third and four factors accounting for 22.5% and 20.5%, and for Figure 2.4, a third factor accounting for 24.2%. (Usually, the dimensionality of the system is one less than the number of classes in the profile (Greenacre, 1993: 14).)

17. Proximity in this case is defined as falling in roughly the same quadrant of the correspondence graph.

18. For Figure 2.4, MacGregor, as the committee chair, is italicized. In just one hearing (monetary policy, 2015), Lord Hollick served as committee chair, but to avoid confusion, his tag is not italicized as he served as committee member for all previous EAC hearings.

19. As can be seen from Appendix 3, King's MPC hearing appearances numbered 10, while Carney's number 6.

20. UK housing policy has become more ideologically contentious as escalating house prices in recent decades have made home ownership increasingly unaffordable. Hence, the provision of 'social housing' for disadvantaged groups has evolved into discussions of appropriate welfare spending by government (Keohane and Broughton, 2013).

Reference

Anstead, N. (2018). "The Idea of Austerity in British Politics, 2003–2013." *Political Studies* **66**(2): 287–305.

Benoit, K. (2020). Text as Data: An Overview. *Sage Handbook of Research Methods in Political Science and International Relations*. L. Curini and R. J. Franzese. London, Sage: 461–497.

Benzecri, J.-P. (1973). L'analyse des données. Tome1: La Taxinomie. Tome 2: L'Analyse des Correspondances (Data analysis. Volume 1 : Taxonomy. Volume 2 : Correspondance Analysis). Paris, Dunod.

Bholat, D., et al. (2015). "Text Mining for Central Banks: A Handbook". *Centre for Central Banking Studies* **33**: 1–19.

Bicquelet, A. (2009). On Referendums: A Comparison of French and English Parliamentary Debates Using Computer-assisted Textual Analysis. Government Department. Wivenhoe, University of Essex **Ph.D.**

Blasius, J. and V. Thiessen (2001). "Methodological Artifacts in Measures of Political Efficacy and Trust: A Multiple Correspondence Analysis". *Political Analysis* **9**(1): 1–20.

Blei, D. M. and J. D. Lafferty (2006). Dynamic Topic Models. *23rd International Conference on Machine Learning*. Pittsburgh, PA.

Blei, D. M. and J. D. Lafferty (2009). Topic Models. *Text Mining: Classification, Clustering, and Applications*. A. Srivastava and M. Sahami. Boca Raton, FL, CRC Press: 71–94.

Bronner, L. (2018). Competition and Communication The Development of Campaigning in Britain from the Second Reform Act to the First World War. Government. London, London School of Economics and Political Science. **PhD** http://etheses.lse.ac.uk/3776/1/Bronner_competition-and-communication.pdf.

Chatsiou, K. and S. J. Mikhaylov (2020). Deep Learning for Political Science. *The SAGE Handbook of Research Methods in Political Science and International Relations*. L. Curini and R. Franzese. Oxford, Sage Publications, pp. 1053–1077

Greenacre, M. and T. Hastie (1987). "The Geometric Interpretation of Correspondence Analysis". *Journal of the American Statistical Association* **82**(398): 437–447.

Greenacre, M. J. (1984). *Theory and Applications of Correspondence Analysis*. London, Academic Press.

Greenacre, M. J. (1993). *Correspondence Analysis in Practice*. London, Academic Press.

Greenacre, M. J. and L. G. Underhill (1982). Scaling a Data Matrix in Low-Dimensional Euclidean Space. *Topics in Applied Multivariate Analysis*. D. M. Hawkins. Cambridge, Cambridge University Press: 183–266.

Grimmer, J. (2010). "A Bayesian Hierarchical Topic Model for Political Texts: Measuring Expressed Agendas in Senate Press Releases". *Political Analysis* **18**(1): 1–35.

Grimmer, J., et al. (2018). Text as Data: How to Make Large Scale Inferences from Language. unpublished paper.

Grimmer, J. and B. M. Stewart (2013). "Text as Data: The Promise and Pitfalls of Automatic Content Analysis Methods for Political Texts". *Political Analysis* **21**: 267–297.

Illia, L., et al. (2014). "Applying Co-occurrence Text Analysis with ALCESTE to Studies of Impression Management". *British Journal of Management* **25**: 352–372.

Keohane, N. and N. Broughton (2013). *The Politics of Housing*. London, Social Market Foundation for National Housing Federation.

Klüver, H., et al. (2015). "Framing in Context: How Interest Groups Employ Framing to Lobby the European Commission". *Journal of European Public Policy* **22**(4): 481–98.

Klüver, H. and C. Mahoney (2015). "Measuring Interest Group Framing Strategies in Public Policy Debates". *Journal of Public Policy* **35**(2): 223–244.

Lahlou, S. (1995b). Vers une théorie de l'interprétation en analyse des données textuelles (Towards a theory of interpretation in text mining). 3rd International Conference on *Statistical Analysis of Textual Data*. S. Bolasco, L. Lebart and A. Salem. Rome: CISU, JADT 1995. **1**: 221–228.

Laver, M., et al. (2003). "Extracting Policy Positions from Political Texts Using Words as Data". *American Political Science Review* **97**(2): 311–331.

Lemercier, C. and C. Zalc (2019). Quantitative Methods in the Humanities: An Introduction (*Translated by Arthur Goldhammer*). Charlottesville, University of Virginia Press.

Osman, N. Y., et al. (2014). "Textual Analysis of Internal Medicine Residency Personal Statements: Themes and Gender Differences" *Medical Education* **49**(1): 93–102.

Ostapenko, L., et al. (2018). "Textual Analysis of General Surgery Residency Personal Statements: Topics and Gender Differences". *Journal of Surgical Education* **75**(3): 573–581.

Proksch, S.-O. and J. B. Slapin (2014). *The Politics of Parliamentary Debate: Parties, Rebels and Representation.* Cambridge, Cambridge University Press.

Quinn, K. M., et al. (2010). "How to Analyze Political Attention with Minimal Assumptions and Costs". *American Journal of Political Science* **54**(1): 209–228.

Reinert, M. (1998). ALCESTE Users' Manuel (English version). Toulouse, Image.

Roberts, M. E., et al. (2014). "Structural Topic Models for Open-ended Survey Responses". *American Journal of Political Science* **58**(4): 1064–1082.

Sanders, J., et al. (2018). Themes and Topics in Parliamentary Oversight Hearings: A New Direction in Textual Data Analysis *Statistics Politics and Policy* **8**, 153–194.

Schonhardt-Bailey, C. (2008). "The Congressional Debate on Partial-Birth Abortion: Constitutional Gravitas and Moral Passion". *British Journal of Political Science* **38**: 383–410.

Schonhardt-Bailey, C. and E. Yager (2012). "Yes, Ronald Reagan's Rhetoric was Unique— But Statistically, How Unique?" *Presidential Studies Quarterly* (September): 482–513.

Schonhardt-Bailey, C. (2013). *Deliberating American Monetary Policy: A Textual Analysis.* Cambridge, MA, MIT Press.

Schonhardt-Bailey, C., et al. (2021). The Accountability Gap: Deliberation on Monetary Policy in Britain and America During the Financial Crisis, London School of Economics and Political Science, Working Paper.

Slapin, J. B. and S.-O. Proksch (2008). "A Scaling Model for Estimating Time-Series Party Positions from Texts". *American Journal of Political Science* **52**(3): 705–722.

Slapin, J. B. and S.-O. Proksch (2014). Words as Data: Content Analysis in Legislative Studies (DOI: 10.1093/oxfordhb/9780199653010.013.0033). *Oxford Handbook of Legislative Studies* S. Martin, T. Saalfeld and K. W. Strøm. Oxford, Oxford University Press: 1–14.

Tyrie, A. (2015). *The Poodle Bites Back: Select Committee and the Revival of Parliament.* Surrey, Centre for Policy Studies.

Vallès, D. W. (2015). The Contours of Political Discourse: Deliberating the Patient Protection & Affordable Care Act. Department of Government. London, London School of Economics and Political Science. **PhD**.

Weale, A., et al. (2012). "Debating Abortion, Deliberative Reciprocity and Parliamentary Advocacy". *Political Studies* **60**: 643–667.

Weller, S. C. and A. K. Romney (1990). *Metric Scaling: Correspondence Analysis.* London, Sage Publications.

Yager, E. and C. Schonhardt-Bailey (2007). *Measuring Rhetorical Leadership: A Textual Analysis of Margaret Thatcher's and Ronald Reagan's Speeches.* Annual Meeting of the American Political Science Association, Chicago.

3

Nonverbal Behaviour in Parliamentary Hearings on Economic Policy[1]

3.1 Introduction

In Chapter 2, we examined the content of both parliamentary and congressional hearings as legislators seek to hold central bankers and Treasury ministers to account for both policies and decision-making processes. Using quantitative text analysis, we find systematic differences in deliberative accountability between (a) types of economic policies, and (b) parliamentary chambers. Assuming that deliberative accountability is of highest quality when legislators ask questions that are focused, pertain to relevant statutory obligations, and are not motivated by partisan or electoral self-interest, *and* witnesses respond *directly* and fully to these questions, we find that monetary policy hearings in the Treasury Select Committee deliver the best results, fiscal policy hearings deliver the worst results and the results for financial stability hearings fall somewhere in between. Yet, this simple comparison among policy types and chambers needs to consider (a) the contextual setting, and (b) the possible overall quality of deliberative accountability across the system. For example, accepting that fiscal policy is also subject to political accountability (that is, chancellors, unlike central bankers, may be voted out of office in elections), we may discount the relatively poorer level of deliberative reciprocity between parliamentarians and Treasury ministers. For monetary policy and financial stability, where policymakers are independent and not directly subject to political accountability, it is reasonable to set the threshold higher for quality in deliberative accountability, since this is the only formal setting for accountability. We find that monetary policy does indeed appear to achieve a higher quality, but less so for financial stability. Reciprocity in financial stability hearings appears to have been compromised in the past both by deficiencies in technical expertise by parliamentarians, as well as the lure of financial scandals, for which political and media awareness offers greater rewards to politicians.

Deliberative Accountability in Parliamentary Committees. Cheryl Schonhardt-Bailey, Oxford University Press.
© Cheryl Schonhardt-Bailey (2022). DOI: 10.1093/oso/9780192847874.003.0003

Across parliamentary chambers, we find that in monetary policy, MPs tend to be more adept than peers at juggling multiple themes. From a different perspective, this same finding might also be interpreted as peers being better able to focus in depth on a particular theme. In either case, both committees exhibited clear evidence of deliberative reciprocity in monetary policy hearings, although arguably this is greater in the Commons.

However detailed the analysis of the content of these hearings may be, we have as yet no understanding of the 'mood' of these hearings. Specifically, what exactly *is* conveyed both to others in the hearings themselves and to outside audiences through the more intangible language of the 'body'—for example, the use of facial expressions, vocal cues, and gestures? Chapter 2 offers an understanding of *what* was said, but not *how* it was said.

This chapter is divided into two parts, each with a unique approach to gauging the effect of nonverbal behaviour in deliberative accountability, within the context of parliamentary hearings. In part one, about a third of the total 37 hearings on monetary policy, financial stability, and fiscal policy analysed in Chapter 2 are subjected to an extensive manual coding exercise. This part of the chapter focuses on nonverbal behaviour at the level of the parliamentary committee (Treasury Select Committee in the Commons and Economic Affairs Committee in the Lords) and the type of economic policy (monetary policy, financial stability, fiscal policy). This approach enables an explicit link back to the findings from the quantitative text analysis, which is also largely at the level of committee and policy type.

In Part two of this chapter, I employ an experimental approach to explore nonverbal behaviour at a more granular level. The experiment is intended to gauge the extent to which nonverbal cues (particularly relative to verbal cues such as logic, data and reasoning) affect judgments about how well a witness responds to questions by parliamentarians, his persuasiveness and his overall competence. As the experiment is conducted in a controlled environment, explicit hypotheses are tested as part of this research design. Hence, this section is distinct from the empirical approach adopted elsewhere in this work.

The first section of Part one reviews the relevant literature on nonverbal communication and posits reasons why we might anticipate an important role for such communication in deliberative accountability. Each part of the chapter then presents its own research design, expectations, and findings.

PART 1: Nonverbal Behaviour at the Level of the Committee and Policy

3.2 Why is Nonverbal Behaviour Important?

The findings in Chapter 2 are instructive as to the depth and breadth of arguments used by policymakers in their defence of policy actions. Yet while text analysis is effective in empirically measuring the deliberative *content*, it provides no information as to the *delivery* of these arguments within a deliberative setting. In short, the written record provides us with the semantic content of deliberation (the 'what' of deliberation) but not the underlying interpersonal dynamic of the committee hearing (the 'how' of deliberation). Measuring nonverbal behaviour promises a means to gauge better both the emotive tone of the arguments and the nature of the intentions of the witnesses appearing before each committee—witnesses whose credibility and intentions with respect to public policy are being judged by parliamentarians. It is this interactional dynamic that this chapter seeks to assess. We expect that by studying this interactional dynamic, we may better capture more nuanced aspects of our three metrics, especially that of *respect*. The second part of the chapter also yields insight into just how far nonverbal communication impacts persuasion in the context of deliberative accountability. While persuasion is not one of our three metrics of quality (for reasons discussed in Chapter 1), as a potential product of the deliberation, it provides a more nuanced measure of the extent to which parliamentarians and audiences outside Parliament are influenced as the deliberative context varies.

To be sure, the study of nonverbal communication in political contexts is extensive. For example, televised debates of national leaders are frequently used to examine the effects of nonverbal communication on political attitudes and responses (Maurer and Reinemann, 2013, Bucy and Gong, 2016, Gong and Bucy, 2016). While the effects of visual cues by political leaders are noted in political election campaigns (Bucy and Grabe, 2007, Bucy and Grabe, 2008, Stewart, Bucy et al., 2015), to date little attention has been paid to the role of nonverbal communication in legislative committee hearings.

Methodologically, the goal here is to bring research from interpersonal communication studies, political psychology, and political ethology (behaviour) into the study of committee deliberation and to show that nonverbal communication can play an important role in government accountability. Indeed, there are strong biological and cognitive reasons why information gleaned from nonverbal means should be evaluated on par with that from verbal communication. To name but a few, the human brain is both more specialized and faster in processing visual information than it is in processing written/verbal information, and cognition is easier for the former than for the latter (Grabe and Bucy, 2009: 275). Verbal language is also a relatively recent phenomenon in human history (in written form, only 5,200 years) relative to the millions of years of history of visual perception. In short, the evolutionary development of the brain suggests that its adaptive ability to absorb visual information is far more advanced (in evolutionary terms) than for written and spoken communication (Grabe and Bucy, 2009: 12). Elsewhere, communication scholars have long argued that verbal and nonverbal behaviour work together in the process of communication (Knapp and Hall, 2010: 11, 20). Empirical investigations into the quality of deliberation in public policy accountability that focus solely on verbal exchanges thus risk missing the role of nonverbal behaviour in shaping such fundamental features as the credibility and trustworthiness of witnesses being held to account for their policy decisions. More broadly, these investigations risk studying just a portion of the actual messages that are being conveyed.

Moreover, nonverbal messages from witnesses may influence—either consciously or not—the attitudes and behaviours of select committee members, particularly in the form of persuasion. As Bucy notes, nonverbal behaviour 'may prime later judgments about political viability and shape the criteria by which [in this chapter, witnesses] are evaluated' (Bucy, 2011: 197). In legislative committee settings, where verbal deliberation is the focus, nonverbal communication may be pivotal in the acceptance or rejection of arguments proffered by policymakers. Nonverbal communication may also contribute to more traditional approaches to understanding political conflicts. For instance, in the traditional Lowi policy typology (Lowi, 1964, Lowi, 1972), where political relationships and conflicts are shaped by people's expectations of policy outputs, one might expect to find more ideological/partisan conflicts in fiscal policy hearings than in either monetary policy or financial stability hearings, as the former aligns with clear partisan cleavages whereas the last two policies are less overtly partisan in orientation (aligning, as we have seen, with findings in the previous chapter). Additionally, a pertinent feature of the UK parliamentary system is that in fiscal policy hearings, backbench parliamentarians (the legislature) hold frontbench parliamentarians (the executive) to account, which invariably generates more partisan tension than in hearings between parliamentarians and unelected (and ostensibly nonpartisan) experts such as central bankers. Hence, while one might expect (as we found in Chapter 2) the argumentative *content* of fiscal policy discussions to be more ideological and partisan than for monetary policy or financial stability, neither Lowi nor his followers explored how perceptions and judgments of this content might be influenced by the *delivery* of this content, and so this aspect of the policy divide is as yet unexplored.

3.3 The Significance of Nonverbal Communication in Parliamentary Hearings

Broadly speaking, persuasion may be the product of (1) the content of the argument (for example, its logic, its evidence, whether it difficult or easy to understand (Cobb and Kuklinski, 1997)); (2) the way in which it is structured or framed (Druckman, 2001, Druckman, 2004); or possibly (3) the way in which it is delivered. It is in the delivery of an argument that nonverbal cues become potentially relevant. While persuasion is not measured directly in this chapter, I do examine the nonverbal context (for example, combative versus relaxed) considering the potential for persuasion to occur. That is, I examine the extent to which nonverbal behaviour may facilitate the persuasiveness of an argument or a committee witness more generally, as well as how this behaviour may affect the deliberative process.

Psychologists have long noted two modes of thinking, one that is instinctual and 'operates automatically and quickly, with little or no effort and no sense of voluntary control', and one that is methodical and deliberative, thereby taking time, mental effort and concentration (Kahneman, 2011: 20–21). By focusing on nonverbal communication, we are allowing for the influence of 'fast' thinking and behaviour on our 'slow' decision-making processes—particularly in the form of persuasion. For instance, as a component of nonverbal communication, rapid appearance-based assessments of candidates (linked to competence and dominance) are shown to be a strong predictor of electoral success (Olivola and Todorov, 2010). Indeed, if we interpret nonverbal communication as a form of 'fast' thinking and behaviour, the visual stimuli inherent in this form of communication may well outweigh the slower, rational, and verbal forms of communication. In reviewing both the evolutionary and biological bases of the visual processing of information, Grabe and Bucy note that '(c)ontrary to the preferences of political theorists for a rationally engaged public that relies on reason and deliberation to make informed decisions, visual experience remains the most dominant mode of learning' (Grabe and Bucy, 2009: 12–13).

Beyond affecting the persuasiveness of speakers and their arguments, there are other reasons to anticipate nonverbal communication to be a fruitful avenue of research. One reason is that whereas speech is deliberate and some-times scripted, nonverbal communication is far less conscious: 'People are formally trained in their verbal behaviour in schools. Nonverbal communi-cation is less obvious, as in subtle facial expressions and barely perceptible changes in voice tone, and people are not typically formally trained in their nonverbal communication' (Matsumoto, Frank et al., 2013: 8). Admittedly, politicians and officials often undergo some media training before giving ev-idence in parliamentary hearings (as well as for other official engagements), and most are practiced public communicators. Hence, we might expect their nonverbal communication (as well as their verbal communication) to be more controlled. It is nonetheless unlikely that such training entirely negates the tendencies of these individuals to allow their own innate mannerisms and emotions to find expression. Consequently, even subtle facial expressions, ges-tures, and other signals such as voice may provide important insights into not only the intentions of committee members, but also the competence, trustworthiness and credibility of the witnesses who are being held to account.

3.4 Interpretations of Nonverbal Communication and How They Apply to Hearings

3.4.1 Emotions versus signals

The extent to which nonverbal behaviour 'signals' the strategic intentions of the sender is disputed, particularly in the literature on facial expressions. On the one hand, such behaviour might serve as a visual manifestation of an indi-vidual's emotions—that is, a spill over or leakage of some discernible internal emotion(s) (Izard, 1997). Core emotions are said to be 'associated with unique physiological signatures in both the central and autonomic nervous systems', and they are, moreover, 'expressed universally in all humans via facial expres-sions regardless of race, culture, sex, ethnicity, or national origin' (Matsumoto and Hwang, 2013: 25). Seven emotions—anger, disgust, fear, joy, sadness, sur-prise and contempt—are each said to produce unique and identifiable facial expressions (Ekman, 2004). This causal link between the face and internal emotions, however, has been challenged on several fronts, including the cate-gorization of complex emotions into single facial expressions and the tendency to overlook *context*.

In contrast to the 'emotions' view of faces, a second interpretation is that facial expressions are employed as social devices to manage interpersonal and intragroup encounters. This approach stems in part from animal communication, where animals 'signal' a behavioural intent—such as to attack or to appease—as a means to negotiate conflict and cooperation with other animals (Yik and Russell, 1999, Rendall, Owren et al., 2009). This behavioural ecology approach maintains that both intention and context are essential to the interpretation of facial expressions (Fridlund, 1994). For example, an angry face conveys a readiness to attack while a contemptuous face is a way to express superiority (Fridlund, 1994: 129). And yet, some facial expressions, like smiling, may in fact convey a combination of emotions—for example, a genuine ('felt') smile may signify a willingness to befriend or to play, but a feigned ('false') smile may signify readiness to acquiesce or appease, or a phony smile may mask some underlying negative emotion (such as anger) (Stewart, Bucy et al., 2015: 76). Contempt can also be conveyed in a 'controlled half smile' by which an individual signals tolerance but not acceptance of some other group member (Stewart, Bucy et al., 2015: 77).

The social and political significance of facial expressions may thus be categorized as intent to attack or threaten (anger face), reassurance or willingness to socially bond (happiness), appeasement (sadness), or intention to flee/submit (fear), and each has been identified in the facial expressions of televised politicians (McHugo, Lanzetta et al., 1985, Bucy and Grabe, 2008, Stewart, Bucy et al., 2015). The socio-political significance of this typology becomes clear when it is subsumed into two broader typologies of social interaction or behavioural types—agonic and hedonic (Masters and Sullivan, 1989). In agonic interactions, the actors are in direct competition for power, and so to maintain social order, one might submit to or appease the threatening actor. In hedonic encounters, actors are more relaxed (even playful), in pursuit of social bonding and alliance building or to reassure/reinforce social status. Facial expressions (and other nonverbal behaviour, such as posture (Bull, 1987)) are thus indicative of a dominance hierarchy (Bucy and Grabe, 2008) and can serve to signal either cooperative or noncooperative intent. For instance, in a one-shot anonymous prisoner's dilemma game, contempt expressions have been found to predict defection by the sender, while genuine smiles signify cooperative intention (Reed, Zeglen et al., 2012). An important caveat to the behavioural ecology approach is that nonverbal messages conveyed by a communicator do not elicit identical emotional responses in all receivers, as the effect of the nonverbal signal is shaped by prior attitudes and the context in which the behaviour occurs (Bucy and Grabe, 2008). Moreover, some people are simply better at 'decoding' the signals of nonverbal behaviour, as studies of gestures have shown (Beattie, 2016: 100).

The emotions and behavioural ecology interpretations are sometimes depicted as if they are in conflict, with disagreement on facial expressions
including 'their clarity, specificity, extent of their innateness and universality,
and whether they relate to emotions, social motives, behavioural intentions, or
to all three' (Izard, 1997: 71). Nonetheless both rely on the evolutionary literature (for example, Darwin (Darwin, 1872 (2009))) and, in the end, converge on
the assessment that facial expressions function to communicate information
(Izard, 1997: 71).

3.4.2 Facial Expressions, Vocal Cues, and Gestures in Parliamentary Oversight

Once investigation turns to the empirics of nonverbal communication, the
analytical and methodological framework encounters significant hurdles, not
least of which is the appropriateness of the data to be examined. One might,
for example, begin quite broadly by measuring the static visuals of the setting,
such as the committee room, seating arrangement, lighting, temperature, and
so on, as some communications scholars have done (Knapp and Hall, 2010).
For simplicity, here the focus is on three primary forms of dynamic nonverbal communication: *facial expressions*, *vocal cues*, and *body movement/gestures*.
These key aspects of communication are shown to be highly effective in gauging behaviour by political actors whose appeals to voters are being televised
(Grabe and Bucy, 2009), although the largest attention in the literature has
been given to facial expressions.

The political significance of facial expressions is aptly summarized by Stewart and colleagues: 'The *face has long been appreciated as a focal point of
attention by those competing for positions of power* and then for maintaining
influence once power has been attained. In large part, this is caused by the
ability leaders have in communicating their emotional state and behavioural
intent nonverbally to followers ...' [italics added] (Stewart, Bucy et al., 2015:
48). The previous section focused predominantly on facial expressions for the
simple reason that competition for power (and jockeying for political advantage) is a subtext of parliamentary committees that seek to hold government
to account. As noted in Chapter 1, these hearings depict to varying degrees
an adversarial form of deliberation. While there is no overt competition concerning policy per se, accountability contains an element of competition over
the influence and direction of policy decisions. In the case of unelected central bankers, there is a recognition that the independence of the central bank
is not absolute—typically governments set the goals while central banks have

discretion over how to pursue these objectives (that is, independence to choose the appropriate instrument(s)) (Blinder, 1998). Moreover, it is by parliamentary statute that the Bank of England's Monetary Policy Committee (MPC) and Financial Policy Committee (FPC) exist and as the ultimate law-making body, Parliament could abolish these independent committees.

Thus, when central bank experts appear before parliamentary committees, they are invariably cognisant of the limits of their independence. In contrast, the situation is more overtly competitive in fiscal policy hearings. The primary witness in these proceedings is the chancellor of the Exchequer, who—like members of the Treasury Committee—is himself a member of Parliament. There is no statutory independence given to either the Treasury or to the chancellor. Moreover, as noted earlier, fiscal policy is inherently more partisan in nature than monetary policy, thus exacerbating the competitive tone of these hearings. We might therefore expect fiscal policy hearings to feature more competitive (agonic) nonverbal facial expressions, and monetary policy and financial stability hearings to showcase expressions of a more reassuring (hedonic) nature. Employing a behavioural model of leader-follower interactions (Stewart, Méhu et al., 2015), we might expect dominant individuals (leading committee members) to invoke threatening facial expressions (for example, anger) and the *presumed* subordinate (the chancellor) to display more submissive or appeasing emotional expressions like sadness or fear. (Select committees may presume that witnesses from the government—for example, the chancellor—are in a subordinate role when being held to account before the committee; however, as part of the executive, the chancellor himself may dispute his subordinate role before the committee.)

A non-competitive setting would predict different facial expressions: dominant individuals (committee members) should seek 'to enhance group affiliation by reassuring subordinates [here, witnesses from the Bank of England] through facial displays of happiness, while subordinates ... will display submissiveness through appeasement gestures such as sadness' (Stewart, Méhu et al., 2015: 192). The presumed motivation in both settings and by both sets of actors is to regulate relations within the group (here, committee members and witnesses) and for each set of actors to maintain its status within the group setting (Masters and Sullivan, 1989: 128); nonverbal behaviour thus functions to regulate intragroup relations.

Turning to vocal cues, research (and consensus) on the emotional significance or interpretation of vocal expressions is less developed than for facial expressions (Frank, Maroulis et al., 2013: 63). Indeed, scientific research into the voice is said to be in 'its infancy' (Dumitrescu, 2016: 658). Nonetheless, identifiable characteristics of nonverbal vocal cues include pitch, loudness, the quality or 'timbre' of the speaker's voice, rate of speech, amount of time spent speaking, response time (how long it takes person A to respond to person B), time spent pausing between words, and errors in speech (Frank, Maroulis et al., 2013: 58–59). Such characteristics are relevant for parliamentary committee deliberations inasmuch as listeners better remember (and are more persuaded by) information if the pitch and amplitude are varied, and persuasion is further increased when the speaker pauses less frequently, spends less time in his or her responses, and speaks more quickly (Frank, Maroulis et al., 2013: 67). An alternative focus of research is on the vocal cues of audiences, including laughter and booing of presidential debates audiences (Stewart, Eubanks et al., 2016, Stewart, 2010), or the link between the interruptions by Supreme Court justices during oral argument and their judicial voting behaviour (Kimmel, Stewart et al., 2012). Others have examined Supreme Court oral argument even more closely, with attention given to such features as speech rate, speech disturbances, the valence of expression and related factors (Schubert, Peterson et al., 1992), and vocal cues between a justice and a lawyer (Beňuš, Levitan et al., 2012).

Beyond facial expressions and voice, gestures and body movement make up a third influential mode of nonverbal communication. Among other functions, gestures help to illustrate speech (for example, pointing and saying 'there'; nodding and saying 'yes') or serve as 'emblems' in place of words (for example, thumbs up for 'okay,' shoulder shrugging for 'I don't know/care') (Matsumoto and Hwang, 2013: 76–79). In contrast to the biological underpinnings for facial expressions and vocal cues, however, emblematic gestures are culturally learned and therefore are less clear-cut to study and interpret. Illustrators may serve a more universal purpose by communicating greater intensity: as Bull notes, 'a speaker can pick out particular words or phrases which may be important in his communication, and highlight them with some kind of illustrative body movement' (Bull, 1987: 33). Illustrators may also serve as a visual means for viewers to track the flow of speech and, with this greater stimulation, better comprehend speech (Rogers, 1978). Alternatively, illustrators might actually convey more about the speaker's emotions regarding message content or attitudes towards one's audience (Bull, 1987: 34). Studies have also found systematic effects on voters' evaluations from differences in the use of gestures by female and male politicians (Everitt, Best et al., 2016), although in the present study, women do not feature prominently either as witnesses (where the two governors and the chancellor are male) or as committee chairs (again, both are male).

For the purposes of this chapter, in which the focus is on nonverbal communication in a deliberative (verbal) context, two difficulties in measuring and coding gestures are relevant. First, viewers are not equally adept at capturing the informative content of gestures: 'research has ... demonstrated that some people seem to miss out on ... information in the gesture channel almost completely; others are tuned in to it and quite unconsciously process this important information along with the speech itself' (Beattie, 2016: 123). Second, viewers of gestures are highly selective about which gestures are actually 'seen', in part because our natural focus is on the face, to which attention gravitates (Beattie, 2016: 150). In any case, the study of gestures in politics is increasingly capturing the attention of researchers across many disciplines, including political science, history, philosophy, and psycholinguistics (Manning, 2007, Braddick, 2009, Casasanto and Jasmin, 2010, Stewart, Eubanks et al., 2016).

3.5 Measuring Nonverbal Communication in Parliamentary Committee Hearings

The purpose of the present research is unique in that it seeks to capture the interactional dynamic of the deliberation between a series of questioners (parliamentarians) and a series of witnesses, particularly as collective groups. Unlike many empirical investigations of nonverbal behaviour discussed above, the subjects of investigation here are engaged in a reciprocal form of communication: rather than giving speeches, they are asking and answering questions— they are not directing their words and actions *at* some passive audience but rather engaging *with* and reacting to one another. This means that the empirical focus is the exchange between two actors (a committee member and a witness), repeated with new sets of actors (or a new committee member and the same witness), for the duration of each committee hearing.

A casual observer might easily dismiss nonverbal behaviour in parliamentary hearings, concluding that what really matters is the verbal arguments and discussion. Even anecdotal evidence illustrates that this is not necessarily the case. In March 2014, one hearing raised the spectre of a possible major transformation in the conduct of the Bank of England's MPC meetings, through a substantial increase in the transparency of policymaking discussions. During this hearing, Treasury Select Committee Chairman Andrew Tyrie queried Paul

Fisher (Executive Director for Markets and member of the MPC) and Mark Carney (Governor of the Bank of England) on whether the Bank stored the verbatim transcripts of the MPC meetings, once these were summarized and published as minutes. The exchange became fodder for MPs and other Bank observers who have sought greater transparency from the Bank. Media attention given to this hearing illustrates the awareness of nonverbal behaviour, with references to 'a very frightened appearing Paul Fisher', a committee chair (Andrew Tyrie) exclaiming '(i)n a booming, outraged voice', and Governor Carney who 'appeared to be attempting to suppress amusement' and 'then breaking out in a full smile' (Martens, 2014). Examples of media and press attention to nonverbal behaviour in select committee hearings are not difficult to find, but no attempt has yet been made to examine this behaviour more systematically.

3.5.1 Coding of Nonverbal Behaviour in Parliamentary Hearings

A pilot study for coding nonverbal behaviour was completed using five full hearings (each with a duration around two hours), from which a simplified coding scheme was devised. Using this scheme, three research assistants (RAs) (one with a doctorate and more than 15 years of research experience, and two second-year undergraduates) then independently coded specific nonverbal expressions and behaviour of key individuals for 12 hearings (totalling 23 total hours of video footage, all of which is publicly available from the UK Parliament website at https://www.parliament.uk/). These hearings are a representative sample of the 37 total hearings on monetary policy, financial stability and fiscal policy in the Commons Treasury Select Committee and the Lords Economic Affairs Committee, over the 2010–15 Parliament (see Appendix 1).

   In Chapter 2, the complete set of 37 hearings were analysed using quantitative text analysis. Here, the 12 coded hearings were selected in reasonably evenly distributed intervals across the 2010–15 timeframe, while factoring into account (a) the inherent imbalance in the distribution of hearings across types of witnesses (27 total hearings for Bank of England officials on monetary policy and financial stability versus ten total hearings for the chancellor on fiscal policy) and across chambers (30 total hearings in the TSC and seven in the EAC), and (b) that the Lords committee held no hearings specifically on financial stability during the 2010–15 Parliament. Thus, for Bank of England witnesses, eight hearings were selected (six for monetary policy and two for financial stability), and for the chancellor, four hearings. Across chambers, 10 were from the Commons and two were from the Lords.

Before beginning coding, the RAs underwent four on-line training courses on micro expressions and subtle expressions (all obtained from the Paul Ekman Group [https://www.paulekman.com/micro-expressions-training-tools/]) and in each of the on-line tests were required to achieve a success rate of at least 75%. The training focused particularly on identifying the seven basic emotions (joy/happiness, surprise, anger, contempt, sadness, fear, disgust), which are identifiable in facial expressions. The test stimuli were provided in the training packages. The RAs were also given a practical text-book (Borg, 2011) on 'body language' to review and use as a reference for the gesture coding.

The coding proceeded as follows. For each hearing, each MP or peer's 'turn' in asking questions was treated as a 'deliberative exchange'. A single delibera-tive exchange may consist of between 5 to 10 minutes of questions and answers between a committee member and a witness.[2] For each exchange, three basic dimensions were coded: facial expressions, vocal cues, and gestures/posture. The coding scheme is summarized in Appendix 5. Facial expressions such as anger, contempt and happiness were measured as single instances (counts) and then tallied for each of the participants in the deliberative exchange. Sim-ilarly, vocal cues, such as variations in volume, speed, and pauses in speaking were also tallied by individual and across each deliberative exchange, as were gestures such as leaning forward, nodding, or shaking the head. The bulk of the coding that is reported here is based on broad areas of agreement among the three coders. The threshold for agreement rests not on the numeric scores (counts) themselves but rather on the *relative* weights of the different types of witnesses (elected minister for fiscal policy versus unelected experts for mon-etary policy and financial stability) and of the two parliamentary committees (Commons versus Lords). As such, the coding is used largely as a qualita-tive assessment of the impact of nonverbal communication in parliamentary oversight hearings.

Some attention is also given to where the coders disagreed. To be sure, measures for coding should avoid incurring inconsistencies arising from hu-man idiosyncrasies (Hayes and Krippendorff, 2007), and to the extent that the agreed results reported are based upon a simple 100% agreement that one set of witnesses or committee exhibited *relatively more* nonverbal cues (anger, hap-piness, and so on) than the other set of witnesses or committee, the bulk of the coding results do not report as findings any inconsistencies among the coders (and so a measure such as Krippendorff's Alpha is not used). Studies do not usually discuss differences among coders (although exceptions include: Schubert and colleagues, who comment on a coder's 'idiosyncratic tendency to over code' (Schubert, Peterson et al., 1992: 49); and Bucy and Gong, who discuss specific techniques for improving intercoder reliability and precision (Bucy and Gong, 2016: 55–58)), yet—as discussed earlier—receivers of non-verbal messages do not necessarily respond in similar ways, as these signals are conditional on pre-existing attitudes and the situational context of the be-haviour, and some individuals are simply more adept than others in discerning the meaning of the signals. Finally, 'stereotypical' university undergraduates have been criticized for being 'socially compliant' and 'more likely to be mer-curial in their attitudes because of lack of self-knowledge' (Stewart, Salter et al., 2009: 57). While this complaint is made in reference to undergraduates as research participants, the authors nonetheless argue that different cultural groups (and by inference, different age groups) vary in their perceptions of nonverbal communication (Stewart, Salter et al., 2009: 58). It is worth, then, al-lowing here for the possibility that—in spite of having received the same train-ing in coding nonverbal behaviour—a meaningful difference may still emerge between younger coders (aged 20–22) and another older coder (in his 40s).

Underlying the coding exercise was a premise that nonverbal behaviour helps to capture the extent of interest in the topic or the intensity of the dis-cussion. (This is akin to motivational activation (Lang, Newhagen et al., 1996, Lang, Sanders-Jackson et al., 2013).) Witnesses who are more nonverbally ex-pressive in hearings may be making greater effort to persuade the committee members (as studies of the use of gestures have shown (Bull, 2003 (2014): 28)), or certain facial expressions may be expressing latent emotions.

Informed researchers in nonverbal communication may note that software is available for automatically coding facial expressions (for example, Visage, FaceReader, AFFDEX, OpenFace, iMotions, to name but a few), and plausibly such software could be used in this instance, rather than human coders. There are three rebuttals to this argument. First, humans still outperform comput-ers in interpreting the nuances and context of facial expressions, although the capacity of automation is no doubt rapidly evolving (Lewinski, 2015). Second, no software yet (of which I am aware) automatically codes facial expressions, vocal cues *and* gestures as a whole package. Third, software that codes all rel-evant aspects of nonverbal communication may well be around the corner; nonetheless, this does not negate the importance of obtaining human coding of the various categories, as observed in real-world settings. Human coding may serve to first map the contours of nonverbal expression in parliamentary hearings, and subsequent automation may then rely on such human coding as a baseline. In short, human coders may initially define the contours of nonverbal cues in parliamentary hearings, and software may subsequently refine or even challenge these outright.

A further response is that the coding of the hearings is the first half of this chapter's approach to studying empirically nonverbal behaviour in parliamentary hearings. The second part of this chapter uses an experimental approach to further extend the analysis of nonverbal behaviour.

3.6 Findings: Nonverbal Communication in Parliamentary Committees

3.6.1 The Context

Again, the focus here is on the delivery rather than the content of the discourse in the parliamentary hearings. Nonetheless, to understand the delivery, it is useful to summarize once again the analysis of the full verbatim transcripts of the 37 oversight hearings on monetary policy, financial stability, and fiscal policy during the 2010–15 Parliament. Variation in deliberation was found (1) between types of witnesses and types of economic policies, (2) between MPs and peers in their respective committees, and (3) in partisan influence across different policy areas.

First, it was found that oversight varies between (a) members of the Bank of England's Monetary Policy Committee and Financial Policy Committee on monetary policy and financial stability and (b) Treasury ministers and officials—primarily Chancellor George Osborne—on fiscal policy. The key difference is that hearings with Bank officials tend to exhibit greater reciprocity in deliberation, whereas those on fiscal policy exhibit more of a 'talking across' one another phenomenon. In monetary policy, both MPs and peers tend to enter exchanges with MPC members on each theme discussed. In these hearings, many members on both sides of the table are able and willing to engage in discussion on multiple themes rather than focusing on just one. In fiscal policy, the chancellor tends to speak to one theme, whereas committee members focus on other themes, and individually, these committee members tend not to focus on more than one theme. Deliberation in financial stability hearings exhibits more of a committee-level reciprocity—that is, FPC members and MPs speak to the same set of themes, but there is more topic specialization among the witnesses than in monetary policy.

Second, deliberative reciprocity is evident for both sets of committee hearings on monetary policy; however, in the Commons committee, members tend to speak to multiple themes, whereas in the Lords committee, peers tend to focus on one theme.

Third, in the Commons, partisanship appears to vary across policy areas. In monetary policy hearings there is virtually no cleavage between the two main parties, whereas in fiscal policy, MPs of the minority party (Labour) tend to be more extensive in their questioning of the Conservative chancellor. For financial stability, a small amount of partisanship could be discerned in the greater tendency of Labour members to speak to the housing issue.

3.6.2 Results

Table 3.1 provides the summary findings for the nonverbal coding. In Appendix 6, Tables 6A through 6C provide the details for the coding. Table 3.1 reports *only* where all three coders agreed on the *relative weights* of the mean scores across the witness type or the committee type. (In cases of a tie in the scores across groups, the determination of coder agreement relied on agreement of rankings by the other two coders.) These summaries correspond to Appendix 6 Tables 6A—6C, in which the findings highlighted in each table (in bold or underlined) represent only where the coders agreed, and in italicized brackets, the degree to which the mean score of one witness or group type was greater than another.

Table 3.1 begins with the aggregate means (corresponding to Appendix 6, Tables 6A and 6B), as grouped by witness type (Bank of England or Her Majesty's Treasury [HMT]); and by legislative chamber (Lords, Commons). The scores are presented for both the parliamentary committee members and the witness, and they aggregate across all the three types of nonverbal communication analysed here (facial, vocal and gesture). At the most aggregate level, fiscal policy hearings—in which the chancellor is the one key witness (with only marginal interjections from Treasury officials)—exhibit more intense nonverbal behaviour than hearings with Bank of England officials. For the facial expressions, the committee members in both chambers (MPs and Lords) and the witnesses have more coded facial expressions in fiscal policy hearings than Bank of England hearings. The same is true for witnesses when it comes to gesture scores. Finally, across chambers, peers score higher on vocal scores than do MPs.

What does this mean? For one, in fiscal policy—where ideological/partisan conflicts are more in evidence as redistributive effects are discussed—we find

Table 3.1 Summary Findings from Nonverbal Coding.

Classification	Comparative Scores, by Committee or Policy
Mean Scores	
Total mean scores for facial, vocal and gestures	(Treasury) Fiscal Policy > (Bank of England) Monetary Policy & Financial Stability
Mean Facial scores	
All Committee members (Commons TSC + Lords EAC)	(Treasury) Fiscal Policy > (Bank of England) Monetary Policy & Financial Stability
Witness	(Treasury) Fiscal Policy > (Bank of England) Monetary Policy & Financial Stability
Mean Gesture scores	
Witness	(Treasury) Fiscal Policy > (Bank of England) Monetary Policy & Financial Stability
Mean Vocal scores	
Committee members	Lords Economic Affairs > Commons Treasury Select
Facial Scores, by Emotion	
Anger	
All Committee members (Commons TSC + Lords EAC)	(Treasury) Fiscal Policy > (Bank of England) Monetary Policy & Financial Stability
Witness	(Treasury) Fiscal Policy > (Bank of England) Monetary Policy & Financial Stability
Contempt	
Witness	(Treasury) Fiscal Policy > (Bank of England) Monetary Policy & Financial Stability
Witness to Questioner	(Treasury) Fiscal Policy > All Committee members (TSC + EAC)
Happy	
Witness	Lords Economic Affairs > Commons Treasury Select
Witness	(Treasury) Fiscal Policy > (Bank of England) Monetary Policy & Financial Stability
Sad	
Witness	(Bank of England) Monetary Policy & Financial Stability > (Treasury) Fiscal Policy
Committee members	Commons Treasury Select > Lords Economic Affairs
Witness	Commons Treasury Select > Lords Economic Affairs

in the aggregate, more intense nonverbal behaviour than in monetary policy or financial stability. Bridging these findings with the textual analysis of the transcripts, we note that in fiscal policy hearings, not only do committee members and witnesses tend to 'talk across' one another, they also become quite animated in doing so—perhaps in frustration with the failure to engage in a more reciprocal dialogue. In both monetary policy and financial stability, where testimony centres more on technical language, the deliberative exchange is far less animated and emotionally charged between questioner and witness. Simply put, Chancellor Osborne's testimony is more partisan in orientation, while that of the Bank's experts is more technical, and, by implication, partisan language conveys more emotive cues than technical language. During fiscal policy hearings, the parliamentarians in both the Commons and Lords tend to reciprocate in kind with their own more frequent use of facial expressions. Moreover, Osborne also tends to use hand movements more frequently than Bank experts, which may suggest that he seeks to persuade his fellow parliamentarians to a greater extent than did officials from the central bank. (Notably, while all the coders observed Osborne's frequent hand movement, one coder scored these movements considerably higher, which supports Beattie's earlier observation that some people are simply more attuned to 'seeing' gestures than others.)

Across chambers, peers in the EAC tend to use more vocal cues than MPs in the TSC. Notably, some peers tend to be economic experts in their own right (for example, former chancellors, such as Nigel Lawson, or financiers and ministers, such as Michael Forsyth) and the questioning tends to be more discursive—that is, peers tend to spend more time in phrasing and elaborating on their questions before allowing witnesses to respond. This finding aligns with anecdotal observations and elite interviews with committee members that greater discursiveness from peers is likely to produce more vocal cues.

The second section of Table 3.1 (corresponding with Appendix 6 Table C) summarizes the mean scores for selected facial expressions, focusing on anger, disgust, contempt, happiness, and sadness. A key emotion expressed in these facial expressions by both parliamentary committee members and Treasury witnesses (predominantly Chancellor Osborne) is *anger*. This emotion is, by comparison, exhibited far less frequently in hearings with Bank experts. Importantly, anger is expressed by *both* the committees and the witnesses in fiscal policy hearings. One further emotion—*contempt*—is also more prominently expressed by witnesses in fiscal policy hearings than in Bank of England hearings. Moreover, focusing on the fiscal policy hearings, we also observe that the witnesses (again, predominantly, the chancellor) exhibit greater contempt than do the parliamentarians who are engaged in questioning. In short, fiscal policy hearings unleash higher levels of anger by questioners and witnesses alike than Bank oversight hearings. In addition, witnesses tend to exhibit contempt toward committee members, but this does not appear to be returned by the committee members toward the witnesses.

Turning to reassuring or *happy* facial expressions, the comparison across chambers suggests that witnesses (both Bank and Treasury) appearing before the Lords committee tend to be more congenial than those appearing before the Commons. Conversely, for expressions of sadness, both committee members and witnesses are more rueful in the Commons committee than in the Lords committee. This does seem to suggest a difference in interactional dynamic between the two committees, with a more reassuring dynamic in the Lords hearings (by witnesses and committee members) and more concern or appeasement ('sadness') in the Commons hearings. Observers of deliberative norms in both committees note that because partisanship is less acute in the Lords committees, these hearings tend to be relatively more relaxed than those in the Commons committees (Norton, 2016), which may help explain this finding. Evidence for this derives both from my own interviews with MPs, peers and policy experts, as well as from other published accounts: 'The absence of an absolute majority, the presence of a sizeable body of peers with no party affiliations and the appointed nature of the House (members not seeing one another as electoral threats) have resulted in a less adversarial approach and fewer divisions than in the Commons' (Norton, 2016: 129). Arguably, MPs generally hold career aspirations and are not as established as are peers, and thus we might draw upon a behavioural model of nonverbal communication for an interpretation of this finding (for example, the 'challenger' style (aggressive) versus the 'power holder' style (more confident, assured) (Broom, Koenig et al., 2009)).

From the behavioural model of leader-follower interactions discussed earlier, one is tempted to depict the TSC as a competitive setting and the EAC as non-competitive. Some aspects of this model seem to apply—for example, the anger by parliamentarians in the Commons committee and the sadness/appeasement of Bank officials in this same committee. But the goal of maintaining social order through fear/submission does not appear to hold for the chancellor in fiscal policy hearings; rather, he mirrors the anger of the committee members and adds to this contempt. Bank officials also do not respond with fear to the anger of the committee members, although their nonverbal expressions of sadness/appeasement are less overtly combative than the chancellor's contemptuous expressions. In short, the expectation of the behavioural model for nonverbal behaviour is that actors will adapt their behaviour to regulate social relations. The interesting finding here is that the chancellor does not appear to respond as expected in either a competitive setting (fear) or a non-competitive setting (appeasement), whereas central bankers respond in *both* committees along the lines of what would be expected in a non-competitive setting. This is not to say that the context of deliberative accountability for central bankers is entirely cooperative and amicable since the nonverbal expressions of parliamentarians is 'anger' towards central bankers. Thus, the context is clearly adversarial, but from the central bank witnesses, the anger is not reciprocated.

There is, however, one final observation which appears out of place—that is, the higher happiness/reassurance displays by Treasury witnesses, relative to Bank experts. At first, this does not accord with the parallel findings of more anger and contempt by Treasury witnesses in these hearings. An intuitive interpretation is the tendency of politicians to be somewhat disingenuous in 'putting a positive spin' (literally, by smiling) on politically sensitive budgetary news. To explore this further, Figure 3.1 presents still photos of Chancellor Osborne which were taken from the coded hearings. The contrast is between the top row and the bottom row (but ignoring his notable weight loss (Dominiczak, 2015)). The 'smirk' in Osborne's smile has been noted previously by journalists (Fenton, 2016), and this element can be seen in the smiles on the first row. The bottom-row smiles are quite different in being more genuine. More specifically, these bottom-row smiles resemble the enjoyment smile (also known as the 'Duchenne' smile, named after Duchenne de Boulogne (Ekman, Davidson et al., 1990)), which accords with feelings of happiness or amusement, but may also be signalling cooperation (Stewart, Bucy et al., 2015). In the top row, Osborne's teeth are less in evidence, and the muscles surrounding the eyes are not contracted. Inasmuch as an enjoyment smile is evidenced by a display of teeth as well as muscle contraction surrounding the eyes (Bucy, 2011), the lack of these features suggests more of a smirk, or disingenuous smile.

Figures 3.2a and 3.2b examine differences in the distributions of facial expression coding. The top and bottom distributions ('J' and 'R') are from the two undergraduate coders, while the distribution by 'G' is from the older coder (with over 15 years of experience in empirical political science research). Both the undergraduates code the happy scores of the hearings with the chancellor

Fig. 3.1 The Smiles of Chancellor George Osborne.

Source: All 6 images were obtained as screenshots from video hearings obtained from https://
parliamentlive.tv, with usage permied by the Parliamentary Recording Unit. As screenshots, the
resoluon is constrained.

(HMT) relatively higher than all other facial expressions (and coder 'R' tends
to over code, as seen in the vertical scale; Figure 3.2b thus provides an enlarged
version of these scores). In contrast, coder G produces a wider array of facial
expression scores, which indicates more scores for anger, contempt, and surprise, and less for happiness. While it is highly unconventional to note what
appear to be idiosyncratic differences among coders, both the nature of Osborne's smiles and the contrast between the innate experience of the coders
suggest that the degree of contempt and anger by Osborne agreed upon by all
three coders (from Table 3.1) might in fact be greater, if perhaps the undergraduate coders had received more extensive training in the specific nature
of Osborne's false smiles. At the very least, Figures 3.1, 3.2a and 3.2b suggest
that more could be done to capture more accurately the genuine versus the
controlled expressions of Chancellor Osborne.

Fig. 3.2a Distributions of Facial Expression Scores Among Coders.

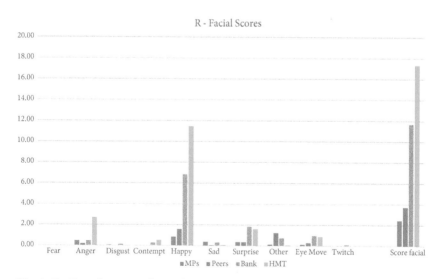

Fig. 3.2b Distributions of Facial Expression Scores—R only.

3.7 Discussion and Conclusion to Part One

The quotations at the beginning of Chapter 1 presage the findings of nonverbal behaviour in the committee hearings. Speaking from his experience as a central banker, Alan Blinder emphasizes that unelected (independent) central bankers are morally accountable to the public and are thereby obliged to explain themselves. In their appearances before the parliamentary select committees in the UK, central bankers convey this acquiescence to parliamentarians in their nonverbal facial expressions. Conversely, the quote by the TSC chair Andrew Tyrie characterizes a particular fiscal policy hearing as having 'pretty vigorous exchanges' in which 'the Government was forced to explain its actions.' The description suggests a heated (threatening) tone in the room and a competition for control over policy decisions or outcomes. This, too, fits well with the documentation of anger expressed by parliamentarians and the chancellor over fiscal policy, although it may not have anticipated the clear finding of contempt by the chancellor toward the committee members. In short, the findings in this part of the chapter accord with the observations of those intimately involved in committee oversight hearings.

This section also builds upon the quantitative text analysis of the deliberative content of the hearings in Chapter 2. The analysis of the verbal content of these hearings found that in fiscal policy hearings, committee members would focus on a certain array of thematic concerns, while the witness (namely the chancellor) would seek to address his own topic(s). As a process, questioners and witness would effectively talk past one another. The content of fiscal policy hearings is also more partisan in orientation than either monetary policy or financial stability. From this coding of the nonverbal communication in these hearings, certain findings complement our understanding of the verbal content: angry/threatening expressions by parliamentarians (shared by the witness) together with the contempt by the witness run parallel to the partisan clashes and failure of both questioners and witness to establish a *shared* discourse around common themes (that is, there is more talking *past* one another than talking *with* one another; the witness tends to avoid answering the question asked, and instead provides a response which is unrelated or diversionary in nature). This nonverbal behaviour of each side may reflect latent emotions of anger and contempt by both backbench and frontbench parliamentarians. Yet bearing in mind that these hearings are not one-shot episodes but occur with regularity throughout the life of the parliamentary session, these expressions may also signal ongoing animosity and a continuous struggle for control over fiscal policy priorities by members of the legislature versus members of the executive. As such, committee members may be signalling their willingness to remain vigilant in questioning ('attacking') the priorities and processes of the Treasury, while the chancellor is also signalling his resistance to this seeming challenge to his authority and competence. In this context, there appears to be little agreement as to who is situated where in the dominance hierarchy between the committee members and the Treasury. Confrontation between backbench and frontbench parliamentarians (legislature versus executive) persists—which is in accordance with behavioural/ethological principles—though the expectation that each set of actors will seek to maintain social order does not appear to apply.

In the monetary policy hearings with Bank officials, the verbal content exhibits very little discernible partisanship, and for each theme in the hearings, both committee members and Bank officials engage with each other—that is, Bank of England officials respond more directly to the questions of committee members, thereby creating a shared thematic discourse. The assessment of nonverbal behaviour in these hearings accords with this verbal content, in that these witnesses display more appeasement ('sad') expressions towards both sets of committee members, suggesting that central bankers perceive these hearings as non-competitive encounters. From the behavioural ecology approach, this behaviour appears to signal a willingness to cooperate with (and defer to) Parliament. While parliamentarians are clearly adversarial, central bankers in monetary policy and financial policy hearings respond deferentially.

The comparison of nonverbal behaviour across the two chambers further complements the analysis of the verbal content. From the transcripts, it was found that in the Commons committee, MPs tended to divide their speaking time across several themes whereas in the Lords committee, each peer tended to focus on one theme (typically one that fell into that peer's area of expertise). The finding of a higher incidence of reassuring facial expressions in the Lords committee is thus a feature of a more relaxed, less confrontational discourse in this committee, where peers are also at liberty to engage witnesses in themes of greatest interest to them.

Finally, this first part of the chapter has neither sought nor obtained a precise quantification of nonverbal behaviour in committee hearings; rather, it has explored the relative occurrence of expressive displays and extent to which systematic differences are identifiable between types of witnesses and types of questioners in the real-world setting of parliamentary oversight. Additionally—and unconventionally—this analysis has made transparent a contrast between more inexperienced, young coders and a more experienced, older coder, with the former less able (or willing) to differentiate the genuine or phony nature of smiles by Chancellor Osborne. Bearing in mind criticisms levelled against the overreliance on undergraduates in empirical research, it is worth noting that false smiles may be an aspect of nonverbal coding which requires far more extensive training and expertise to accurately code. Ultimately, however, the goal here is to gauge the extent to which the interactional dynamic of fiscal policy hearings differs from hearings with central bankers, and the extent to which contrasts are observed in nonverbal behaviour between parliamentary committees. To that end, we have found clear differences.

PART 2: Nonverbal Behaviour at the Individual Level: An Experimental Approach

3.8 Introduction

The first half of this chapter sought to gauge the influence of nonverbal behaviour using extensive hand coding of facial expressions, vocal cues, and gestures. The second half takes a very different approach to gauging the effect of nonverbal behaviour in select committee deliberations. In a controlled experiment subjects were asked to give impressionistic responses to nonverbal behaviour, having viewed/listened to selected clips from the twelve hearings coded in the first part of this chapter. The experiment measures the extent to which nonverbal cues—alongside verbal reasoning—shape perceptions of the witness as competent and persuasive. The intent is to isolate as much as possible the independent effect of nonverbal behaviour on the perceptions of the deliberative process, and particularly subjects' impressions of the overall credibility of the witness who is being held to account by the parliamentary committee.

3.9 Two Mechanisms for Assessing the Effect of Nonverbal Behaviour

The experiment set out two separate mechanisms for assessing the independent effect of nonverbal behaviour in committee hearing deliberations. The first draws upon the classic case of the 1960 first presidential debate between John Kennedy and Richard Nixon, from which a so-called 'myth' has developed surrounding the differing assessments of the candidates by television viewers (who could see the candidates) and radio listeners (who could only listen to them) (Vancil and Pendell, 1987). While dramatic differences in appearances did indeed exist between the two candidates (with Kennedy appearing younger, healthier and more attractive than the older, physically ailing and less attractive Nixon), the effect that these differences had on audiences' assessments of the debate winner is disputed (Vancil and Pendell, 1987, Druckman, 2003). Druckman's experimental reanalysis of the Kennedy-Nixon debate directly challenges the scepticism cast upon the effect of the television visuals by Vancil and Pendell's survey of the evidence. Druckman's reanalysis of the Kennedy-Nixon debate creates two groups of participants (randomly assigned). The subjects in the first group watched (and listened to) the debate while subjects in the second group only listened to an audio version of the same debate. Druckman's finding of a significant difference in assessment of the debate winner between viewers and listeners-only provides the basis for the first mechanism used in my experiment. That is, participants were randomly assigned either to a group that watched (and listened to) clips from parliamentary committee accountability hearings or a group that listened to an audio version of these same clips. Viewers would thus be exposed to all three forms of nonverbal behaviour discussed earlier in this chapter—facial expressions, gestures, and vocal cues—while listeners would be exposed only to vocal cues. To the extent that, as Grabe and Bucy argue, 'visual experience remains the most dominant mode of learning' (Grabe and Bucy, 2009: 12–13), I expect to find a significant difference between viewers and listeners-only in their assessments of the witness. In summary, I hypothesize that:

> H1: A significant difference will exist between viewers and listeners-only with respect to subjects' assessments of (a) how well the witness addresses questions; (b) his competence; and (c) his persuasiveness.

I also expect viewers to be more likely than audio-only subjects to pick up on, and thus mention, nonverbal cues as they make their assessments of the competence and persuasiveness of witnesses (bearing in mind that audio-only subjects may still rely on vocal cues for their judgements). I thus hypothesize that:

> H2: Viewers of the hearings will be significantly more likely than audio listeners to mention nonverbal cues in their open-ended explanations of the reasons given for their assessments of the witness as competent and/or persuasive.

Table 3.2a VIDEO CLIPS USED IN EXPERIMENT, BY NONVERBAL EXCHANGE DYNAMIC.

Parliamentary Committee Member Question Style	Witness Response Style	
	Combative	*Appeasing*
Contentious	1: Mann (MP) & Osborne Norman (MP) & King	2: MacGregor (Lord) & King Mudie (MP) & King
Conciliatory	3: Tyrie (MP) & Carney Tyrie (MP) & Osborne	4: Fallon (MP) & Osborne Hollick (Lord) & King Lawson (Lord) & Osborne

The second mechanism for assessing the independent effect of nonverbal behaviour builds upon the behavioural ecology approach (discussed in Part one of this chapter), where nonverbal cues serve as signals of communication. This social *interaction* aspect of nonverbal behaviour is measured with reference to the 'nonverbal exchange dynamic' between the questioner and the witness in each clip—namely, the extent to which the exchange is contentious or conciliatory. An expert in nonverbal communication[3] independently analysed and categorized each video clip by (a) the style of questioning by the committee member (contentious or conciliatory), and (b) the response style of the witness (combative or appeasing).

Table 3.2a shows the classification of the videos into a two-by-two table: contentious questioner/combative witness (cell 1); contentious questioner/appeasing witness (cell 2); conciliatory questioner/combative witness (cell 3); and conciliatory questioner/appeasing witness (cell 4). Each of the four cells is thus used to generate a new variable ('video category'), which offers a single measure of the nonverbal exchange dynamic that reflects the unique content of each of the clips—and in particular, the degree to which the nonverbal exchange is, broadly speaking, conflictual. Very simply, the videos in cell 1 are judged as most conflictual and those in cell 4 the least conflictual. In cell 2 the questioner is judged as relatively more aggressive than the witness, whereas in cell 3 the witness is the more aggressive actor.

While this categorization relies on the judgment of an expert in nonverbal communication, a reasonably simple—and independent—check can be made by linking the categories back to the hand-coding of the full hearings by research assistants (from Part one of this chapter). To do this, I extracted the individual coded data for facial expressions for the specific clips used in this experiment. Relying on the codes of the senior research assistant, I compiled the unstandardized counts for the three facial expressions which (arguably) best capture the tension between the questioner and witness—that is, anger, disgust, and contempt. For each video clip, I compiled the averages for the questioner and witness (combined) and for each separately. These are given in Table 3.2b. From the counts of these facial expressions, we can see that the relative differences in these cell values marry up well with the designated nonverbal exchange dynamic. That is, where we would expect the greatest conflict (cell 1), the mean is the highest. And, where one actor is deemed more aggressive than the other (cells 2 and 3), we can see that the relative means of the questioner and witness reflect this disparity. The one slight exception to our expected values is the cell 4 mean for the questioner and witness, which is slightly larger than that for cell 3, but it is nonetheless considerably less than for cells 1 and 2. Overall, the hand-coded facial expressions align well with the expected nonverbal exchange dynamic in Table 3.2a, thus lending confidence to the robustness of this measure.

While this dynamic is expected to shape the views of subjects as to the overall competence of the witness, no prior expectation is made as to the form or direction of these views. I thus hypothesize that:

H3: A significant difference will exist among the four types of nonverbal exchange dynamic with respect to subjects' assessments of (a) how well the witness addresses questions; (b) his competence; and (c) his persuasiveness.

(and)

H4: The nonverbal exchange dynamic will influence subjects' open-ended explanations of the reasons given for their assessments of the witness as competent and/or persuasive.

3.10 Experiment Set-up and Procedure

For the experiment[4] I randomly assigned 120 university students to one of two groups. Eighty subjects watched a series of video clips (which were selected from the parliamentary hearings previously coded in Part one of this chapter). The remaining forty subjects (the control group) only *listened* to recordings of these same hearings. The audio-only cohort was shown still photos of both the questioner and the witness during each clip, as the pilot study for this experiment suggested some difficulty in identifying speakers without at least some

Table 3.2b HAND-CODING OF FACIAL EXPRESSIONS FOR VIDEO CLIPS, BY NONVERBAL EXCHANGE DYNAMIC[a].

Parliamentary Committee Member Question Style	Witness Response Style	
	Combative	*Appeasing*
Contentious	**1:** (Anger + Disgust +Contempt) Questioner and Witness Mean = 9 Questioner Mean = 5 Witness Mean = 4	**2:** (Anger + Disgust +Contempt) Questioner and Witness Mean = 5.5 Questioner Mean = 3 Witness Mean = 2.5
Conciliatory	**3:** (Anger + Disgust +Contempt) Questioner and Witness Mean = 3 Questioner Mean = 1 Witness Mean = 2	**4:** (Anger + Disgust +Contempt) Questioner and Witness Mean = 3.7 Questioner Mean = 2 Witness Mean = 1.7

[a] Raw codes are from senior research assistant coder

visual aid. The participants were informed that the study sought to gauge deliberation in parliamentary hearings, but were *not* informed that the focus of
the study was nonverbal communication.[5] Subjects were informed that their
final payment would be deducted by one-third if they failed to correctly answer
two very simple questions—based on the content of the videos—at the end of
the experiment. This was intended to incentivise them to pay close attention
to each of the video clips. Furthermore, to sustain the participants' attention,
prior to each clip, they were asked to identify (from a list of eight) the two
key topics that were discussed in each hearing. After viewing/listening to the
clip, they were asked a series of questions concerning their impressions of witnesses' competence and persuasiveness in responding to the questioner, and
finally were given space to explain their assessments in their own words (see
questionnaire template, Appendix 7).

While all subjects viewed/listened to all the nine clips, and answered the
subsequent questions for each clip, the sequencing of the clips was randomized
among the subjects (to mitigate a conditioning bias associated with a particular
sequence of clips—see Appendix 8, which also provides the rationale for selection, timings and content of each clip). The nine video clips (totalling about
45 minutes) include six from the Treasury Select Committee (three on fiscal
policy, three on monetary policy/financial stability) and three from the Lords
Economic Affairs Committee hearings. The clips contain one of three witnesses: George Osborne (former Chancellor of the Exchequer), Mervyn King
(Bank of England Governor, 2003–13) and Mark Carney (Bank of England
Governor, 2013–20).

Following completion of the nine videos (and the set of questions after
each video), subjects met in focus groups of five to discuss their individual
impressions of the witnesses. Each subject was asked by a research assistant
(who remained in the meeting room) to evaluate Osborne, King and Carney
according to his (1) likeability; (2) competence; and (3) persuasiveness. Following these discussions, participants returned to their computer stations, and
were asked whether the group discussion changed their initial impressions of
each witness (Osborne, King, Carney), and if so, why, or why not. This post-
group element sought to gauge the extent to which social persuasion may have
prompted participants to alter their initial assessments of the witnesses. As
the potential for nonverbal cues to have an indirect effect on the judgments
of an audience—that is, indirectly through discussions with others—did not
appear to have been significant, the results for this part of the experiment are
not reported here. However, as other intriguing results are found, Appendix 9
reports this aspect of the experiment.

3.11 Predictor Variables, Outcome Variables, and Stages of Analysis

3.11.1 Stage One

Analysis of the experimental data was structured in three stages (see Table 3.3a for the percentage frequency distributions of all the relevant variables). Stage one sought to test whether statistical differences in subjects' assessments of the witnesses (measured by the ordinal outcome variables) exist between the two key predictor variables—that is, group type (viewing vs audio-only) and across the four categories of nonverbal exchange dynamic. Three ordinal outcomes captured the initial assessments of witnesses by the subjects, namely, *how well he addressed* the questioner, *his persuasiveness* in responding to questions, and finally his *overall competence* (again, see Appendix 7 for the questionnaire template).[6] Stage one of the analysis thus tests whether viewing the clip (as opposed to hearing it only) or the nonverbal exchange dynamic between the questioner and witness (contentious or conciliatory questioner; combative or appeasing witness) had a statistically significant effect on how well subjects thought the witness answered the questions, how persuasive he was and his overall competence.

3.11.2 Stage Two

Stage two derives from the open-ended question pertaining to each video clip (Appendix 7). This question sought to query subjects' rationale behind their three-part assessment of the witness—that is, participants were asked to provide in their own words their explanations for their closed-ended evaluations. They were asked: 'Based only on the video clip you just viewed/heard, explain why you think [George Osborne / Mervyn King / Mark Carney] was persuasive - or not - AND why you believe [George Osborne / Mervyn King / Mark Carney] was competent - or not'. To analyse these open-ended questions, I (together with assistance from a policy expert who has testified before both the TSC and the EAC for many years) manually coded all the open-ended responses for the nine videos. Together, we read each explanation for why the participant evaluated the witness as he/she did, and then created three variables which we coded dichotomously, depending on whether it was mentioned in the response: (1) *competence* (including his knowledge); (2) *verbal reasoning*

Table 3.3a VARIABLE LIST (WITH FREQUENCIES).

VARIABLES FOR STAGES 1 AND 2

STAGE 1: TESTS OF DIFFERENCES IN ORDINAL OUT-
COMES BETWEEN CATEGORIES OF PREDICTOR
VARIABLES
STAGE 2: GAUGING EFFECTS OF PREDICTOR
VARIABLES ON REASONS GIVEN FOR ORDINAL
RESPONSES (OPEN-ENDED)
Key predictor variables:

Group Type
   (viewing [66.7%], audio only [33.3%])

Nonverbal exchange dynamic

   1. contentious questioner + combative witness
      [22.2%]
   2. contentious questioner + appeasing witness
      [22.2%]
   3. conciliatory questioner + combative witness
      [22.2%]
   4. conciliatory questioner + appeasing witness
      [33.3%]

Ordinal outcome variables

Addressed Well (witness addressed concerns of questioner
   very well: strongly disagree [4.4%], disagree [24.3%],
   agree [51.1%], strongly agree [20.3%])
Persuasive (arguments of witness were persuasive:
   strongly disagree [4.9%], disagree [24.2%], agree
   [51.1%], strongly agree [19.8%])
Competence (rate competence of witness as: poor [2.3%],
   below average [10.2%], average [30.9%], above average
   [35.0%], very good [21.6%])

**Open-ended reasons given for ordinal responses, coded
dichotomously [% mentions]**

Why: from competence [51.7%]
Why: from verbal reasoning [95.3%]
Why: from nonverbal [19.1%]

Control variables

Student status (undergraduate [43.3%], *postgraduate*
   [56.7%])
Gender (male [46.7%], *female* [53.3%])
English speaker (from UK, Canada or USA) [16.7%]
Partisanship (left of centre [26.7%], *no leaning* [60.8%],
   right of centre [12.5%])

(which entailed a more specific use of language, reasoning, logical argument); and (3) *nonverbal cues*. For each of these variables, a positive or negative mention of the trait may have signified an endorsement or criticism of the speaker (for example, 'he was competent' or 'he lacked competence'), but the slant of the comment was not coded. To illustrate, the following statements provide examples of the three coded responses (bearing in mind that a statement could score '1' for more than one variable).

Competence:
A little bit of doubts here and there but the intent to clarify his arguments made him appear to be more persuasive and knowledgeable about the topic of concern.

Doesn't really answer the question in my opinion. Not competent because no actions taken to improve welfare despite higher welfare spending.

He made a joke, and even challenged Mr Mudie: 'how on earth are we not independent?' By asking this question he is showing competency, as if his argument is the only one which is valid.

Here, Mervyn King was not as persuasive because it was George Mudie who was leading the whole conversation. King did not have good answers to Mudie's questions and his knowledge on the issues mentioned did not seem strong throughout the video, hence it made him incompetent in this conversation. Likewise, the 10-year remark was somehow inappropriate, and it looked like King wanted to answer the question by referring to the number of years in charge and he did not actually answer the question.

Verbal reasoning:
George Osborne was not clear in his explanation, and misled Michael Fallon. He then had to clarify in his earlier explanation.

I think George Osborne was persuasive in this clip as his answers were direct, without much extra unnecessary information. I think the 'straight to the point' attitude suggests high competency as it shows he knows the answers and is aware of all the possible concerns.

Mr. Carney gave very clear answers. I liked the fact that he organized his arguments by utilizing signposts. I also appreciated the fullness of his answer. He seemed to give answers that not only answered the question directly, but that also responded to the underlying assumptions and premises being questioned.

On the business cycle turns question, Mr. Carney was able to accept limits of institutional ability. Mr. Carney offered evidence to the validity of the Bank of England's stress tests. He also offered evidence to the ability of the Bank to choose meaningful and challenging tests, which will reveal banks as too risky. Mr. Carney aptly answers, and shows competency by relating the rationale of policies of the Bank.

Nonverbal cues:
He was still being persuasive, but he stammered a lot in this clip which makes him slightly discredited.

(Audio only group)

His body language was convincing, as far as persuasion goes. As regards … competency, in addition to his body language, he exposed ideas in a clear and detailed fashion.

(Viewing group)

He looked prepared on the topics because he reported several facts and numbers. However, there were several hesitations in his speech and he frequently avoided eye-contact with the listener. This reduced his persuasiveness.

(Viewing group)

He did not look very serious. From the first point he started talking it looked as if he was laughing and as if he does not take the problem of climate change seriously. His response thereafter was rather generic. I did not find him very persuasive and due to his generic response, I mark his competency as average.

(Viewing group)

Notably, nonverbal cues could also be evident in the audio-only cohort, as seen in the first quoted comment above, which cites the vocal cue of 'stammering' as a trait that lessened Osborne's persuasiveness. It thus bears repeating from the discussion preceding Hypothesis 1 that while facial expressions and gestures are clearly observed only by the viewing group, vocal cues could not be so easily isolated. Thus, the effect of nonverbal communication which this study isolates in the two groups is limited more specifically to facial expressions and gestures, while vocal cues permeate both groups.

In contrast to Stage one, Stage two sought to gauge the *effect* of the key predictor variables (group type [viewing/audio-only] and nonverbal exchange dynamic) in each video on subjects' explanations for *why* they assessed each witness as they did. These open-ended assessments thus comprised three further outcome variables: (1) *why: from competence*, (2) *why: from verbal reasoning* and (3) *why: from nonverbal cues*. The third outcome variable is used to test Hypotheses 2 and 4. The variables capturing mentions of competence and verbal reasoning are included as exploratory measures, but with no stipulated priors.

From Table 3.3a, the vast majority (95 per cent) of subjects included some aspect of verbal reasoning in their explanation why they assessed the witness as they did. Nonetheless, nearly one-fifth (19 per cent) mentioned some form of nonverbal behaviour in their explanation. For a better overview of their overlapping nature, Table 3.3b provides a three-way crosstabulation of *why: from competence, why: from verbal reasoning* and *why: from nonverbal cues*. The counts for this table are in repeated measures format[7] so that the N=1080 (120 subjects x responses to nine clips, with some loss from missing responses). Notably, 114 (10.6 per cent) of the responses included mentions of *all* three reasons—that is, competence, verbal reasoning, nonverbal cues—while 15 (1.4 per cent) responses mentioned none of these.

The regression analysis for Stage two also included four control variables: the *student's status* (undergraduate or postgraduate, as a proxy for maturity), *gender*, his or her *partisanship* (left of centre, no leaning, right of centre), and whether the subject came from an *English-speaking* country (from the United Kingdom, Canada or the United States). The characteristics of the 120 participants were reasonably diverse. For example, both post-graduates and undergraduates participated, with a distribution of 57 per cent to 43 per cent; slightly more females than males participated (53 per cent and 47 per cent); and most (61 per cent) were centrist or with no particular

Table 3.3b Cross tabulation of *Why: from Competence* with *Why: from Verbal*, with *Why: from Nonverbal* as Layer Variable (in counts of responses, repeated measures format).

Why: from nonverbal			Why: from verbal reasoning		Total
			No mention of verbal reasoning	Mentions verbal reasoning	
No mention of nonverbal cues	Why: from competence	No mention of competence	15	417	432
		Mentions competence	25	413	438
	Total		40	830	870
Mentions nonverbal cues	Why: from competence	No mention of competence	7	80	87
		Mentions competence	4	114	118
	Total		11	194	205
Total	Why: from competence	No mention of competence	22	497	519
		Mentions competence	29	527	556
	Total		51	1024	1075

ideological leaning, 27 per cent were left of centre and about 13 per cent were right of centre.

The last control variable—*English-speaking*—requires more discussion. As background, when considering the characteristics of the participants, it is important to note that their responses are meant to proxy those of parliamentarians. That is, since the broader goal of this work is to gauge deliberation in legislative hearings, the intent of this experiment is to capture the effect of nonverbal behaviour on parliamentarians within these hearings—bearing in mind that parliamentarians are themselves (intended to be) representative of the larger population. Setting aside any judgment as to the representativeness of parliamentarians, it is worth noting two ways in which the participants of this experiment may differ significantly from parliamentarians: their nationality and their age. In terms of nationality, about 9 per cent of the subjects were from the UK, and the rest were from 32 other countries (whereas in 2016, about 11 per cent of parliamentarians were of immigrant origin (English, 2016) and in the UK more broadly, about 14 per cent of the population were born abroad ((NA), 2017)). This means that, relative to British parliamentarians, the participants of this study may have been less familiar both with the English language, and with UK politics and political institutions. Nonetheless, while non-UK students may have been less at ease with the English language, all the students possessed sufficient language skills to be studying at university in the English language, and so the language issue is likely to be minimal. As for their familiarity with UK politics and political institutions, one might also argue that, in the absence of parliamentarians serving as subjects of this study (surely a tall order), any set of student participants could not be expected to have the same knowledge of parliamentary politics as that held by parliamentarians themselves. Moreover, as the focus of this experiment is on nonverbal behaviour, one might also argue that parliamentary knowledge is less important than simple human observation. And finally, although the multi-national diversity of the participants may be a drawback in terms of familiarity with the UK Parliament, this diversity is also an advantage in allowing us to gauge the effect of *nonverbal* communication across different languages and cultural norms, thus allowing us to potentially broaden our inferences from this study.

A second characteristic that distinguishes the participants from parliamentarians is their age: 52 per cent were aged 18 to 22, 40 per cent were 23 to 29 and 8.3 per cent were over 30. In contrast, the average age for a member of the UK

Parliament in 2015 was 50, and it was 40 years of age for the average Briton in 2018 (Carter and Swinney, 2018). While this may limit the inferences drawn from this study, it is one that is shared by many academic studies that rely on university students for laboratory experiments.

3.12 Analysis and Results

The raw data from the experimental test were converted into repeated measures format (N=1,080), thereby maximizing the leverage of the responses across the nine videos. Turning to the evaluations in Stage one (*address well*, *persuasiveness* and *competence*), a Levene's test was used to assess the null hypothesis of equal variances, and significant differences were found for both *address well* (p < .05) and *persuasiveness* (p < .01).[8] The alternative rank-based nonparametric Kruskal-Wallis H test was used to gauge whether statistically significant differences in how well the witness responded to the questioner (*address well*), how persuasive he was (*persuasive*) and how competent he was (*competent*) exist between (a) the viewing and the audio-only groups; and (b) the four types of nonverbal exchange dynamic categories (Table 3.2a) between the committee member and the witness. The null hypothesis of this test is that the mean ranks of the groups[9] are the same.[10]

Significant differences in the viewing/audio-only groups are found for the assessments of *how well the witness responded* to the questions of the committee member, χ^2 (1) = 5.24, p = 0.02 with a mean rank of 554.6 for the watching cohort and 512.3 for the listening-only cohort. No statistically significant differences are found between the two groups for assessments of the witness's *persuasiveness* (χ^2 (1) = 1.20, p = 0.27) or *competence* (χ^2 (1) = 1.24, p = 0.27). Similarly, for the median test statistic, the variable *how well the witness responded* is significant, but the other two variables are not (i.e., *how well the witness responded* obtained χ^2 (1) = 4.36, p = 0.04; *persuasiveness* χ^2 (1) = 0.19, p = 0.67; and *competence* χ^2 (1) = 0.01, p = 0.92).

Turning to the second predictor variable—nonverbal exchange dynamic—we find statistically significant differences among the four categories for all three outcome variables:

- For assessments as to *how well the witness responded* to the questions of the committee member, χ^2 (3) = 41.97, p = 0.00 with a mean rank of 451.7 for cell 1, 539.1 for cell 2, 620.5 for cell 3, and 547.3 for cell 4. The median test statistic obtains χ^2 (3) = 13.65, p = 0.00.

- For assessments of *persuasiveness*, χ^2 (3) = 33.89, p = 0.00 with a mean rank of 463.5 for cell 1, 550.39 for cell 2, 614.9 for cell 3, and 535.6 for cell 4. The median test statistic obtains χ^2 (3) = 8.52, p = 0.04.
- And, for assessments of *competence*, χ^2 (3) = 27.13, p = 0.00 with a mean rank of 471.7 for cell 1, 575.1 for cell 2, 601.1 for cell 3, and 522.9 for cell 4. The median test statistic obtains χ^2 (3) = 10.35, p = 0.02.

In sum, statistically significant differences are found between the viewing and audio-only groups with respect to assessments of how well the witness responded—that is, the mean ranks of subjects exposed to the effects of facial expressions and gestures (the viewing cohort) are significantly higher than those who only listened to the videos in terms of their assessments of how well the witness address the questioner. However, no significant difference is found for his overall competence or his persuasiveness. The significance of just one of these assessment measures lends support to Hypothesis 1 (a), but not to Hypothesis 1 (b) or (c), and so the effect of viewing the hearings (as opposed to listening only) is not as powerful as anticipated.

More striking, however, are the significant differences found between the four categories of the nonverbal exchange dynamic for all three of the outcome variables.[11] This finding lends strong support to Hypothesis 3 (a), (b) and (c). Particularly intriguing is the finding that across all three outcome variables (addressed the questioner well, persuasiveness, competence), the mean ranks for nonverbal exchange category 3—conciliatory questioner and combative witness—are the highest, suggesting that subjects gauged the witness as performing the 'best'. This finding suggests that a combative stance is likely to be an effective way for a witness to persuade an audience as to his competence. Importantly, however, the combative stance seems only to work effectively when the questioner is not also aggressive, since we also find that across all three outcome variables, the mean ranks for video category 1— contentious questioner and combative witness—are the lowest of the four categories. This suggests that highly conflictual exchanges—where the actors are together confrontational/combative—lead audiences to perceive the witness as having performed the 'worst'. Recalling the central focus of this work on the adversarial context of deliberative accountability, it is thus intriguing that the audiences do not assess *excessive* conflict in a favourable light. When the questioner and witness are both conflictual, audiences rank the performance of the witness quite poorly. Yet at the same time, audiences do rate *some* conflict favourably—but only when the source is from a combative witness facing a conciliatory questioner. This helps to shed some light on our question from Chapter 1—that is, would people recognize quality deliberation if they saw it? The finding here is that people do not view excessive conflict as quality deliberative accountability—or more precisely, they judge the person being held to account unfavourably when this witness faces a contentious questioner. It would thus appear that quality in deliberative accountability is judged in part by the extent to which the witness faces a contentious questioner.

Stage two of the analysis sought to gauge the *effect* of the key predictor variables (group type [viewing/audio-only] and nonverbal exchange dynamic) on subjects' open-ended explanations *why* they assessed each witness as they did. The three outcome variables were: *why: from competence, why: from verbal reasoning* and *why: from nonverbal cues*. Whereas in Stage one the task was to assess whether closed-end (ordinal) assessments of the performance of witnesses were associated with either (a) participants' exposure to facial expressions and gestures (group type), or (b) the degree of nonverbal confrontation between questioner and witness (nonverbal exchange dynamic), in Stage two, we seek to gauge whether the underlying reasons (open-ended replies) given by participants for their assessments of witnesses might also be associated with our two nonverbal predictor variables. In Stage two, a form of generalized linear model—a generalized estimating equations model (GEE)[12]—is employed, given that the data are in repeated measures format and the outcome variables are binary. Table 3.4 reports the results from the regressions for the effects of group type on the three outcome variables: competence, verbal reasoning and nonverbal cues, including as controls the four demographic variables—student status (undergraduate/postgraduate), gender, partisanship and English speaking. No significant effect is found between the two groups with respect to mentions of competence or verbal reasoning (and none was hypothesized). However, as anticipated in Hypothesis 2, we do find a statistically significant effect ($p < .05$) of group type on whether subjects mention nonverbal behaviour in their open-ended explanations (regression C). This suggests that subjects who viewed hearings (as opposed to those who listened only) were more likely to mention nonverbal cues like eye contact, head movements, or types of facial expressions in their reasons for assessing the witness as they did, which lends clear support for Hypothesis 2. In other words, subjects who viewed the hearings (relative to those who only listened to the hearings) were more likely to explain their reasons for assessing witnesses as they did in terms of nonverbal cues. This is striking, as one could

Table 3.4 Generalized Estimating Equation Regressions[a] for Effect of Group Type on Open-Ended Explanations for Assessments of Witnesses, using Repeated Measures (N subjects = 120; N responses = 1080).

Parameter[b]	A. Response = Why: from Competence		B. Response = Why: from Verbal Reasoning		C. Response = Why: from Nonverbal Behaviour	
	Unstandardized coefficient	S.E.	Unstandardized coefficient	S.E.	Unstandardized coefficient	S.E.
GROUP TYPE (0) Audio only (1) Audio & Viewing	0.24	0.29	−0.20	0.48	0.51	0.26*
STUDENT STATUS (1) Undergraduate (2) Postgraduate	−0.55	0.27*	−0.01	0.61	0.23	0.28
GENDER (1) Male (2) Female	0.10	0.28	−0.82	0.55	0.35	0.26
ENGLISH SPEAKING (0) No (1) Yes	0.12	0.40	1.53	1.03	0.05	0.36
PARTISANSHIP (reference category is Right leaning, coded as 1)[b] (−1) Left leaning	0.10	0.43	−0.19	0.76	0.27	0.40
(0) Centrist/No leaning	0.51	0.39	0.18	0.58	0.75	0.39
INTERCEPT	−0.50	0.58	−4.36	1.17***	0.61	0.53

	Model effects: Wald χ^2 (df)	Model effects: Wald χ^2 (df)	Model effects: Wald χ^2 (df)
Quasi Likelihood under Independence Model Criterion[c]	1520.94	428.46	1056.80
Corrected Quasi Likelihood under Independence Model Criterion	1473.29	408.10	1036.24
Included cases	1075	1075	1075
GROUP TYPE	0.70 (1)	0.17 (1)	3.89 (1)*
STUDENT STATUS	4.24 (1)*	0.00 (1)	0.67 (1)
GENDER	0.13 (1)	2.25 (1)	1.80 (1)
ENGLISH SPEAKING	0.08 (1)	2.22 (1)	0.02 (1)
PARTISANSHIP	2.76 (2)	0.43 (2)	5.01 (2)
INTERCEPT	2.57 (1)	67.87 (1)***	72.32 (1)***

*$p < .05$. **$p < .01$. ***$p < .001$. [a] GEE fitted with a logit link function, a binomial probability distribution for the dependent (response) variable with the highest value as the reference category, and an unstructured working correlation matrix. [b] GEE usually lists the parameter of the reference category, although as this parameter is redundant, it is set to zero. For simplicity, this redundant parameter is not listed here. [c] The kernel of the log quasi-likelihood function is used.

conjecture that viewing a hearing (rather than simply listening to it) might allow a greater understanding of the nature of the arguments or the intellectual rationale given by the witness, if for no other reason than participants might pay closer attention to the words of the witness if these participants could 'see' the witness in action (so to speak). This is not, however, what we find. Participants who viewed as opposed to those who listened only to the hearings were not more likely to explain their reasons for assessing witnesses' persuasiveness or competence in terms of verbal reasoning or logical argument, but rather in terms of the 'body language' they observed. Again, returning to our question from Chapter 1, judgments on deliberative accountability are clearly related to whether the reasons offered for decisions taken are observed visually or not. This is a subtle but important critique of much of the current literature by deliberative scholars who have not (yet) fully appreciated the impact of nonverbal communication in reason-giving deliberative discourse.

Notably, across the regression results for the three outcome variables (columns A, B and C), one control variable—the student as an undergraduate or postgraduate—is significant for mentions of competence and is negatively signed. This indicates that undergraduates were more likely than graduates to mention aspects of competency in their reasons for assessing witnesses.[13]

In contrast to the group type variable, the nonverbal exchange variable captures a more nuanced aspect of nonverbal behaviour, as it is based on the degree of confrontation or conflict between the questioner and witness. For this predictor variable, I first analysed the four-part categorization of this variable, using the GEE approach. This revealed two distinct patterns of significance among the four categories. One pattern showed a significant effect of the witness being 'combative' (cells 1 and 3, Table 3.2a) as opposed to 'appeasing' (cells 2 and 4) on the verbal reasoning outcome variable. A second pattern showed a significant effect of the questioner being 'contentious' (cells 1 and 2, Table 3.2a) as opposed to 'conciliatory' (cells 3 and 4) on the nonverbal behaviour outcome variable. To simplify the GEE regression and the interpretation of results, I created two dichotomous variables from the exchange dynamic predictor variable: contentious questioner (0) versus conciliatory questioner (1); and appeasing witness (0) versus combative witness (1). The first of these dummies bisects the two rows in Table 3.2a while the second bisects the two columns. These two dummy variables are included in the regression models in Table 3.5, along with the control variables. As seen in regression F, the questioner dummy is negatively signed and highly significant ($p < .001$), which suggests that in video/audio clips where the questioner

Table 3.5 Generalized Estimating Equation Regressions[a] for Effect of Video Category on Open-Ended Explanations for Assessments of Witnesses using Repeated Measure (N subjects = 120; N responses = 1080).

Parameter[b]	D. Response = Competence		E. Response = Verbal Reasoning[d]		F. Response = Nonverbal Behaviour	
	Unstandardized coefficient	S.E.	Unstandardized coefficient	S.E.	Unstandardized coefficient	S.E.
EXCHANGE DYNAMIC DUMMY FOR QUESTIONER (0) Contentious Questioner (1) Conciliatory Questioner	−0.10	0.09	−0.40	0.26	−0.57	0.14***
EXCHANGE DYNAMIC DUMMY FOR WITNESS (0) Appeasing Witness (1) Combative Witness	0.08	0.11	0.86	0.30**	0.14	0.15
STUDENT STATUS (1) Undergraduate (2) Postgraduate	−0.56	0.27*	−0.01	0.55	0.23	0.28
GENDER (1) Male (2) Female	0.09	0.28	−0.96	0.47*	0.32	0.27
ENGLISH SPEAKING (0) No (1) Yes	0.07	0.39	d		0.04	0.34
PARTISANSHIP (reference category is Right leaning, coded as 1)[b] (−1) Left leaning	0.05	0.43	−0.65	0.73	0.20	0.41
(0) Centrist/No leaning	0.47	0.39	0.50	0.55	0.75	0.40
INTERCEPT	−0.31	0.53	−3.29	0.61***	0.94	0.52

Continued

Table 3.5 *Continued*

Parameter[b]	D. Response = Competence	E. Response = Verbal Reasoning[d]	F. Response = Nonverbal Behaviour
Quasi Likelihood under Independence Model Criterion[c]	1519.22	412.55	1048.83
Corrected Quasi Likelihood under Independence Model Criterion	1479.91	402.30	1030.54
Included cases	1075	1075	1075
	Model effects: $Wald\ \chi^2\ (df)$	*Model effects:* $Wald\ \chi^2\ (df)$	*Model effects:* $Wald\ \chi^2\ (df)$
EXCHANGE DYNAMIC DUMMY: *Contentious Questioner*	1.35 (1)	2.35 (1)	17.30 (1)***
EXCHANGE DYNAMIC DUMMY: *Combative Witness*	0.53 (1)	8.04 (1)**	0.89 (1)
STUDENT STATUS	4.35 (1)*	0.00 (1)	0.65 (1)
GENDER	0.10 (1)	4.20 (1)*	1.46 (1)
ENGLISH SPEAKING	0.03 (1)		0.02 (1)
PARTISANSHIP	2.63 (2)	4.53 (2)	5.36 (2)
INTERCEPT	2.85 (1)	139.02 (1)***	57.54 (1)***

*$p < .05$. ** $p < .01$. *** $p < .001$. [a] GEE fitted with a logit link function, a binomial probability distribution for the dependent (response) variable with the highest value as the reference category, and an unstructured working correlation matrix. [b] GEE usually lists the parameter of the reference category, although as this parameter is redundant it is set to zero. For simplicity, this redundant parameter is not listed here. [c] The kernel of the log quasi-likelihood function is used. [d] Model collinearity prevented inclusion of English Speaking for the Verbal Reasoning response variable.

is contentious, subjects are more likely to reference nonverbal cues in their explanations for why they assessed the witness as they did. Conversely, in clips where the questioner is conciliatory, subjects are less likely to reference nonverbal cues in these explanations. The effect of the mode in which the questioner conducts himself is, moreover, the only variable in the regression which is significant for references of nonverbal behaviour. This finding strongly supports Hypothesis 4, and moreover, it targets which form of the nonverbal interaction influences subjects' open-ended replies. The key appears to rest with the degree of confrontation by the questioner, regardless of whether the witness responded in a combative or an appeasing manner. Succinctly put, when a questioner is contentious, respondents are more likely to mention nonverbal behaviour by the witness, and when the questioner is conciliatory, respondents are less likely to mention nonverbal behaviour by the witness. For deliberative scholars, this highlights the critical role for gauging the degree to which the deliberative discourse is conflictual. For accountability scholars, this suggests that the process of accountability is shaped by the nonverbal behaviour of those holding policymakers to account—the more aggressive the behaviour, the more the attention of the audience is drawn to the responding nonverbal behaviour of the policymaker. More to the point, when the questioner appears to be riling the witness, does the witness remain calm or does he become riled?

But what exactly is it about the contentious or conciliatory nature of the questioner that appears to prompt more mentions of nonverbal behaviour? To gain a better understanding of these results, I extracted two subsets from the complete dataset of subjects' open-ended responses. The criteria for selection were the questioner type (conciliatory/contentious) and whether the subject mentioned any nonverbal cues. Specifically, the first subset comprised cases in which the questioner type is conciliatory and nonverbal behaviour is not mentioned, and the second subset comprised cases in which the questioner type is contentious and the subject mentioned nonverbal behaviour. Essentially, these are the two extremes of the correlation between the exchange dynamic dummy variable for the questioner and the nonverbal behaviour response variable (from regression F, Table 3.5). Using quantitative text analysis,[14] I conducted a 'specificity analysis', which allows one to compare the language used in a subset of a corpus with the larger corpus or alternatively to compare the language used in two subsets of a corpus. Moreover, the analysis specifies the words and phrases (Elementary Context Units) that are used more or less frequently in each subset and assigns statistical significance to the unique vocabulary. The details of this analysis are given in Appendix 10.

In summary, when a questioner is *not* riling the witness, observers pay more attention to the witness's verbal responses (Appendix Table 10a), but when the questioner appears to be riling the witness, observers pay more attention to the nonverbal responses of the witness (Appendix Table 10b). The textual analysis thus reveals that in cases when the questioner is conciliatory and no mention is made of nonverbal behaviour, participants in this study explain their assessments of witnesses in terms of logic and reasoning—for example, 'they were sensible approaches', 'the rationale of policies of the Bank', 'he used the statistic', 'he brings out the environmental policies sensibly'. Notably, Mark Carney is strongly associated ($p < .05$) with this category, and among the statistically top words are 'stress' [referring to stress tests], 'target', 'problem' and 'solution'. In contrast, in the subset of cases when the questioner is contentious and participants mention nonverbal cues, subjects refer to the calm and/or confident demeanour of the witness as he faced difficult questions, or they noted the defensive manner of the witness (with statistically significant words including 'defensive', 'look', 'manner' and 'confident'). The top phrases provide a sense of the descriptions used by subjects: 'Mervyn King remained calm, polite and composed ... even through the accusations of George Mudie'; 'he seems confident in his recommendations and corrects what Norman is trying to get at. His demeanour is calm and quiet (too quiet?), and he gets noticeably defensive (in body language and voice)'; 'when pressed or questioned, he remained calm and again answered directly'. In a few cases, even though subjects were asked to give their reasons for assessing *witnesses* as they did, they pointed to the nonverbal cues of the *questioner* (for example, 'John Mann looks a bit angry and he can't agree with George Osborne'), but nonetheless were characterizing the confrontational nature of the questioner vis-à-vis the witness. Finally, while Mark Carney is associated with the first subset of cases (as noted above, at $p < .05$) Mervyn King is associated ($p < .001$) with this second subset. George Osborne is not statistically significant for either subset of comments, as he appears to straddle the two subsets.

For the verbal reasoning outcome variable, the effect of the nonverbal exchange between questioner and witness is quite different. As shown in Table 3.5 (regression E), it is the behaviour of the witness that has a highly statistically significant effect ($p < .01$) on the verbal reasoning outcome variable and is positively signed. This suggests that in video/audio clips where the witness is combative, subjects are more likely to reference verbal reasoning in their explanations why they assessed the witness as they did. Conversely, when the witness is appeasing, subjects are less likely to reference verbal reasoning in these explanations. While this paper has not stipulated any expectations for the verbal reasoning outcome, this finding is nonetheless important to an understanding of the role of nonverbal behaviour in parliamentary committee hearings—namely, it appears that when a witness is combative, more atten-tion is given to his verbal argumentation, and when a witness is appeasing, less attention it seems is given to his verbal argumentation.

Two final remarks from Table 3.5 are noteworthy. As was evident from Table 3.4 (regression A), undergraduates are significantly more likely to ref-erence competence in their explanations. In addition, male subjects are sig-nificantly more likely to reference verbal reasoning in their explanations than female students. (The coefficient for gender is similarly signed for the group type model (regression B) but is not statistically significant.) The partisan ori-entation of subjects and whether they came from an English-speaking country does not appear to have any effect in any of the explanation regression models.

In sum, the results for the nonverbal exchange dynamic suggest that when they are asked to provide their reasons why they offered their initial assess-ments, the degree of nonverbal confrontation between the questioner and witness tends to shape their mentions of both what was said (relative to an appeasing witness, a combative witness tends to draw the attention of the viewer/listener more to verbal argumentation) and how it was said (relative to a conciliatory questioner, a contentious questioner draws attention more to nonverbal behaviour in the interaction). In both cases, it would seem that more or less confrontation between questioner and witness (as well as whether it is the questioner or the witness who is driving the confrontation) appears to influence whether observers are more likely to focus on the logic and ratio-nality of the witness's argument *or* on his body language. These findings are intriguing not only for deliberative scholars, who do not appear to have ex-amined the extent to which nonverbal communication shapes the attention given to the reasons and arguments given in deliberative discourse. But the findings are also central to the focus of this work on the adversarial context of deliberative accountability.

3.13 Conclusion

It is worth pausing to reflect on the substance of our findings from both the coding of nonverbal behaviour and the experiment. What have we learned, and more to the point, how do these findings contribute to our understanding of deliberative accountability in parliamentary committee hearings?

Broadly speaking, the aim of this chapter was to measure empirically the effect of nonverbal behaviour in parliamentary accountability hearings. It sought to do so both at the level of the parliamentary committee and policy type, and at the individual level. At the more aggregate level, comparisons were made between (a) the more confrontational Commons committee and the more relaxed Lords committee, and (b) the animosity and struggle for dominance in fiscal policy hearings (with 'angry' questioners and a 'contemptuous' chancellor as witness) versus the more non-competitive atmosphere in monetary policy hearings (where central bankers appear to be appeasing 'angry' parliamentarians). These findings could be linked directly back to the textual analysis of the hearing transcripts, allowing us insights into the apparent correlation between deliberative encounters in which the actors talk past one another and evidence is found of nonverbal cues of anger and contempt. In contrast, hearings in which parliamentarians and witnesses share a discourse around common themes (i.e., reciprocal deliberation) appear to be correlated with less hostile and more appeasing body language between questioner and witness. The present research does not allow us to posit any direction of causality—for example, does talking past one another lead to angry body language or do latent feelings of anger/contempt lead to an unwillingness to engage in reciprocal dialogue? Nonetheless, the correlations found between verbal and nonverbal behaviour offer a first step in bridging the *what* and the *how* of deliberative accountability.

The experimental part of this chapter sought to explore whether nonverbal cues influence judgments as to the performance of a witness appearing before a parliamentary hearing. Thus, the experiment sought to address in part the question of what people judge to be quality in accountability, by focusing on their assessments of the persuasiveness and competence of policymakers being held to account. Participants were exposed to nine selected clips from the previously coded hearings, and then asked to render judgments (both in ordinal and open-ended responses) as to the overall competence and persuasiveness of the witness in each hearing. Two mechanisms were employed to operationalize nonverbal behaviour: first, a random separation of subjects into two groups—one that only listened to selected clips from the hearings and the second that could also watch the questioner and witness in each clip (*group type*); and second, a four-part categorization of the nine hearing clips based on the degree of contention between questioner and witness (*nonverbal exchange dynamic*).

The findings strongly suggest that nonverbal cues are pivotal for understanding and gauging deliberation in committee settings. However, they also reveal that studying nonverbal behaviour in deliberative settings is quite different from studying it in the speeches of politicians. In deliberative accountability settings, the *nonverbal exchange dynamic* between questioner and witness is critical. It is this dynamic that is seen to have demonstrated the most powerful effect of nonverbal cues. Why is this important? The reader may recall that participants in the experiment were intended to serve as proxies for parliamentarians, with the motivation of the experiment being to gauge the extent to which a questioner might perceive a witness to be persuasive/credible or not, based in part upon nonverbal cues. However, perhaps the most intriguing finding from this study is that in deliberative accountability, it is essential to measure nonverbal cues in terms of the degree to which the questioner challenges the witness (is he confrontational or conciliatory?) and the degree to which the witness offers a robust response (is he combative or appeasing?). That is, the parliamentarian is a partner to the witness in a nonverbal exchange, and it is the tone of this exchange (rather than simply the observation of the witness by the parliamentarian) that is found to be most significant. For deliberative scholars, this points to the importance of not only considering the role of nonverbal communication alongside deliberative discourse, but also capturing the interpersonal communication dynamic, particularly in terms of the adversarial nature of the interaction.

The body language between questioner and witness is seen to have shaped the judgments of participants in the study in both their ordinal responses and in their open-ended explanations. For instance, the degree of confrontation between a questioner and a witness (as measured by whether the questioner was conciliatory or confrontational, and whether the witness was appeasing or combative) was found to have a highly significant effect on all three measures of the performance of the witness (quality of response, persuasiveness, competence). Importantly, a witness was gauged as performing 'best' when his body language portrayed a robust response to a non-confrontational questioner (that is, his nonverbal behaviour was combative while his questioner was conciliatory). In highly conflictual exchanges (where both the questioner and the witness are confrontational/combative), subjects judged the witness as performing the 'worst'. This last finding suggests that in exchanges where both parties are confrontational, the potential for persuasion by an audience is highly compromised. This aversion to highly confrontational interactions has implications for how we understand accountability. From Chapter 1, we noted the 'accountability explosion' but we also noted that despite more accountability, the public does not appear to have acquired more trust or confidence in government. The finding from this chapter—that people judge excessive conflict in an accountability hearing as reflecting poorly on the persuasiveness and competence of the policymaker—could help to explain why more accountability (if highly conflictual) could make the public less satisfied with and less trusting of government officials.

Additionally, in subjects' own explanations for why they responded as they did on the ordinal measures, the confrontational nature of the body language between questioner and witness is highly significant in its effect on an audience's judgment of the witness. In cases where the questioner is contentious, the audience is more likely to observe and mention the nonverbal behaviour in the witness—and in particular, the calm/confident demeanour of a witness (or his defensive manner in) facing difficult questions. In cases where the questioner is conciliatory, the audience is less likely to mention nonverbal behaviour by the witness, and instead refer to the logic and reasoning in the witness's responses. While this study did not set out to gauge the effect of verbal reasoning on persuasiveness, the analysis of the open-ended responses sheds light on the importance of verbal reasoning relative to nonverbal cues, as each shapes judgments on persuasiveness. Specifically, the confrontational nature of the body language between questioner and witness is seen to affect the degree of attention given by the audience to the verbal argumentation of the witness. When the witness is combative, more attention is given by the audience to his verbal reasoning and logic, whereas when the witness is appeasing, less attention is given to these arguments.

While the interactional dynamic between questioner and witness exhibited the most significant results, the effect of viewing the hearings—as opposed to only listening to them—was seen to have generated some notable findings. In the ordinal responses, where subjects simply ranked the performances of the witnesses, a significant difference was found between the two groups in how well the witness responded to the questioner. And, in the explanations given by subjects for their ordinal assessments of the witnesses, it was found that subjects who viewed the hearings (relative to those who only listened to the hearings) were significantly more likely to explain their reasons for assessing witnesses as they did in terms of nonverbal cues like eye contact, head movements, or facial expressions. In other words, the visual effect of seeing the witness give testimony appears to shape an audience's judgments on the witness's competence and persuasiveness in favour of nonverbal cues, while judgments based on verbal reasoning or logical argument exhibit no effect from the visual stimuli.

Notes

1. The first half of this chapter derives from my earlier article (Schonhardt-Bailey, 2017). This section is reprinted with permission, as per Cambridge University Press guidelines and direct correspondence with the editor of *Politics and the Life Sciences*.

2. The term 'deliberative exchange' should not be confused with the 'turn-taking' concept, which is sometimes understood to consist of an individual speaker taking a turn in a conversation, in a back-and-forth series of turns for an entire conversation (Bull, 2003 (2014): 86).

3. Erik Bucy is the Marshall and Sharleen Formby Regents Professor of Strategic Communication in the Department of Advertising at Texas Tech University, and his work on nonverbal communication is extensive (for example, (Grabe and Bucy, 2009) and (Bucy, 2011)).

4. Conducted in 2015 at the LSE Behavioural Research Lab. The LSE Behaviour Research Lab operates a database of participants (about 2,100). A brief overview of the experiment and a request for participants is circulated a few days prior to the experiment; they are then selected on a first come basis.

5. Participants provided informed consent, as prescribed by the UK Economic and Social Research Council (ESRC).

6. The questions on how well the witness answered questions and his persuasiveness deliberately forced the participant to make a judgement one way or the other (strongly disagree or disagree, versus agree or strongly agree), whereas the third question allowed a 'middle' assessment of *average*.

7. Stage two adopts a repeated measures design, given that the tests on each subject were repeated—that is, all 120 subjects were exposed to the videos [or audios] and were asked the same set of questions.

8. The null hypothesis of equal variances was thus rejected, which—together with the ordinal nature of the outcome variables—made the use of a one-way ANOVA parametric test inappropriate.

9. The groups are: viewing vs audio-only; and contentious/combative vs contentious/appeasing vs conciliatory/combative vs conciliatory/appeasing.

10. While the Kruskal-Wallis H test does not assume that the data for each group of the outcome variable are normally distributed, to allow one to compare medians, it does assume that the distributions of scores within each group of the test (independent) variable have the same shape or variability. Histograms for each of the ordinal outcome variables (*address well*, *persuasiveness* and *competence*) were compared for both the group type (viewing/audio) and the nonverbal exchange dynamic (four types) and were found to have the same shapes. Hence the results that follow include both the mean and median comparison (i.e., the null hypothesis for the medians of the groups is also tested).

11. As mentioned, the one-way ANOVA is an inappropriate method; however, notably, the same variables are statistically significant in both one-way ANOVA and Kruskal-Wallis H tests.

12. For repeated measures data with binary response variables, the method of generalized estimating equations (GEE) (Liang and Zeger, 1986, Zeger and Liang, 1986) allows

flexibility and can produce robust and reliable parameter estimates (Homish, Edwards et al., 2010). The GEE is a quasi-likelihood approach which allows one to model correlated responses by relying on working correlation matrix structures, which corrects for within-subject correlation (a conservative unstructured working correlation matrix is selected here, as this requires no assumption about the degree of correlation between pairs of observations). (Tests on the consistency of GEE estimates comparing the unstructured working correlation matrix with others finds that the interpretation of the results does not, however, vary significantly (Owusu-Darko, Adu et al., 2014). The unstructured matrix estimates (and includes in the estimation of the variances) 'all possible correlations between within-subject responses' (Ballinger, 2004: 133).)

GEE allows the researcher to choose the model form from a variety of possibilities (Ballinger, 2004). A binary logistic model is used for this analysis, thereby enabling a binomial distribution with logistical link. (The latter 'is the standard linking function for binary dependent variables' (Ballinger, 2004: 131).) The value of GEE, as Ballinger notes, is that its 'estimates are the same as those produced by OLS regression when the dependent variable is normally distributed and no correlation within response is assumed' (Ballinger, 2004: 130).

13. This finding is open to conjecture but is not explored further in this chapter.
14. The software which facilitates this is T-LAB 2017 version 3.2.2.7. As noted earlier, previous research has demonstrated consistency between thematic automated text analysis software such as T-LAB and Alceste, and topic modelling (Sanders, Lisi et al., 2018)

Reference

Ballinger, G. A. (2004). "Using Generalized Estimating Equations for Longitudinal Data Analysis." *Organizational Research Methods* 7(2): 127–150.

Beattie, G. (2016). *Rethinking Body Language: How Hand Movements Reveal Hidden Thoughts*. London, Routledge.

Beňuš, Š., et al.(2012). *Entrainment in Spontaneous Speech: The Case of Filled Pauses in Supreme Court Hearings*. Proceedings of the 3rd IEEE Conference on Cognitive Infocommunications, Kosice, Slovakia.

Blinder, A. (1998). *Central Banking in Theory and Practice*. Cambridge, MA, MIT Press.

Borg, J. (2011). *Body Language: How to Know What's REALLY Being Said*. Harlow (UK), Pearson Education Limited.

Braddick, M. J., ed. (2009). *The Politics of Gesture: Historical Perspectives*. Oxford, University of Oxford Press.

Broom, M., et al. (2009). "Variation in Dominance Hierarchies Among Group-Living Animals: Modeling Stability and The Likelihood Of Coalitions." *Behavioral Ecology* 20(4): 844–855.

Bucy, E. P. (2011). Nonverbal Communication, Emotion, and Political Evaluation. The *Routledge Handbook of Emotions and Mass Media*. K. Döveling, C. v. Scheve and E. A. Konijn. London, Routledge: 195–220.

Bucy, E. P. and Z. H. Gong (2016). Image Bite Analysis of Presidential Debates. *Exploring the C-Span Archives: Advancing the Research Agenda*. R. X. Browning. West Lafayette, IN, Purdue University Press: 45–75.

Bucy, E. P. and M. E. Grabe (2007). "Taking Television Seriously: A Sound and Image Bite Analysis of Presidential Campaign Coverage, 1992–2004." *Journal of Communication* **57**(4): 652–675.

Bucy, E. P. and M. E. Grabe (2008). "'Happy Warriors' Revisited: Hedonic and Agonic Display Repertoires of Presidential Candidates on the Evening News." *Politics and the Life Sciences* **27**(1): 78–98.

Bull, P. (2003 (2014)). *The Microanalysis of Political Communication*. London, Routledge.

Bull, P. E. (1987). *Posture and Gesture*. Oxford, Pergamon Press.

Carter, A. and P. Swinney (2018). "Where Are the UK's Youngest and Oldest city Populations?". https://www.bbc.com/news/uk-43316697 Retrieved 5 November 2018, pp. 1–5.

Casasanto, D. and K. Jasmin (2010) "Good and Bad in the Hands of Politicians: Spontaneous Gestures during Positive and Negative Speech." *PLoS ONE* **5**:1–5

Cobb, M. D. and J. H. Kuklinski (1997). "Changing Minds: Political Arguments and Political Persuasion." *American Journal of Political Science* **41**(1): 88–121.

Darwin, C. (1872 (2009)). *The Expression of the Emotions in Man and Animals: Definitive Edition*. New York, London, Harper Perennial.

Dominiczak, P. (2015). David Cameron Praises George Osborne for his Weight Loss. *The Telegraph*. London, 26 Jan 2015.

Druckman, J. N. (2001). "On the Limits of Framing Effects: Who Can Frame?" *Journal of Politics* **63**(4): 1041–1066.

Druckman, J. N. (2003). "The Power of Television Images: The First Kennedy-Nixon Debate Revisited." *Journal of Politics* **65**(2): 559–571.

Druckman, J. N. (2004). "Political Preference Formation: Competition, Deliberation, and the (Ir)relevance of Framing Effects." *American Political Science Review* **98**(4): 671–686.

Dumitrescu, D. (2016). "Nonverbal Communication in Politics: A Review of Research Developments, 2005-2015." *American Behavioral Scientist* **60**(14): 1656–1675.

Ekman, P., et al. (1990). "The Duchenne Smile: Emotional Expression and Brain Physiology II." *Journal of Personality and Social Psychology* **58**(2): 342–353.

Ekman, P. (2004). *Emotions Revealed: Understanding Faces and Feelings*. London, Phoenix (Orion Books Ltd).

English, P. (2016) Pathways to Power Workshop: The Political Representation of Citizens of Immigrant Origin in Seven European Democracies (https://www2.le.ac.uk/departments/politics/research/pathways/pathways-to-power-workshop).

Everitt, J., et al. (2016). "Candidate Gender, Behavioral Style, and Willingness to Vote: Support for Female Candidates Depends on Conformity to Gender Norms." *American Behavioral Scientist* **60**(14): 1737–1755.

Fenton, S. (2016). George Osborne Failed to Suppress a Smirk at the Mention of More Austerity Cuts During PMQs: The Chancellor Failed to Suppress a Smile as His Plans to Enact More Austerity Cuts Were Quoted During PMQs. *Independent*. London, 6 March 2016.

Frank, M. G., et al. (2013). The Voice. *Nonverbal Communication: Science and Applications*. D. Matsumoto, M. G. Frank and H. S. Hwang. Thousand Oaks & London, Sage: 53–74.

Fridlund, A. J. (1994). *Human Facial Expression: An Evolutionary View*. San Diego, Academic Press.

Gong, Z. H. and E. P. Bucy (2016). "When Style Obscures Substance: Visual Attention to Display Appropriateness in the 2012 Presidential Debates." *Communication Monographs* **83**(3): 349–372.

Grabe, M. E. and E. P. Bucy (2009). *Image Bite Politics: News and the Visual Framing of Elections*. Oxford, New York, Oxford University Press.

Hayes, A. F. and K. Krippendorff (2007). "Answering the Call for a Standard Reliability Measure for Coding Data." *Communication Methods and Measures* **I**(1): 77–89.

Homish, G. G., et al. (2010). "Analyzing Family Data: A GEE Approach for Substance Use Researchers." *Addictive Behaviors* **35**(6): 558–563.

Izard, C. E. (1997). Emotions and Facial Expressions: A Perspective from Differential Emotions Theory. *The Psychology of Facial Expression*. J. A. Russell and J. M. Fernández-Dols. Cambridge, Cambridge University Press: 57–77.

Kahneman, D. (2011). *Thinking Fast and Slow*. UK, Penguin Books, Allen Lane.

Kimmel, C. M., et al. (2012). "Of Closed Minds and Open Mouths: Indicators of Supreme Court Justice Votes during the 2009 and 2010 Sessions.". *The Forum* **10**(2): Article 3.

Knapp, M. L. and J. A. Hall (2010). *Nonverbal Communication in Human Interaction, 7th edition*. Boston, Wadsworth Cengage Learning.

Lang, A., et al. (1996). "Negative Video as Structure: Emotion, Attention, Capacity, and Memory." *Journal of Broadcasting & Electronic Media* **40**(4): 460–477.

Lang, A., et al. (2013). "Motivated Message Processing: How Motivational Activation Influences Resource Allocation, Encoding, and Storage of TV Messages." *Motivation and Emotion* **37**(9): 508–517.

Lewinski, P. (2015). "Automated Facial Coding Software Outperforms People in Recognizing Neutral Faces as Neutral from Standardized Datasets." *Frontiers in Psychology* **6**: 1–6.

Liang, K.-Y. and S. L. Zeger (1986). "Longitudinal Data Analysis Using Generalized Linear Models." *Biometrika* **73**(1): 13–22.

Lowi, T. J. (1964). "American Business, Public Policy, Case Studies, and Political Theory." *World Politics* **16**: 677–715.

Lowi, T. J. (1972). "Four Systems of Policy, Politics and Choice." *Public Administration Review* (July/August): 298–310.

Manning, E. (2007). *Politics of Touch: Sense, Movement, Sovereignty*. Minneapolis, University of Michigan Press.

Martens, P. (2014). "Bank of England Drops a Bombshell on Parliament: It Shredded Its Crisis Era Records." *Wall Street on Parade: A Citizen Guide to Wall Street* **March 12 2014**.

Masters, R. D. and D. G. Sullivan (1989). "Nonverbal Displays and Political Leadership in France and the United States." *Political Behavior* **11**(2): 123–156.

Matsumoto, D., et al. (2013). Reading People: Introduction to the World of Nonverbal Behavior. *Nonverbal Communication: Science and Applications*. D. Matsumoto, M. G. Frank and H. S. Hwang. Thousand Oaks & London, Sage: 3–14.

Matsumoto, D. and H. S. Hwang (2013). Body and Gestures. *Nonverbal Communication: Science and Applications*. D. Matsumoto, M. G. Frank and H. S. Hwang. Thousand Oaks & London, Sage: 75–96.

Matsumoto, D. and H. S. Hwang (2013). Facial Expressions. *Nonverbal Communication: Science and Applications*. D. Matsumoto, M. G. Frank and H. S. Hwang. Thousand Oaks & London, Sage: 15–52.

Maurer, M. and C. Reinemann (2013). Do Uninvolved Voters Rely on Visual Message Elements? A Test of a Central Assumption of the ELM in the Context of Televised Debates. *ECPR General Conference*. Bordeaux.

McHugo, G. J., et al. (1985). "Emotional Reactions to a Political Leader's Expressive Displays." *Journal of Personality and Social Psychology* **49**(6): 1513–1529.

(NA) (2017) Population of the UK by Country of Birth and Nationality: 2016 (Latest Population Estimates for the UK by Country of Birth and Nationality, Covering the Period From 2004 to the Year Ending 2016). *Statistical Bulletin*

Norton, P. (2016). Legislative Scrutiny in the House of Lords. *Parliament: Legislation and Accountability*. A. Horne and A. L. Sueur. London, Bloomsbury: 117–136.

Olivola, C. Y. and A. Todorov (2010). "Elected in 100 Milliseconds: Appearance-Based Trait Inferences and Voting." *Journal Of Nonverbal Behavior* **34**: 83–110.

Owusu-Darko, I., et al. (2014). "Application of Generalized Estimating Equation (GEE) Model on Students' Academic Performance." *Applied Mathematical Sciences* **8**(68): 3359–3374.

Reed, L. I., et al. (2012). "Facial Expressions as Honest Signals of Cooperative Intent in a One-Shot Anonymous Prisoner's Dilemma Game." *Evolution and Human Behavior* **33**: 200–209.

Rendall, D., et al. (2009). "What do Animal Signals Mean?" *Animal Behaviour* **78**: 233–240.

Rogers, W. T. (1978). "The Contribution of Kinesic Illustrators Toward the Comprehension of Verbal Behaviour Within Utterances." *Human Communication Research* **5**: 54–62.

Sanders, J., et al. (2018) Themes and Topics in Parliamentary Oversight Hearings: A New Direction in Textual Data Analysis Statistics, *Politics and Policy* **8**, 153–194

Schonhardt-Bailey, C. (2017). "Nonverbal Contention and Contempt in U.K. Parliamentary Oversight Hearings on Fiscal and Monetary Policy." *Politics and the Life Sciences* **36**(1): 27–46.

Schubert, J. N., et al. (1992). "Observing Supreme Court Oral Argument: A Biosocial Approach." *Politics and the Life Sciences* **11**(1): 35–51.

Stewart, P. A., et al. (2009). "Taking Leaders at Face Value: Ethology and the Analysis of Televised Leader Displays." *Politics and the Life Sciences* **28**(1): 48–74.

Stewart, P. A. (2010). "Presidential Laugh Lines: Candidate Display Behavior and Audience Laughter in the 2008 Primary Debates." *Politics and the Life Sciences* **29**(2): 55–72.

Stewart, P. A., et al. (2015). "Strengthening Bonds and Connecting with Followers: A Biobehavioral Inventory of Political Smiles." *Politics and the Life Sciences* **34**(1): 73–92.

Stewart, P. A., et al. (2015). "Sex and Leadership: Interpreting Competitive and Affiliative Facial Displays Based on Workplace Status." *International Public Management Journal* **18**(2): 190–208.

Stewart, P. A., et al. (2016). ""Please Clap": Applause, Laughter, and Booing during the 2016 GOP Presidential Primary Debates." *PS: Political Science & Politics* **49**(4): 696–700.

Vancil, D. L. and S. D. Pendell (1987). "The Myth of Viewer-Listener Disagreement in the First Kennedy-Nixon Debate." *Central States Speech Journal* **38**(1): 16–27.

Yik, M. S. M. and J. A. Russell (1999). "Interpretation of Faces: A Cross-cultural Study of a Prediction from Fridlund's Theory." *Cognition and Emotion* **13**(1): 93–104.

Zeger, S. L. and K.-Y. Liang (1986). "Longitudinal Data Analysis for Discrete and Continuous Outcomes." *Biometrics* **42**(1): 121–130.

4

A View from the Inside

4.1 Introduction

The two previous chapters have explored the content of deliberative accountability using quantitative text analysis and then its delivery, using coding of
nonverbal behaviour and a controlled laboratory experiment. This chapter
adds one further methodology to this multi-method approach, namely a
qualitative analysis of in-depth elite interviews with key parliamentarians, parliamentary staff, Bank of England officials and Treasury officials who have
had direct experience of the oversight hearings in the Treasury Select Committee (TSC) and Economic Affairs Committee (EAC). Critical insights and
analyses are drawn from twenty-three in-depth elite interviews. The result is
an unprecedented analysis of the quality of deliberative accountability in the
hearings of these select committees, as perceived by both the questioners and
witnesses.

Importantly, these interviews elicit more impressionistic and contextual interpretations from the individuals who actively participated in the hearings,
thus allowing us a unique insight into how individuals personally involved in
the process interpret the value and quality of accountability and deliberation
in these hearings. While quantitative text analysis can provide a statistically
concise assessment of the content of the hearings, it cannot offer clear answers as to 'why' participants behaved and responded in the ways that they
did, nor can it probe the thought processes of these participants. Interviews
provide a much better means by which to probe the 'why' questions, as well
as the thinking behind their words and actions. These data additionally allow us to better understand how the participants perceive the influence of
nonverbal communication (both their own and others) during the hearings.
Finally, the interviews offer a check on the results obtained from the quantitative text analysis—for example, in asking respondents directly: 'do these results
accord with your experience—and why or why not?' Hence, one purpose here
is to 'triangulate' the analysis along the lines suggested by Gaskell and Bauer
(Gaskell and Bauer, 2000), by incorporating an independent method—that is,

Deliberative Accountability in Parliamentary Committees. Cheryl Schonhardt-Bailey, Oxford University Press.
© Cheryl Schonhardt-Bailey (2022). DOI: 10.1093/oso/9780192847874.003.0004

elite interviews—to corroborate the results from the use of other methods to study deliberation.

Elsewhere I have combined text analysis with the use of in-depth elite interviews with the monetary policymakers and politicians who contributed to generating the political texts under investigation (Schonhardt-Bailey, 2013). These interviews were found to offer differing perspectives on key concepts and issues. Of course, just like any other data sample, the inferences that we can draw from the interviews are contingent upon the quality of our sample of interviewees. In this regard, I do not claim to have a fully representative sample of participants from all the parliamentary hearings; rather, I have obtained a *reasonably good* sample of relevant and informed participants, as based on the composition of their extensive experience and pivotal roles in the hearings. These interviewees are listed in Table 4.1, and are grouped into three broad categories—parliamentarians and parliamentary staff, Bank of England officials, and Treasury officials.

As an overview, the sample consists of *three chairmen of the two parliamentary committees* (Tyrie, McFall, Hollick); *six MPs with experience serving on the TSC* (Tyrie, McFall, Pearce, Norman, Garnier, Thurso); *three peers with experience serving on the EAC* (McFall, Hollick, Forsyth); *four parliamentary clerks or advisors* (whose anonymity is preserved); one Bank of England governor (King); *two Bank of England deputy governors* (Bean, Tucker); *eight Bank of England members of the MPC and/or FPC*, including the 'Interim' FPC[1] (King, Bean, Tucker, Fisher, Barker, Turner, Cohrs, Kohn); and *two senior Treasury officials* (Macpherson, O'Donnell). Moreover, among the interviewees are one with experience both as a member of one of the parliamentary committees and as a witness from the Bank of England's Financial Policy Committee (Turner); one with experience testifying before the two US congressional oversight committees, in addition to experience testifying before the TSC (Kohn); and one with experience in testifying before parliamentary committees both on fiscal policy (in her capacity as representing the Confederation of British Industry) and on monetary policy (Barker). While very few women were participants of any sort in the context of these parliamentary hearings, the study nonetheless includes three women interviewees (Pearce, Barker, and a parliamentary clerk). Only where the context of the quote is inextricably linked to the identity of the official are the remarks of interviewees who agreed to attribution disclosed.

The interviews were conducted between 2013–2017, which allowed the inclusion of key participants who had recently stepped down from their official positions and therefore tended to be more open and franker than current office

Table 4.1 Details of Interviews.

NAME	DATE OF INTERVIEW	PLACE/MODE	BACKGROUND OF INTERVIEWEE (relevant positions in UK Parliament, Treasury, and/or Bank of England)
PARLIAMENTARIANS AND STAFF			
ANDREW TYRIE, MP (Conservative)	4 September 2013	Portcullis House, Parliament	Chair of Treasury Select Committee, 2010–17
LORD MCFALL (John Francis McFall, The Rt Hon. the Lord McFall of Alcluith), MP and Peer (Labour)	16 March 2016	House of Lords, Parliament	As MP Chairman, Treasury Select Committee, 2001–2010; then Member, Economic Affairs Committee, 2012–2015
TERESA PEARCE, MP (Labour)	10 May 2016	Portcullis House, Parliament	Member Treasury Select Committee, 2011–15
JESSE NORMAN, MP (Conservative),	8 January 2014	Portcullis House, Parliament	Member Treasury Select Committee, 2010–15
MARK GARNIER, MP (Conservative)	6 June 2016	Parliament	Member Treasury Committee, 2010–16
LORD THURSO (John Archibald Thurso, The Rt Hon. the Viscount Thurso; MP (Liberal Democrat)	31 May 2016	Café, 30 John Islip Street, London	Member Treasury Select Committee 2006–15
LORD HOLLICK (Clive Richard Hollick, The Lord Hollick), (Labour)	5 May 2016	Phone interview	Chair of Economic Affairs Committee 2014–17 (Member since 2010)
LORD FORSYTH (Michael Bruce Forsyth, The Rt Hon. the Lord Forsyth of Drumlean), MP and Peer (Conservative)	11 May 2016	House of Lords	Member Economic Affairs Committee 2008–13, and 2015- (Previously MP, 1983–1997)
COMMITTEE CLERK	8 November 2013	Parliament (main site)	Has been working with select committees since 1996.

Continued

Table 4.1 *Continued*

NAME	DATE OF INTERVIEW	PLACE/MODE	BACKGROUND OF INTERVIEWEE (relevant positions in UK Parliament, Treasury, and/or Bank of England)
SENIOR COMMITTEE STAFF	13 May 2016	Portcullis House, Parliament	Treasury Select Committee Staff
COMMITTEE CLERK	9 January 2014	7 Millbank, Parliament	Deputy Principal Clerk
COMMITTEE ADVISOR (House of Lords)	28 February 2014	Not specified, to retain anonymity	Requested anonymity
COMMITTEE CLERK (House of Commons)	9 January 2014	7 Millbank, Parliament	Requested anonymity
BANK OF ENGLAND OFFICIALS			
THE LORD KING (Mervyn King, Baron King of Lothbury)	24 May 2017	London School of Economics	Governor, Bank of England, 2003–2013, Member of both MPC (1997–2013) and Interim FPC (2011–13)
SIR CHARLIE BEAN	17 November 2014	London School of Economics	Deputy Governor, Bank of England, Member MPC (2000–14), and Member FPC (2011–14)
SIR PAUL TUCKER	5 June 2017	London School of Economics	Deputy Governor, Bank of England (2009–2013), and Member MPC (2002–2013) and Member FPC (2013)
PAUL FISHER	5 May 2016	Bank of England	Executive Director for Markets (2009–14), Bank of England Internal Member MPC (2009–14) and Member Interim FPC (2011–13)
DAME KATHARINE BARKER (Kate Barker, Dame Katharine Mary Barker)	23 May 2016	London School of Economics	External Member MPC (2001–10). Notably, in her capacity as housing expert and representing the CBI, she has also testified on fiscal policy.

Continued

Table 4.1 *Continued*

NAME	DATE OF INTERVIEW	PLACE/MODE	BACKGROUND OF INTERVIEWEE (relevant positions in UK Parliament, Treasury, and/or Bank of England)
LORD TURNER (Adair Turner, Baron Turner of Ecchinswell)	24 May 2016	INET Foundation, London	Member Interim FPC, 2011–2013 as Chairman of FSA (2008–13), and a Crossbench member of House of Lords since 2005 (and Member, Economic Affairs Committee for 2 years). In these positions he has both testified before the Economic Affairs Committee *and* served on it.
MICHAEL COHRS	6 June 2016	Café, Brompton Rd, London	Member, Interim FPC, 2011–13
DONALD KOHN	21 June 2017	London School of Economics	Member Interim and Permanent FPC 2011–18, Vice Chairman Federal Reserve, 2006–10. As Vice Chairman of Federal Reserve (and previously as Federal Reserve Board Governor), has testified many times before US congressional oversight committees.
TREASURY OFFICIALS			
LORD MACPHERSON (Nicholas Macpherson, Baron MacPherson of Earl's Court)	22 March, 2016	UK Treasury	Permanent Secretary to the Treasury, 2005–2016
LORD O'DONNELL (Gus O'Donnell, The Lord O'Donnell GCB)	27 September 2016	71 High Holborn, London	Cabinet Secretary (highest official in the British Civil Service), 2005–11, Permanent Secretary to the Treasury, 2002–2005

holders. All the interviews were conducted by the author of this work. The average length of each interview was about an hour and with the exception of the parliamentary staff, all agreed to be named as interviewees. All but three of the interviewees agreed to be recorded and their interviews used for the purposes of this work, although several preferred their comments not to be attributable. For this reason, in most instances, quotes or remarks will be simply attributed to 'committee clerk', 'Bank of England official', 'EAC member', and so on. Moreover, given the limited number of interviews, Bank of England officials (other than Governor King) who agreed to have their remarks attributed are nonetheless anonymized, since revealing them would compromise the anonymity of other Bank officials.

4.2 Interviewing Approach and Question Template

While the methods and findings from Chapters 2 and 3 have contributed substantially to understanding many aspects of the quality of deliberative accountability, they are nonetheless *indirect* methods. That is, they have not tapped into the considerations and thinking of either the parliamentarians or their witnesses. In this chapter, the intent is to obtain a more *direct* measure into why parliamentarians and witnesses in oversight hearings said what they said and behaved as they did. This is achieved through a series of open-ended questions to the participants themselves (and committee staff).

Broadly speaking, the questions sought to illicit responses on seven aspects of the oversight hearings: (1) the role that select committees have come to play in holding government agencies to account, as it has developed from their modern creation in 1979; (2) assessments of the interviewees as to the quality of deliberation and accountability in select committee hearings; (3) the motivations and intentions of the parliamentarians who serve on these committees; (4) the extent to which partisanship varies across policy type (fiscal, monetary, financial stability); (5) how deliberation varies across chambers (Commons, Lords), and to the extent that the interviewee is knowledgeable of practices in other countries (like the US), how deliberation in the UK might differ to that experienced in other legislatures; (6) the role that individual personalities play in the conduct of oversight; and (7) the role that nonverbal communication and gender play in the oversight hearings.

Table 4.2 lists the specific questions asked of interviewees, though notably, while these questions constituted the template for the interviews, the conversational style often broadened the discussion into related topics.

Table 4.2 Questions to Parliamentarians and their staff, Bank of England officials, and Treasury officials.

Questions	Relevance
1. I would like to hear your views as to how you think deliberation in the TSC has evolved since the beginning of the modern select committees (1979)? How would you assess any changes?	Historical Development of Select Committees and their Importance
2a. Broadly speaking, would you say that hearings are a good venue for holding the Bank and Treasury to account? As background, we can think of accountability working in at least two ways: (1) directly, via deliberation in hearings; and (2) outside hearings, perhaps consciously or subconsciously, where some decision or action may be decided upon depending on how it might be defended in a later TSC hearing (i.e., serving as a 'brake' to some actions).	Conceptual Understanding of Accountability
2b. If one purpose of deliberation is to persuade, how well do you think witnesses (BoE or Treasury) are/have been at persuading TSC or EAC members towards a particular stance, or policy decision?	Quality of Deliberation
3. What do you think is the motivation of TSC and EAC members?	Motivation/Purpose of Committee Members
4a. I'm interested in your insights into the findings from textual analysis of 2010-15 hearings (TSC, EAC).	Check on findings from Textual Analysis
<ul><li>Hearings with BoE officials exhibit greater reciprocity, whereas fiscal policy exhibits a 'talking across' one another (Fiscal policy: chancellor speaks to one theme; committee members focus on other themes).</li><li>Deliberation in financial stability exhibits more 'committee-level' reciprocity (and more specialization).</li><li>Partisanship: virtually absent in monetary policy; fiscal policy exhibits clear partisanship (financial stability: small amount).</li><li>TSC vs EAC (in monetary policy): MPs each tend to speak to multiple themes, while peers focus on one theme each.</li></ul>	

Continued

Table 4.2 *Continued*

Questions	Relevance
4b. To what extent does partisanship shape the discussion—particularly in regards to BoE officials vs Treasury witnesses?	Quality of Deliberation
4c. Very generally, do you think there is a different agenda and feel to the oversight process when it is Bank of England officials before the TSC, as opposed to chancellor and senior Treasury officials?	Perceived differences between policy types (or unelected vs elected officials)
5a. Broadly speaking, how would you assess the differences in the deliberative process between MPs in the TSC and Lords in the EAC?	Quality of Deliberation
5b. In comparing the UK with other countries (e.g., US) how would you assess deliberation in the TSC?	Quality of Deliberation in Comparative Perspective
6. Are there some members who might be seen as (or see themselves as) mavericks and if so, how would you assess their role in the committee?	Quality of Deliberation
7a. Do you think that you have ever (consciously) taken note of the 'body language' of witnesses (smiles, vocal cues, any form of nonverbal communication) during the hearings? How relevant do you think nonverbal communication is to the hearings?	Delivery (Nonverbal Communication)
7b. What role, if any, do you think gender plays in the hearings?	Quality of Deliberation

4.3 Themes in Interviewees' Responses

4.3.1 History and Importance of Select Committees

Question 1 from Table 4.2 sought to elicit possibly unique perceptions on how interviewees assessed the importance of select committees, and particularly their importance in Parliament and vis-à-vis the UK executive. Overwhelmingly the interviewees remarked on the growing importance of select committees, particularly in the wake of the 2010 reforms. For Andrew Tyrie (former Chairman of the TSC), this meant that his constituency had become 'the whole of the Commons' (that is, all members of Parliament, not just MPs from his own party)—which strengthens the nonpartisan nature of the committee. One committee clerk assessed the 2010 reforms as giving 'greater confidence to committee chairs' and making them 'more assertive'. A member of the TSC described the effect of the 2010 reforms more from the perspective of a committee member:

> [Since the reforms of] 2010, [the TSC] ... has much more power. It used to be in the gift of the Whips ... so as a government member of the committee you had to be loyal and as an opposition member you had to be effective in opposition and if you weren't the whips would shift you. Or if you really enjoyed being on the Treasury Committee and you rebelled ... they would take you off that and put you on the Lavatory Cleaning Committee or something, whatever they could find. So clearly it was a measure of the pressure the whips could put you under. [TSC member]

And, from the perspective of the governor of the Bank of England, the importance of the reforms is that it lessened the incentives for partisan divides:

> I think the Treasury select committee, as with other select committees, gained in self-confidence because they could see its role was very important but what made it important was the ability to keep the committee together and not split on party lines. [King]

With respect to the EAC, a similar ethos of nonpartisanship is expressed: '[the EAC] is seen as having influence, it is seen as adding a valuable body of evidence on a particular topic and being completely unafraid to ask awkward questions. It comes to unanimous conclusions and doesn't split along party lines' [EAC member].

Apart from partisanship, one official from the Bank remarked on the added impact of the financial crisis on the TSC, noting that the crisis had shone a spotlight on the activities of the committee:

> I think the crisis has given a big rise to the chair of the Treasury Committee in terms of the public. I think before the crisis nobody would have cared much about the Treasury Committee; it wouldn't have appeared much in the news, unless something sensational happened, it wouldn't have got reported. The chair of the Treasury Committee is now a big, powerful figure in a way that it wasn't before [… *and relative to other committees*], the Treasury Committee is the sort of daddy of them all now. [Former Bank of England official]

Other parliamentarians went so far as to assert that the power of select committees has come at the expense of debates on the floor of the House of Commons:

> Select Committees … through the progress [they have] made, have a life and a vitality of their own, and the main cross-examination and the main policy formation is done in Select Committees now rather than the House, on the floor of the House, so the floor of the House has become devalued. If you want to change [things it is] in the Select Committees. [EAC member]

> I think people are beginning to see the importance of a select committee because what happens in the Chamber is virtually irrelevant most of the time. What happens in select committee rooms can change things; it can change things. It can have … a huge effect because it is a cross-party group; the power of that report is much more powerful than that motion so I think select committees are beginning to understand their own power, which is good. I'm a big advocate of select committees, I think they do really good, interesting work. It is where you get in-depth scrutiny, it is where you can change things, [and] you can actually have a massive effect on policy. If a policy comes out and a select committee report says 'this is hopeless', that has an effect, it changes things, whereas a vote in the Commons, which we [the opposition party] always lose never changes anything. [TSC member]

The consensus was that select committees had certainly increased in importance, so that in the view of one Bank of England official the select committee system 'has, in subtle and not-so subtle ways, shifted a bit of power back to Parliament away from the executive'. Yet, at least one senior official with many years of experience appearing before parliamentary committees maintained 'I still think the executive in this country gets a pretty easy ride'.

4.3.2 Accountability and Deliberation in Oversight Hearings

The second thematic category is the broadest and most extensive, as it explores the views of interviewees on concepts that are central to deliberative accountability, namely, (1) the role and purpose of accountability, (2) the quality of deliberation in select committee hearings, (3) the extent to which accountability in these hearings is improved based on the reasons offered by decision makers, (4) whether persuasion emerges as a product of the deliberative process, and (5) the constraints imposed on the decision of policymakers themselves, in anticipation of appearance before accountability hearings. (These aspects of accountability and deliberation were largely addressed in questions 2a, 2b, and to a small extent, question 5b, from Table 4.2.)

4.3.2.1 Accountability

While this work has explored accountability from a number of different perspectives, these interviews provide the first perspective from those responsible for the accountability process in UK economic policy making. To begin, how did the interviewees define accountability and its actual purpose in the parliamentary hearings? According to one MPC member, the fundamental purpose of accountability is to 'question the decisions' of the policymakers:

> I suppose the point is, if it weren't for those sessions, nobody is questioning the decisions. There is nobody there to question the decisions, so if for example … if you vote one way, if you vote for a rate cut, and three months later … you stop voting for a rate cut, there is always a bit in the [MPC] minutes about it. Maybe you'll make a speech about it but it is an opportunity for somebody outside to say 'well, what did you think you were doing? What has really changed your view? Are you embarrassed about it?' You know, to really question you about your speeches, to try and enlarge information. Now, whether that is really holding you accountable or not I don't know because I suppose what could go wrong here? … Do you organize the Bank properly so that you get the right information? Do you use sensible models? How do your models perform? How do they work? How else could you be held accountable? Are you really aiming at the target or are you aiming off and if you

are aiming off, then why? Can you talk about that? They do that quite well. Do you really have a free level of debate on the committee? Is it really nine people? They do that pretty well. [MPC member]

As this MPC member notes, sometimes questioning the decisions entails questioning the organization—in this case, the internal organization of the Bank of England. On this point, former Governor King differs, arguing that accountability in policy-decision making should *not* extend to the internal organization of the Bank (for example, strengthening the Court of Directors, which is responsible for resourcing), but rather the actual decision-making outputs:

(T)he biggest disagreement I had with [TSC Chairman] Tyrie, on other things there were no disagreements, but on this there was, because I said to him 'Look, if you want to hold us accountable, the Treasury Committee is the place to do it. We make the decisions, we [the Monetary Policy Committee, P.R.A., Financial Policy Committee] have been appointed by the Government ... You invite us along, put questions to us, we have to defend what we've done, and anyone else in the country or world can write about it and say we are right or wrong. The idea that the people on the Court of the Bank should form judgments on whether we've made right or wrong decisions is crazy ... They are not the Treasury Committee, or the people's representatives, elected to hold us to account. [The Court cannot] ... hold the Bank of England to account in a way the Treasury Select Committee can because it doesn't have the information or the time to hold us to account. Holding someone to account doesn't require a full-time job; it requires the ability to ask the right questions and you can employ outside people to write reviews on us if you want, or get us to hire people to write reviews, which are published, which is what we did but the members of the Court . . ?' I said to Tyrie, 'let's suppose they produce a report saying 'the MPC set the wrong level of interest rates'. What do you conclude from that? Do you conclude that the Court is better at setting interest rates than the MPC, in which case they ought to be on the MPC, or if you conclude they are not, why ... are they being asked to write a review? They are not monetary policy experts. What you should do is to make sure the Bank has to commission a report from outside, genuine experts on what we've done on monetary policy, and they publish their report and we respond, and we have a debate in front of you at the Treasury Committee. [King]

King's opposition to the TSC encroaching on the Bank's governance arrangements helps us better to understand a key theme obtained from the text analysis of the TSC transcripts in Chapter 2—that is, the thematic class on the *monetary policy decision-making process*. For this theme, TSC chair Andrew Tyrie was highly significant, but given Governor King's clear opposition to the TSC questioning the governance of the Bank's Court, it is not surprising that the MPC is found not to have engaged (statistically) on this theme.

One former Bank of England official assessed accountability in the TSC hearings quite unfavorably, as this member noted an inherent mismatch of intentions between the questioners and the witnesses:

> So they are set up to hold us accountable, we both agree on that. We go along often thinking that they are to hold us to account for the technical decisions we have made on monetary policy—I don't think they are. I think what they are actually doing is holding us to account for the political consequences of the technical decisions we have made, and so I think you get this mismatch because and it is to be expected, they don't know the technical anywhere near as well as we do, in the Commons certainly, and you can tell that in the questions they ask, the fact that they can't do follow-up questions and so on. But they know politics a hell of a lot better than we do and a lot of the questions, particularly from the mavericks, are trying to make some political point out of the technical issue that is at hand … The chair has his own political agenda … and I think that is the best way to understand this slight adversarial view of it in that our officials are there trying to give technical answers to what they would see as technical questions, and the other side are busy trying to make political points out of asking political questions. [Former Bank of England official]

Turning to the responses of the members of the TSC, the purpose of accountability was interpreted somewhat differently. For one TSC member, it meant 'understanding the judgments' of economic policymakers:

> Broadly speaking, the TSC work(s) on the basis of trying to find out the facts and trying to solicit opinions, bearing in mind that very often there aren't any facts. There are judgements that have been made based on interpretation of data which is quite different to a concrete fact and therefore understanding the data being used and understanding the judgments applied to it are as important as knowing what the facts were. [TSC member]

For another TSC member, one purpose of accountability is to get policy experts to explain themselves, but in language that is comprehensible to politicians (and the public): 'we need to try and bring the geeks back to normal language'—that is, to 'get them out of the thinking up there, and explain how exactly does it work? Is it hitting the targets? Is it achieving the things we want it to achieve?' This member also notes that 'the media circus' surrounding hearings 'is distracting' as it encourages parliamentarians to 'play to the media'. The member argues that accountability is inherently dull, but important:

> [It] is about hard work … when they get down to the nitty-gritty and do the real hard work at drilling down, looking at the stats, finding out what the background is, making sure what you are trying to achieve you will achieve, where the problems might be, what has happened in other countries, all of that sort of stuff is really, really interesting but it is dull. No-one wants to see that on TV but that's the interesting work.

As a final note on accountability, one anecdote from a TSC member provides a unique insight into the process. While accountability may often be seen as deliberate, purposeful, and carefully crafted, occasionally, it is simply opportunistic and accidental:

> [Adam Posen and I] used to meet for dinner from time to time and … having a discussion with him about it, he said 'Boy, you asked the right question' and I said 'What are you talking about' and he said 'You asked the question' and it was something to do with some interpretation and it was a complete accident … I [had] settled on [a particular] sentence … I just seemed to think 'What does that mean?' and I asked Adam Posen 'There is this question here: what do you think of it?' He told me afterwards what I had stumbled on was a sentence that had been arrived at after a monumental argument in the MPC largely between Adam and Mervyn [King] and that when I asked that question it was like 'either he is inside track or' and it was a total accident. Adam, of course, thought I had done it on purpose. [TSC member]

4.3.2.2 Deliberation

While deliberative democracy theorists provide a number of different criteria for what constitutes 'good' and 'bad' deliberation, these interviews offer a unique perspective from those who are actually 'deliberating'. A common thread, certainly among the committee members, is that the deliberative process in the accountability hearings is meant to educate parliamentarians, but in some cases, also educate central bankers. One Bank of England official provides a particularly clear description of this educational function for parliamentarians:

> The thrust of questioning in the Treasury Committee on monetary policy has … very much focused on understanding the rationale of policy, and … trying to bring out why people voted in a particular way and what their thinking was. I don't even remember anyone explicitly saying we were wrong to vote for interest rates or anything like that. It was very rare that an MP would say anything like that. They may bring out the consequences of policy, for example on Quantitative Easing, when there were quite of lot of questions on the distributional consequences of Quantitative Easing … but it was never considered as Quantitative Easing hitting pensioners or 'don't you think it is the wrong thing to do' or whatever. It was, 'What are the consequences?'—and trying to get a better understanding. They may go on to say 'well should these issues be taken account of in how policy is formed' but never in the way of actually saying 'you have made the wrong decision'. In that sense, there was never any question of the Bank's independence in making that decision. It was more, 'was the Bank aware of the consequences of the decision?' and was it taking account of all the relevant factors in making that decision. [Bank of England Official]

We can link these comments back to the remarks of the previous Bank official who perceived a mismatch in accountability expectations, with MPC members expecting to be held accountable for technical decisions and TSC members expecting to hold the Bank to account for the political consequences of technical decisions. Notably, there is a balance to be struck between what some Bank officials perceive as the appropriate pushing of MPC members to be cognizant of potential political consequences of MPC decisions (for example, distributional consequences of quantitative easing) and what others might perceive as inappropriate pushing of the Bank into explicitly partisan areas or highly political matters.

In any case, the educational process for parliamentarians requires some foundation of knowledge by the committee members. One way that the committees provide this foundation knowledge is through 'pre-meetings' with independent experts—for example, in advance of the hearing on the Bank's Inflation Report. Having served as an expert at some of these pre-meetings, prior to joining the Bank, a Bank of England official describes their usefulness:

The purpose was to help the parliamentarians understand the arguments in the Report and to give them potential lines of questioning. I have to say that I think that is a very good thing for parliamentarians to do if they want to hold a group of policymakers to account, whether it is central bankers, the Treasury, or whatever. Given that most of them are not specialists, then having a pre-meeting with some independent experts is potentially helpful. [Bank of England Official]

Parliamentary clerks were also keen to stress that the committee members were provided with both training and extensive briefings, in order better to provide the necessary knowledge base for committee members to ask appropriate questions. These briefing documents range from 50 to 150 pages and the TSC staff noted that they produce for the members about two of these briefings per week. The briefings provide a number of areas of enquiry and include various agency reports, news articles and other relevant materials from which the committee members can then draw to press witnesses on particular points.[2] One parliamentary clerk remarked that these briefing documents were fundamental to the deliberative process as members would use them as 'a first base' and would then think through the implications of the background materials, 'thinking of their own questions, scribbling, correcting, tweaking ... and then responding to what the witness says'.

Interviewees had two further observations on what contributed to 'good' deliberation. First, they agreed that both the TSC and EAC were the 'right' size—that is, around eleven to thirteen members. This small size was seen as important for the deliberative process. As will be seen in a later section, mention of the equivalent US congressional committees—with memberships ranging from 55 to 70 plus for the House Financial Services Committee and 23 to 25 for the Senate Banking Committee—surprised some interviewees, as they wondered how deliberation would operate with such large numbers. Second, a couple of members of the TSC thought that the use of social media in the deliberative process could be beneficial. One acknowledged having 'watched Twitter during hearings, because intelligent people will be commenting'. This member then remarked that 'looking on Twitter, [I] would "crowd-source" a question that arises from that ... in the most directly representative way'. Another committee member said that 'I texted mates of mine on dealing room floors saying, "the Governor has just said this: what do you think?" And they would come back'. This use of 'crowd-sourcing' of questions, however, may raise concerns (for example, with respect to transparency, bias, and so on) as to the appropriateness of the 'general public' playing a role in parliamentary hearings.

Turning to aspects of deliberation in the committee hearings that were deemed as 'bad' or undermining the quality of deliberation, interviewees mentioned five items. First, whereas committee clerks defended the expertise and knowledge of members, one MPC member expressed quite the opposite:

> I think 'deliberation' is a very interesting word, it has become very fashionable now. You have these deliberative times where people talk through issues, [but the TSC] never really felt like that, because … it tends to be that they've all got these set questions and they ask their questions and then sometimes, because they don't really understand the answer, they can't ask a follow-up so they just ask their two questions. [*As an example, the member describes an occasion*] where Paul Tucker was asked exactly the same question by two MPs in succession because the second one hadn't been paying attention and bless him, I really admired Paul because … apparently he gave a slightly different answer whereas I would have said 'Haven't I just answered that?' Paul is too polite to do that but I did often feel that their advisors must have been very frustrated because they had probably set them up with this question and probably an idea of why it mattered but the MPs themselves didn't always have the confidence to follow it up [*The member recommends that to improve deliberation, MPs should become better informed*] Become reasonably informed. You don't want them to be total experts, but you want them to be reasonably informed. [MPC member]

It would seem that perceptions of (and perhaps the reality of) the expertise of TSC members varies considerably. For at least one Bank official, the pre-committee educational meetings served to bring some degree of expertise to the table for TSC members, whereas for others, this was clearly deemed insufficient.

Second, one witness felt that the overly aggressive nature of the questioning (in the TSC) harmed the deliberative process:

> These committees are covered by parliamentary privilege. MPs can pretty much say what they like without any come back, while witnesses do not have the same protections as they would in a court of law. If you follow a few of the more heated sessions, you will see some committee members (not all) trying to lead witnesses or put words in their mouth by summarizing in a way which

is not what has been said. And it is very difficult to contradict. You can only answer questions that they are asking, and you can't always explain yourself as you would choose. They will sometimes ask the same question repeatedly even after you've answered it as best you can—seemingly to provoke you into saying something you didn't mean to [say]. They make pejorative comments about witnesses' characters or performance, and in some cases those comments have been career damaging or even ending. There doesn't seem to be any concept of 'natural justice' involved in front of a parliamentary committee. Personally, I think there should be some rights for the witnesses and there should be some sort of code of behaviour we should expect from the questioners. In fact, some can be aggressive, they can make inaccurate assertions, they can lead people to say or imply something they didn't mean, and there is no come-back because it is all under parliamentary privilege. As a witness you have to be polite even if asked a silly or rude question and you must try and answer what was asked, even if it doesn't concern your area of responsibility. They react badly if you say you don't know or don't have a view. It's good theatre but it's not fair on witnesses. [Witness X[3]]

This expectation that witnesses often adopt a stance of appeasement vis-à-vis committee members accords well with the findings in the previous chapter on nonverbal communication. We saw, for instance, that the emotive expressions of TSC members were of 'anger' (in hearings both with the Bank and the Treasury). We also saw evidence of Bank officials matching this anger with expressions of appeasement.

Third—and somewhat in contrast to the above perception that witnesses are expected to answer questions outside their areas of expertise and responsibility—members of both the Commons and Lords committees pointedly remarked that they preferred witnesses to admit when they did not have the answers:

We asked him some obvious questions like 'What does the government mean by affordable housing?' [His answer was] 'Well, you know, it depends what you mean.' Any sentence that starts, 'It depends', usually takes a long time to finish and gets you nowhere, other than to confirm that the witness didn't know the answer. He was sitting next to somebody who answered the questions very precisely, very clearly, and when she didn't know the answer, she said 'Well, we'll come back to you on that' and the contrast between the two of them and the way they came across was … very marked. [EAC member]

You might ask the question, and it is something they haven't thought about beforehand, and you can see them considering and one of the most powerful answers is for somebody to say 'I am not sure about that: I'll get back you. Would it be okay if I wrote to you' because you think, 'yes, they were being honest'.... (T)he worst type of evidence sessions are the ones where they know what you are going to say, you know what they are going to answer, you don't get anywhere. It has wasted everybody's morning, that they walk away thinking 'I came away unscathed' and we think 'well that was a waste of time, we might as well have sent them an email.' [TSC member]

The juxtaposition between witnesses who perceived aggression in the questioning of committee members versus members themselves who seemed to respect the willingness of witnesses to admit when they did not have the answers is noteworthy. Both sides perceive a diminished quality of deliberation when witnesses were pushed on questions for which they had no responsibility or knowledge, although it is apparent that personalities and processes may shape how this manifests in each case.

A fourth source of compromised deliberation is the inability of members to follow a line of questioning to its conclusion. According to one TSC member this stems from the way the committee chair conducts the hearing:

One of the problems with the Treasury Select Committee in particular is the way it is run, [it] doesn't give you [an] opportunity to really dig because the way Treasury runs is the chair chairs it in his very chair-like way but he allocates you very small spaces of what to ask. So he may say 'you have six minutes' so you might be in minute five just getting somewhere and he'll say 'that's it, enough' and he will move on to the next person so you are not allowed to, if you are pulling on a piece of string and it is starting to unravel, you're not allowed to get to the end of it. So it is quite frustrating... What tends to happen on the Treasury Select Committee is people try to look for 'killer' questions rather than proper scrutiny which I think is a real weakness of that committee. [TSC member]

A final *potential* source of poor deliberation—that is, the televised recording of oversight hearings—is disputed among committee members. For one TSC member, the use of cameras encourages grandstanding by members, which lessens the depth and quality of deliberation: 'I do think that people do play to the cameras and I don't think you should because it is very sober and important stuff' [TSC member]. Others conceded the grandstanding incentive but nonetheless argued that the cameras allowed 'more people ... [to become] engaged with what is going on' [EAC member] and thus could be seen as beneficial to both deliberation and accountability.

4.3.2.3 Shades of Opinion

In the UK, multiple members of the MPC and the FPC appear alongside the Governor of the Bank of England in formal oversight hearings. Committee members are thus afforded the opportunity to explore the extent to which members of the MPC and FPC[4] differ among themselves on policy decisions. Whereas the MPC and FPC may come to an agreed policy decision, various 'shades of opinion' may have shaped this final outcome.

One Bank of England official prefaced his response to this aspect of the deliberative process by emphasizing that to understand the importance of 'shades of opinion' one must first accept the underlying premise of the MPC—namely, that of 'one person, one vote':

> One of the key things about the Monetary Policy Committee is that it is a committee of nine individuals and the governor's vote carries no more weight than the others, though a lot of the press coverage is written as though it does carry more weight and that for example, the decision to raise rates is the governor's alone. However, the one person, one vote principle was established right at the outset in 1997. It is clear in statute, and actually the Treasury Committee plays an important role in asking individual members why they are voting in a particular way, and because we had split votes from relatively early on, with Mervyn King as Deputy Governor voting against [then Governor] Eddie George in the first year. We had Mervyn King on the wrong side on many occasions. The whole basis of having a group of nine individuals who vote separately is something that is hard-wired into the DNA of the system. [Former Bank of England official]

Given this context, he argues that this independence of judgement within the committee was something of a leap of faith, as 'it was not at all clear ... that it would actually work' in practice, but then continues to explain why it has indeed worked well:

> When it first started it was not at all clear that having nine independent voting members would actually work well. One of the concerns was that there

would be a discordant cacophony of different views and in fairness when there are occasions when the committee is split, 6 to 3 or 5 to 4 or whatever, you get press reports about fighting like 'ferrets in a sack'. Of course, equally the committee is criticized when it is unanimous, with people saying 'too much Groupthink' and not enough variety of views, or the governor is considered to be too powerful or something like that, so for the press, you can write a critical story whatever the criteria. But one of the key things about why, having the multiple viewpoints has mostly worked well, is because there is a certain understanding that people have of the committee that key documents like the Inflation Report or the Minutes are primarily statements about what the majority is. In the Minutes there is a paragraph, perhaps a bit more, of why minority members think differently, and there may be a little bit in the Inflation Report which says some members hold different views, but the Inflation Report is really the story of the median voter, the middle person on the committee, 'the best collective judgment' as the wording has it. But then of course people give individual speeches and it is generally understood that people will give their own nuances on the outlook. One of the key principles which have mostly but not universally been observed is that when people give their own speeches they don't go out and rubbish other people. They would say 'this is the committee's view but I have a different view', and [it works well] having that sort of communication whereby people are understood to be speaking as individuals but anchor what they say with reference to the centre of gravity on the committee. [Bank of England official]

Governor King echoes this endorsement of the 'shades of opinion' on the MPC, noting that it reflects both 'a well-functioning mature committee' but also one that is guided by a clear statutory remit:

It reflects the pattern of behaviour of the underlying institution so in the Fed they might allow up to a couple of dissents; anything more than that and you are into chaos ... I was in a minority I think three times as governor. It had no impact on the way the committee functioned and if anything I think it strengthened the view that the committee was doing exactly what it was saying it was doing. It wasn't a one-person committee, people did have their views and from time to time it wouldn't be surprising if the governor was in a minority. No one found that awkward or difficult ... The impact was that people thought this was a well-functioning mature committee that can cope with understandable differences of views. [However] where I think we would have been in real difficulty is, if we hadn't been given a clear [statutory] remit. [King]

While this independence of views is valued both inside and outside the Bank, it nonetheless poses challenges to select committees as they question either the MPC or the FPC. The predominant source of frustration among Bank of England officials has been the imbalance in the questions targeted at the governor versus other MPC or FPC members:

All [the committee members] really want to do is talk to the governor but they know they had to have us all there to hold us all to account. So you'd get some questions sort of thrown out to the other officials because they are there, but you'd be lucky to get two in two hours most of the time. Now in the very recent past two or three years … I think they have tried deliberately to be a bit more spread out but for most of the time of the MPC they have focused on the governor and the Lords was even worse. [Former Bank of England official]

They once did this to [MPC external] Danny Blanchflower, and I thought it was just outrageous, because he flew over the Atlantic and went to the House of Lords and they did not ask him a question. Not a question … I think when I went I hardly spoke, and somebody challenged it afterwards and they said, 'Why do you ask people' [to come to hearings] and they said 'because they can'… While the Lords focused on Mervyn [King], almost 100 per cent of the TSC [in previous years] asked nearly all the questions of the governor but latterly they broadened out and made a real point of addressing the questions to more people on the committee and sometimes asking all of us to comment on one thing which I thought was a more fruitful way of finding out what was going on in the committee. [MPC member]

Even while the TSC appears to have targeted its questions more equitably among the Bank of England officials,[5] MPC member Barker comments on her frustration 'because they wouldn't ask you the right questions'. As an external member of the MPC with an expertise in housing, she remarks that 'they would always ask me about the housing market as though I had no knowledge of the exchange rate, or the labour market', or they would always ask Stephen Nickell (a labour market economist also serving as an external MPC member) about the labour market. And so, she concludes, 'it often didn't give you the opportunity to say things you really wanted to say and they never … at the end really said to all of us "Is there anything you haven't said?"' [Barker]

4.3.2.4 Persuasion

A particularly intriguing set of responses came from question 2b on Table 4.2, 'If one purpose of deliberation is to persuade, how well do you think witnesses have been at persuading TSC or EAC members towards a particular stance, or policy decision?'

While the question was consistently posed the same way, interestingly (and perhaps tellingly) both parliamentary clerks and one TSC member tended to misunderstand the direction of persuasion as being one of the TSC persuading either the Bank or the Treasury, rather than the other way around. One committee clerk then went on to differentiate between persuasion and pressure, arguing that the use of persuasion is a subtler process of challenging officials on their policy stances (holding them accountable/demanding explanations) and possibly yielding a changed outcome in the long-term, whereas pressure is something different, and used more selectively. Pressure implies more confrontation on the part of the committee and can only work when it is used rarely/selectively and only when the committee is unanimous [Committee clerk].

Apart from the slight confusion over who was persuading whom, the remaining interviewees expressed a variety of views as to the extent to which TSC members were persuaded by witnesses in oversight hearings. For one Bank official, the premise of the question assumed an intent that did not exist:

> We're not going in there trying to persuade them of anything. They are asking us questions [to] which we are giving our technical answers so we're not going in there trying to persuade them to take a particular view. They say 'Why did you do that?' We explain. I wasn't ever there thinking 'I'm trying to change your point of view on this.' I'm just trying to say 'This is my view. You are asking me what are my views and I'm trying to give [them] to you so you understand.' Now, I think they then absorb some of that and they understand it better. But if they really have a political point they are not going to be shifted by anything we say. Why should they be? But they may understand it better. [Former Bank of England official]

For one MPC member, the premise of the question was valid, yet, the ability of committee members to be persuaded depended on their *willingness* to be persuaded:

> There are some MPs who on some issues were not persuadable but I did think that MPs sometimes shifted their position or views ... They fall into several

camps. There is the camp of people who are not listening; there is the camp of people who are listening and agree with you; there is the camp of people who are listening and who disagree with you and always will; and there is the camp of people who actually don't think about a topic and are genuinely interested in your answer. [MPC member]

From the perspective of Treasury official Macpherson, the Bank of England had demonstrated a consistent track record in its ability to persuade select committees, in part owing to their expertise as technocrats but also their preparedness when they appear before the committees:

I think the Bank of England is a good case study on how you can influence [select] committees. I think generally but not always the Bank has been good at setting out its reasons for what it has done and for the most part I think it is fair to say that senior Bank officials have been treated reasonably respectfully and one of the reasons for that is that they are basically being held to account as technocrats. You can try and apply a political lens to view all of this but it is quite difficult to make that stick, and they are technocrats who know a lot about this subject. I [also] think the Bank is very good at preparing for committees ... When we appoint people, I'm always struck by how well-prepared they are, the support they get in giving evidence on their views. [Macpherson]

Two examples of successful persuasion by the Bank were offered, first by an FPC member and next by Governor King:

Well, the TSC put forward their own views as how Court should function, how the Bank should function ... The TSC wanted a dual board almost like the German dual board structure and the Bank simply said 'No, and here is the reason why not'. And lo and behold the next meeting, the chairman of the TSC said 'And as you know, I don't want to have the German dual board structure'. It was almost like it was lifted, and the chairman of the TSC now owned it and was totally agreeing with the Bank. [FPC member]

I think [I persuaded the committee] on certain aspects on the resolution regime. The first hearing within days of Northern Rock I went along and said there are four things that are wrong and we have to put them right. And all four things were in their report and they were implemented in subsequent legislation so I think we did have quite an impact on persuading them. [King]

4.3.2.5 Oversight as a Brake

A final cut into the broader conceptual themes of deliberation and account-ability is the extent to which expectations of questioning before parliamentary hearings operate to 'constrain' or otherwise serve as something of a 'brake' on the actions or decisions of either the Bank or the Treasury. Views from inter-viewees were somewhat divided on this point. Two committee clerks offered different perspectives. For one, the priority of the TSC is to 'get government [Treasury or Bank] to explain themselves and their policies—changing policy is neither expected nor sought after as a committee goal'. Another clerk ac-cepted that the TSC does indeed constrain policy decision making. This clerk compared oversight to the existence of the Freedom of Information Act; it forces witnesses to ask themselves, 'If I were to get a Freedom of Information request on this, or if I were to be questioned in a select committee on this, would I be able to justify it?'

With one exception—by an MPC member who maintained that the MPC would not have behaved any differently in the absence of the TSC—witnesses were far more in agreement with the sentiment of the second clerk, namely, that accountability hearings force witnesses to consider how they would justify their policy decisions. One Bank official described the brake as 'very real':

> It is very real. I've said that myself and thought that myself and made deci-sions bearing that in mind, sitting there thinking 'what is the right decision to make?' I'm going to be sitting there in front of the Treasury Committee trying to defend this. Is it something I'm happy publicly to be seen trying to defend, and if not, why not? And actually, that is not a bad way of trying to make decisions.... There have been other times when I've said 'Well, this is obviously the right decision, and here are nine reasons for it but I can't possi-bly use seven of those in public.' [*Cheryl Schonhardt-Bailey "What do you do then?"*] Well, use the only reasons I can use in public because they are the ones I'm going to have to go with, and if there are no reasons I can use in public it's a tricky decision to make. If I can't actually explain to anyone why I've made that decision, is it the right decision? [Former Bank of England official]

A similar stance was noted by an FPC member as he reflected on deliberations within the FPC meetings:

> I want to tell you that it never entered into deliberations but that wouldn't be fair; it did in a positive way ... (A)s we sat doing policy in the [Financial Policy] Committee I did occasionally think 'How will this play in front of

the cameras'? and 'Have we really thought it through? Have we explained it correctly in this publication which goes to the public' and 'How are we going to feel when, and it does come up occasionally, how are [we] going to answer the chairman of the TSC when he asks this question'? So, I don't mean that negatively. I don't mean that we are trying to hide and obscure what we were doing. I mean it in a 100 per cent positive way that the accountability was there and I think it is a positive. [FPC member]

One TSC member described this brake as 'the Telegraph test' and argued that it is part of the wider process of accountability:

Oh, I think it is what politicians would call 'the Telegraph test'. If this goes pear-shaped, what is the headline in the *Telegraph* going to be . . ? [Things that in the past were not disclosed are now] discussed publicly. People make speeches, people publish papers, you know, the governor is out there as are all the senior members of the Bank, deputy governors, and as a result there is … evidence of 'I need to think about [this], I'm going to say this in a public forum. 'Whether it be preparation for the Treasury Select Committee or a speech I'm making or whatever … I am absolutely convinced that openness and transparency and that debate that has taken place will make people say 'now, just before I sign off on this decision what's going to be the question the TSC will ask about it?' or 'How is that going to look in our published annual?' 'On that date you voted that way and on that date you voted that way. Could you please explain to the committee why you changed your mind? What [are] the data that obliged you to do that?' Now, there is no trick in that question, but it means that whoever it is gets to then explain how they were thinking and the wider debate is informed by that and that is all a form of accountability. [TSC member]

For Governor King, the effect of the 'brake' was said *not* to have impacted upon MPC decision making, but did come into play when Bank officials grappled with whether or not policy decisions by the Bank extended beyond its statutory remit:

I think there are two dimensions to [the 'brake']. The first one is the quality of the decision: are we doing the right thing? The second is: are we going beyond our remit? And those are two different things. So, on the first I can honestly say that I can't recall any time when people were agonising about monetary policy, deciding what was the right level of interest rates, or the right amount of asset purchases, where anyone thought about 'I'd like to raise interest rates by so much but the Treasury Committee or people in the public will respond badly to that.' I don't think there was any issue of that because the way in which people [on the MPC] would explain themselves if asked publicly were the same questions and the same reasoning that they used in [considering] the right level of interest rates ... And those are the debates in front of the Treasury Committee that exactly mirrored the reasoning that was used in the [Monetary Policy] Committee. So, on that first dimension I don't think it was ever relevant. Where it is relevant, and it is very important in my view is the second one, which is 'are we doing things which go beyond our remit ... (A)re there things that we might do in the financial crisis that would not be within the remit of a central bank?'. Various politicians, either in government or on the Treasury Committee, said 'Well, why don't you do something that has more effect on the economy—buy assets, whether it be bonds or commercial paper or shares, equity shares issued by a small company, to really help them'. I said 'No, because that is not within the remit of the central Bank'. And they said 'Why?' and I said 'Because it is playing with the taxpayers' money and if you buy shares in a company you can lose the money, and that's a decision that may be the right one to take but it's not for us to take. It is not in our remit' ... It cannot be for the central bank because we have no authority to take risks with taxpayers' money. [King]

4.3.3 Motivations of Parliamentarians on Committees

Unlike the US Congress where all representatives and senators serve on at least one (and usually more than one) legislative committee, not all MPs or peers are members of parliamentary select committees. So, it is reasonable to ask, what motivates parliamentarians to serve on a select committee? Perhaps not surprisingly the summary response was that motivations ranged from the more selfless to the more self-serving. Among the more selfless motivations, according to one TSC member, is the desire to put previous experience to use in public service, noting that 'public service is the highest calling a person can have'. This TSC member perceived the broader role of a Member of Parliament in three ways: (1) serving constituents; (2) acting as the representative of constituents in government issues; and (3) play a role in the scrutiny of government (and its agencies). One committee clerk perceived that members of the TSC were driven by 'the thirst for knowledge' and were 'trying to dig deeper into the rigor of the decisions that are made'. Other public service oriented motivations included the duty to inform the House of Commons on the economy as well as serving to 'demystify' the language of financial services for the public. The 'thirst for knowledge' aspect was conveyed on a more personal level by one TSC member, who essentially saw his time on the TSC as an opportunity to obtain an unofficial 'degree level course' in public finance:

> I recognised that it was an influential committee ... I knew that being on a select committee would be something that would be worthwhile doing ... So I was really lucky and I knew just how lucky I was, extraordinarily lucky, and I thought this is one of the most important things that is going to happen to me. Getting elected was brilliant and getting onto the Treasury Committee was absolutely fantastic.... Having not been to university, all through my life I've just picked stuff up as I've went along and to a certain extent I was always slightly chippy about having not gone to university. And I suddenly looked at the Treasury Committee and started looking at the work of it and I thought 'you know what? This is the single most interesting thing that I am ever going to do in my life. It is like going to university. I can learn so much about how the country is run in terms of the fiscal and monetary stuff', and I've treated it as a degree level course in learning about public finance and I have absolutely adored the whole thing so I will always try and get to the meetings. I will never schedule another meeting [that conflicts] with the Treasury Committee. [TSC member]

Others perceived the motivations of TSC members as more self-serving, primarily in gaining recognition as a possible ministerial candidate or simply to gain media attention, particularly in comparison to peers who serve on the EAC:

> I think the Treasury Select Committee is meant to be a place for people to shine. It is meant to be prestigious. It is meant to be, you are elected onto it, it is a feather in the cap to be a member of the Treasury Select Committee. So often people want to spend their time there showing how good they are for their own promotion purposes. Now once you are in the Lords, you are in the Lords, so whereas there is a lot of ego on the Treasury Select Committee I think there is less of that in the Lords. It is more about the work, it is more thoughtful. But there is a lot of ego on the Treasury Select Committee because it is somewhere where you can make your mark and become a minister ...They particularly want to be on the Treasury Select Committee and ... the

Public Accounts [Committee] because those are the two that get the headlines in the papers. People like being in the papers—they do like it. They like
being courted by Newsnight ... There are a lot of people who want to be on
the Treasury Select Committee because it is seen as the top select committee.
[TSC member]

Nonetheless, this TSC member notes that,

Select committee work is very, very valuable and I think it is some of the most
interesting work you do as a backbench MP. Absolutely—it is where you can
make your mark, you can really immerse yourself in a subject, you can really
grind down into a subject and inquire and produce a report that is of value.
[TSC member]

The motivation for members of the EAC tended to focus more on the interest of the peer in the subject matter: '... they are just in interested in the topic, it
is fascinating for them. They get a chance to talk about monetary policy [with
the MPC]' [Former Bank of England official]—although according to one parliamentarian, it also provides people who have 'bees in their bonnet' a 'venue
to pursue it'. Overall, the assessment of most interviewees would accord with
the following from one EAC member:

Well, I think it's bluntly seen as one of the most authoritative and interesting
committees in the House [of Lords] because you can reach into any part of
government because there is always an economic aspect. It tends to attract
members who have considerable expertise and deserved self-confidence. It
doesn't mean to say they are right on everything but they are always well-
prepared and informed. It is analytical, data-driven and evidence-driven. The
EAC style is approachable rather than confrontational. But nevertheless we
are there to get answers and information. Members of the committee are quite
capable of doing that. They are regarded as seasoned, experienced, knowledgeable, and able to frame questions that do elicit valuable information.
Reports by the Economic Affairs Committee do carry a lot of weight within
the Lords and within government, and are followed carefully by specialist
commentators. [EAC member]

The impression one acquires of the EAC is that its members are more in-
nately self-confident (owing in part to their greater relative expertise) than
their colleagues in the TSC. This self-confidence appears to engender a 'style'

of approachability rather than confrontation. This accords well with the analysis of nonverbal behaviour in both committees, in which peers are seen to be more relaxed while MPs exhibit more anger.

4.3.4 Policy Type and Partisanship

Questions 4a and 4b from Table 4.2 sought the views of interviewees both on the findings from the text analysis of the hearing transcripts from the 2010–15 Parliament, and particularly on the degree to which partisanship within the TSC (and less so the EAC, given their unelected status) may have shaped the deliberations with witnesses. As a reminder, the quantitative text analysis found the most conspicuous partisanship in fiscal policy hearings, and the least in the monetary policy hearings. Additionally, deliberative reciprocity between questioners and witnesses was almost non-existent in fiscal policy, but clearly evident in monetary policy hearings. Finally, deliberation in financial stability hearings was seen to exhibit far more specialization of topics by expert witnesses, but at the committee level, more reciprocity than in fiscal policy but less than in monetary policy.

This section is divided into three areas of focus: (1) interviewees' assessments of the extent to which they observed a clear difference in partisanship between fiscal policy and monetary policy hearings; (2) observations regarding the apparent lack of deliberative reciprocity in fiscal policy hearings; and (3) a broader discussion of the unique characteristics of financial stability as it pertains to accountability in Parliament.

4.3.4.1 Fiscal Policy vs Monetary Policy Hearings
The predominant view of the interviewees was that, in spite of the TSC aspiring to achieve cross-partisan unity, partisanship was alive and well during oversight hearings on fiscal policy. For the most part, this was seen to result from the very nature of fiscal policy, as for example, Chairman Tyrie noting that taxation is 'a core function' of governments, so that when governments enact fundamental change (or there is a change of government) this generally necessitates changes in taxation policy. Treasury official Macpherson characterized fiscal policy as essentially 'taking money away from one set of citizens and potentially giving it to another':

> I think generally the mood is different; it is in the nature of tax and spend decisions and fiscal policy more generally that these are the most political of decisions: they are about taking money away from one set of citizens

and potentially giving it to another. In a sense that is why people go into Parliament—it reflects its 1,000-year history. I think it is fair to say it is inevitable discussions around those issues are more political so if you have the chancellor before the Treasury Select Committee, although the committee will play its classic nonpartisan role of asking questions, there is more scope for, it sounds pejorative, political grandstanding, posturing and point scoring ... So, there is more political knock-about and that also feeds through into the cross-examination of Treasury officials because we are officials who are serving a political chancellor of the Exchequer. I think we are regarded as fairer game than impartial independent Bank officials which doesn't mean that the way Bank officials are held to account is non-political or somehow that they get an easy ride but I think there is at least an interest on the part of the committee to hold them to account in a less partisan way. [Macpherson]

External MPC member Barker (who has experience testifying before select committees both on fiscal policy [representing the CBI] and on monetary policy) agreed that partisanship was less evident in monetary policy than in fiscal policy, but remarked that some questions which might be perceived as partisan actually arose from a misunderstanding of the limits of monetary policy on the part of TSC members:

Fiscal policy is a real government-bashing thing whereas monetary policy [is] generally much more straightforward. The main difficulty with monetary policy [is] some of the people not really understanding ... the limits of our remit and our abilities and so [one MP] ... would ask things like 'from what you have said today, what do I say to my unemployed constituents. What are you going to do for them?' The answer to which, dressed up, is nothing. I'm not going to do anything for your unemployed constituents in the short-term. What I am going to do is deliver monetary stability for the country as a whole but the multiple reasons for why your constituents are unemployed are generally nothing to do with me. So that was much more ... straightforward because you can see it is an understanding problem. [Barker]

Recognizing the partisanship in fiscal policy, members of the TSC described the partisan divide in predictable ways:

When the Bank of England comes in front of the committee, the committee tends to act as a pack in a lot better way than it does when it is politicians. The committee tends to divide along political lines so if it is, for instance, the chancellor, then the committee will divide. The opposition just want to beat him up and the ruling party want to give him an opportunity to explain how brilliant everything is so that, the politics seems to come into it when it is politicians in front of us, more than when it is the Bank of England or the governor. [TSC member]

I think unquestionably when you have a politician in front of you, you are going to … probably divide [the committee membership] into three types of questions. You have those loyalists so when the chancellor of the Exchequer comes in front of you the loyalists will be tossing him easy questions in order to try and highlight what a genius George Osborne is. You will have the rebels of the same Party who will be trying to make slightly destabilizing or asking much more pointed questions and then you have the opposition who are asking outright opposing-type questions. [TSC member]

While most respondents agreed that the reason for the partisan nature of fiscal policy hearings was—as Macpherson noted—its inherent distributive and re-distributed nature, one peer noted that the institutional secrecy of the Treasury contributed to partisanship, remarking that of all the Government departments, Treasury 'is by far and away the most secretive'. This respondent voiced frustration that 'the reluctance of the government machine to embrace transparency … inhibits proper scrutiny, it inhibits proper accountability, and it means that citizens mistrust government and government decisions' [EAC member].

4.3.4.2 Reciprocity in Fiscal Policy Hearings
The empirical finding of the fiscal policy hearings (in both the TSC and the EAC) displaying a tendency for the chancellor to speak to one theme and parliamentarians to focus on other themes resonated with interviewees, with the simple explanation being that the chancellor seeks to convey a specific message in hearings, regardless of the questions of parliamentarians:

When the chancellor [appears in hearings], it is clearly much more like he is giving an interview to the media and he is going to answer the question that he wants to be asked and not the one that they want to ask him and it is much more like with a radio or TV journalist asking a politician questions. When you do media training, they advise you [to] ignore the question, work out what you want to say, ignore the questions you are actually asked and answer the ones you want to answer. [Moreover the chancellor] is just going to say what he is going to say and disregard the questions. It is very hard for the committee to get after him because he is the chancellor and he is as much protected by parliamentary privilege as they are. They can't get him. They can do all sorts of things with [un]elected officials for contempt of Parliament or anything else if we don't appear or we don't answer questions or we try to plead silence on something. You can't do that with members of Parliament. [Former Bank of England official]

And, in the words of one TSC member:

The chancellor will come knowing what he wants to say on the record and what he wants to get out there so … it doesn't matter what your questions are … (I)t's like the media trade, you go in, get your three points over, and leave, so when pressed he will answer the question, but he will have his themes. He sees it as a set-piece speech, so he will have his themes that he wants to get over. So no matter what you ask, he will go back to his themes and as I say … it tends to be set-piece that doesn't really get us anywhere at all … He needs to survive, he needs to leave, and as long as there is no soundbites that come out of it that are going to lead the news, that is a success. But where it has got us in terms of the scrutiny and understanding is probably nowhere. [TSC member]

A further cut into the lack of reciprocity came from a Treasury official, who argued that whereas monetary policy is a 'very narrow subject', fiscal policy covers public spending across a whole array of policy areas (health, education, defense, and so on). As a result, 'you would expect there to be much more mismatch' between parliamentarians and the chancellor, since he is 'talking about the whole of government' and 'will want to concentrate on the bits where he thinks it is going well and they will want to concentrate on the bits where they think it is going badly' [O'Donnell].

4.3.4.3 Characteristics of Financial Stability Hearings

The quantitative text analysis revealed that in the financial stability hearings, parliamentarians tended not to engage with the key experts from the Financial Policy Committee, and so in areas of technical expertise, there was little in the way of discernible deliberative reciprocity. It is on this finding in particular that respondents offered intriguing and insightful reasons for why financial stability is an area of policy with unique challenges for accountability.

First, whereas monetary policy has a well-established literature in economics, along with widespread agreement that low inflation supports growth and employment, no such agreement exists for financial stability:

> For example, if inflation is running above target and the Bank raises interest rates, growth slows and unemployment rises, people understand that is the price of getting inflation back under control. There is a reasonable, common understanding of that. We don't have that in the financial stability area and I think this is going to be one of the key issues that will arise in 5, 10 years' time, whenever there are enough people who have forgotten this crisis, and a new lot of people coming in. Between now and then the Bank has to do as much as it can to build a constituency for financial stability in the same way that we built a constituency for low inflation. [Bank of England official]

Second, far more than in monetary policy, financial stability may be said to offer politicians more scope for the possibility of scandals and bank failures, topics which invariably generate more headline news than the day-to-day mechanics of policymaking:

> When it comes to financial stability, the political process likes scandals; it likes disasters or banks collapsing ... but the nitty-gritty of either macro-prudential policy or day-to-day micro-prudential ex-ante, before something bad happens, it doesn't have much political resonance ... To get under the skin of it requires quite a lot of investment and research on the part of the questioner, and you have got to look at it from the MPs' point of view. You are dealing with [witnesses] who are huge experts ... whose lives have consisted of being regulators and so it is quite hard work. I just wonder if deep down those guys are prepared to invest in the knowledge you have to have to hold people to account successfully which is why they fall back on disasters. [Macpherson]

Related to both the above reasons (financial stability as a newer discipline and the attraction of focusing on scandals) is that similar to fiscal policy, financial stability can affect groups or firms quite differently. According to one committee clerk:

> In monetary policy there is more that you can read from an economics masters textbook about the construction of an independent monetary policy and so I think the committee briefing and its approach maybe more formulaic ...

Whereas with financial stability it is a newer discipline and almost anything goes ... With financial stability, you've got 'what is in the best interests of the financial stability of the country' but also we have the question of 'well, is this actually proportionately or disproportionately affecting these particular groups?' You've got the 'is this the dead hand of the FPC that is going to come down on the animal spirits that produce this incredibly dynamic part of the economy to grow?' So you are going ... to have people being pulled in different directions. [Committee Clerk]

Many of these points are linked together in an explanation by former FSA Chairman Turner:

There are two differences [between financial stability and monetary policy] ... In monetary policy you've got a clear objective and a clear set of tools, so you've got the interest rate and then we've got Quantitative Easing, basically two tools, and the objective is the inflation rate that anchors everything ... The MPC has a clear governing statute ... and we have a nice, clear thing called the Inflation Report ... The Inflation Report says 'well, we think this is what we think is going to happen with inflation therefore we've kept interest rates low and therefore we've done this' and ... the whole thing gives itself to a structured conversation ... If the [Treasury] Committee had strong points of view they would be saying 'you are wrong, you are not being tight enough, you are not being loose enough' but at least the discussions of what you could debate about are defined by what monetary policy is and by the fact that there is a clear statutory objective...

...

There is a statutory objective of financial stability but what does financial stability mean? And there are a myriad of tools that you could be using, capital, liquidity, you could be supervising, you could be doing something for the derivative markets ... The objective cannot be definitively defined as to whether you have met it or not. You know if for a year the inflation rate was 2% the Bank of England has perfectly met its objective. You would never know that you'd perfectly met the objective of financial stability and you can never tell how badly or well you've done.... I think that is what changes the nature of debate and makes it much less rooted. [Turner]

Turner then goes on to explain why the lack of clear metrics for measuring success—together with the necessity for some limits on transparency—make parliamentary accountability extremely difficult:

Some of the relevant facts are in the Financial Stability Report but some of them ... cannot in real time or two weeks after real time, be fully revealed to the external world, and this is where a lot of the tension comes from ... What data was considered is pretty coherent in the MPC; there isn't hidden stuff whereas with the FPC there will be some presentations ... which do not end up in the FPC minutes or in the Financial Stability Report and can't. So that is what then produces the tension [in the TSC] ... The objective is just much less clear, the instruments are more multi-faceted; some of the inputs have to be kept secret at least for a period of time. [Turner]

In an entirely different vein, one TSC member describes the difficulty in conducting oversight of financial stability, because there is a lack of clarity in terms of measuring financial stability, but also it is inherently fragile (which he likens both to herding animals and to a nuclear reactor):

[Financial stability] is really much more like putting a herd of sheep or cattle along a road, which is, you do lots of little tiny nudges with your horse and semi-instinctively it kind of all works. You only need one bang and they break and then you are into recovery mode ... whereas with monetary policy you are watching the inflation fan chart and you see it really starting and everyone pulls away and they look at all the things that are making that happen. Basically, the dial has gone red and then they go 'well, look at the labour market, look at this, look at that.' Yes, inflation is going up, we are going to jack up interest rates by half a point or a quarter of a point or whatever is decided. It is a very, it is not binary, but ... it is near as you get to facts and a decision at the end of it.

...

Financial stability: what is financial stability? I mean it its purest sense, nobody loses money but nobody makes money, everybody has the same amount and nothing happens. Well that actually is not what we mean. We want vibrant markets, we want people to make things and make profits and re-invest them and we want people to have more money and be able to spend more money and have better houses and have all the good things. We all want that. So financial stability in itself, it is almost like a nuclear reactor in that you've got something that's very unstable at the heart of it reacting in a way that you control to get the heat and light you want. It is a similar kind of thing in that financial stability is part monetary policy, part markets, part global trade, part foreign policy, part domestic policy, and all of these things are going on. [TSC member]

As a final insight into the challenges that the Treasury Committee face when holding financial stability policymakers to account, another TSC member argues that should 'things go wrong', the blame will invariably fall on the politicians, not the policymakers.

> I've seen surveys and [in] recent ones ... I think only about 10 per cent of people have ever heard of the Financial Policy Committee let alone necessarily understand what it actually does. Yet it was created directly to respond to the accusation that politicians are incapable of taking away the punch bowl when the party gets in full swing and this is what we saw ... We are conscious that at some point people won't be able to get a mortgage, to move to a new job, and they won't blame the FPC for that—they will blame politicians for that. They will assume that something has come from Parliament or the Treasury or the chancellor that will have meant that banks have been tightened up and they won't interpret it as deflating or as FPC deflating a bubble. They will interpret it as banks not doing what they should be doing which is lending ... And that is when it becomes a political problem and a political issue ... If we start turning round and saying 'No, it is the FPC' [it becomes] a blame game, but that is why this is potentially a very, very difficult political area for us. [TSC member]

4.3.5 Institutional Variations (Across Chambers and Across National Legislatures)

4.3.5.1 Lords vs Commons

As noted earlier, the TSC and the EAC each have different remits for conducting oversight hearings. The TSC has the statutory obligation for holding government departments to account, while the EAC adopts a more thematic approach to accountability. Bearing in mind those different remits, the focus here is on the quality of deliberation and overall accountability in the respective committees.

As a whole, the respondents maintained that deliberation in the Lords was 'better' than in the Commons, for a variety of reasons. First, as unelected parliamentarians, members of the EAC were less partisan than MPs, but nonetheless, they did tend to 'have obsessions' or subjects on which they had been working, so that 'they are geared up and they feel confident in that area' [O'Donnell]. Second, there was broad agreement that relative to the TSC, EAC members tended to be far more knowledgeable and have more expertise in economics, which generated more of a dialogue between questioners and witnesses:

> Historically you might have [on the EAC] a former governor of the Bank of England or a former Treasury permanent secretary, certainly a lot of former chancellors of the Exchequer who have been on the other side of the fence and will have quite deep knowledge ... There is less confrontation and more dialogue, that sometimes can be a successful way of getting the executive to share more information, to tell them more about how it actually is ... If I contrast the Commons with the Lords, the fact that you do have experts in the Lords, that fact that the environment is less overtly political means I think that you can have a more equal relationship in terms of the balance of knowledge between those asking the questions and those answering them. [MacPherson]

> Because there is greater knowledge and expertise in the Lords, there is greater relevance in the follow-up questions to witnesses. The Treasury Committee is less well-equipped with follow-up questions. If you have professional knowledge it is easier to continue the conversations. Discussions in the Lords had more of an argument and an exchange on account of the greater professional knowledge of the Lords. [Bank of England official]

This expertise of EAC members created an opportunity to explore areas of interest in more detail, but also lent them a degree of confidence to ask 'stupid questions':

> I would describe it as a series of rifle shots rather than a scatter-gun approach and that's where we decide that there are a number of areas that we really want to dig into and target. We try to dig deeper. Our role is to uncover the thinking behind policies ... and to try to uncover the rationale in contrast [to] the more confrontational approach that sometimes is adopted, and quite rightly adopted, by the Treasury Select Committee. [EAC member]

> [EAC members] are very independent-minded, and also they are grown-up enough, they don't want anything particularly ... and long enough in the tooth in the main to ask a stupid question. I mean I often ask stupid questions and sometimes if you ask a stupid question you actually discover a goldmine. [EAC member]

Overall, then, the tone of the Lords committee is said to be calmer and more deliberative than in the Commons:

[EAC members] are amazingly non-party political in their style so that makes it different. Now it can mean that it becomes you know, bluntly more soporific but it can mean that it can be also more calm and deliberative and [they are] really interested in the answers because I'm asking the question to which I want to know the answer rather than I'm asking the question in order to prove to my constituents that I have asked this question. Because what you get in the Commons [is] 'doesn't this prove that your organisation is not fit for purpose?' You never get that in the Lords, it is just not the style of it, that whole tone and wording you will frequently hear in all of the Commons. [Turner]

Others described the EAC as 'more civilized' than the TSC, and more 'polite': 'the Lords is completely different [from the Commons], and I think more effective. We are very polite to people, we are never rude to people, [although] we can sometimes be a little bit aggressive …' [EAC member].

Commentary on the TSC highlighted a number of features which interviewees perceived as being detrimental to high quality deliberation, namely, the higher turnover of members in the TSC, the lack of in-depth subject knowledge, the tendency to grandstand, and outright rudeness towards witnesses—as evidenced by the following:

Turnover:
There is always a rolling change because personnel change. One of the key differences between the Treasury Committee and their counterparts in the House of Lords is that you can get people come on to [the TSC] and are learning more of the business but they then leave because of political opportunities and promotion to the cabinet or shadow cabinet. Then with the arrival of new less-informed members who do not have the same background knowledge, there is considerable change. So, there is always this continual turnover in the Treasury Committee whereas in the Lords there is less of a turnover in personnel and a lot of people on the Lords Committee have professional knowledge such as former chancellors, distinguished academics, and professors of economics. That makes a difference in the question and answer session. [Bank of England official]

Lack of Knowledge
I think where it suffers [in the TSC] is because most of the members are not experts and they do struggle with the follow-up questions and probing into an answer and probing the weaknesses … I have wondered whether the Treasury Committee could do a better job if it had its own professional advisors there

who could scribble down on a piece of paper, hinting to the committee what the follow-up question should be. Given the sort of people that you have, that is the only way you can really address that. In the Lords, you have got people who actually are in a positon to deal better with the follow-up questions and to go deeper into an issue. Too often in the Treasury Committee you get the question, then the answer from the governor, and then that is the end of the conversation, and you move on to something else without further pushing and testing. [Bank of England official]

Grandstanding/Rudeness

The big difference between the House of Commons and the House of Lords is in the House of Commons, you have far more grandstanding by MPs and sometimes they give the impression that the name of the game is getting on the 9 o'clock news or getting a headline in the newspapers which is fair enough but often they do it by being gratuitously rude and offensive to their witnesses. [EAC member]

Going to the Treasury Committee was like playing a local derby where you know everyone is terribly excited, all the supporters are desperate to have a win rather than a defeat, hostile atmosphere, people being aggressive and so on. [King]

One might discern from these assessments a rather negative view of deliberation in the TSC. Even so, it should be noted that while one Bank official faulted the TSC for its lack of expertise, he nonetheless remarked that the committee 'has more of a feel that the policymakers are responding to the representatives of the people' and that 'what you don't get in the Lords is the same sort of bite for accountability.' Lord McFall (with experience on both the TSC and the EAC) also described the difference in mindset between the two committees: '[in the Lords] you are unelected, your mindset is a scrutiny mindset but you are not there to upset the applecart to the same extent as you are in the House of Commons.' A bite for accountability and a willingness to upset the applecart may well be a perfectly acceptable foundation for deliberation in the TSC. On reflection, it is worth recalling that in the quantitative text analysis we found in monetary policy hearings that TSC members tended to be associated with multiple themes (as did MPC members), whereas in the EAC, members tended to focus more on single themes. This empirical finding fits well with the description of the TSC as taking a scattergun approach and the EAC using more of a rifle shot approach, with the latter enabling a more targeted discourse. Moreover, Governor King's assessment of the TSC as 'like playing a local derby where you know everyone is terribly excited, all the supporters are desperate to have a win rather than a defeat, hostile atmosphere, people being aggressive and so on' also fits with the nonverbal behaviour analysis finding 'anger' in the expressions of TSC members.

Finally, with many years of experience testifying before both committees, Governor King provides a rather more measured view of questioning in the EAC. He notes that in his experience, questions in the 2010–15 EAC lacked follow-up,[6] in part because of the limited time given to the committee hearings. Nonetheless, he maintains that the quality of the questions themselves were of a high standard:

> In the Lords it was a shorter session, so there was a time-limit on it, whereas in the House of Commons you could have been there forever, and I mean we had several hours of sessions at times and we would go and start at 9:30a.m. There might be a ten-minute break in the middle; we could be going to 1:30pm … In the House of Lords it would typically be one hour. What they would do is that each member of the House of Lords Economic Affairs Committee would have one question and they would have rehearsed their questions beforehand, and very often they would have read them out. They'd have discussed it with their advisors. The problem was that although they were good questions, and they were more thoughtful and more substantive than the House of Commons questions, in the House of Lords there was no follow-up … It was just the norm. They didn't follow up their question with a second or third question, partly because of time. So what you would do in the House of Lords, you would get a question that could be quite profound and you'd give a little five-minute lecture and then the next person would ask their question, a different question, so in a sense it wasn't teasing things out and pressing. There was no pressing. People were very polite and they [were] good questions so it was an opportunity to say something thoughtful so the things that we volunteered in the House of Lords Committee were often I think more interesting and more substantive than things that came out in the Treasury Committee. [*Cheryl Schonhardt-Bailey: Because the question itself was more probing?*] The question itself. You see, the House of Commons might be 'Well, don't you think you completely misjudged the economy last month'. The House of Lords might be 'You suggested recently Mr. King that it might be an idea if we had this reform to the structure of banking but wouldn't this be an argument for adopting a

different reform'. And then you would have, it would be more like an academic exchange of view, conducted very politely. [King]

From these comments we can observe something of a trade-off between deliberation and accountability. Whereas the EAC may offer higher quality deliberation, in terms of 'digging deeper' into issues, the TSC may offer higher quality accountability, if by accountability we refer to the democratic link back to voters and constituents. This work has focused on just one aspect of accountability—namely, the explanation-giving aspect of accountability. Importantly, this explanation-giving aspect of accountability may be of higher quality in the unelected Lords committee, but this is not to say that it is necessarily lacking in the Commons committee. Certainly by our measure of reciprocity, the TSC delivers on explanation-giving accountability. The question raised is, are these explanations better given in terms of more rapid-fire, more contentious give and take between questioner and witness, or in terms of lengthier, more intellectually rigorous, and also more relaxed dialogue? The very simple and direct response is that the two are not entirely comparable, and instead they both deliver on distinct aspects of accountability. Overall, this comparative insight into the merits of deliberation in both the Commons' and Lords' committees helps to inform the discussion of a system of deliberative accountability, as presented in Chapter 1. The argument set out anticipated variations in the quality of deliberative accountability across different contexts, but it also argued for a wider lens in order to properly assess the system of accountability for economic policy decision making. Here, we can see that each chamber delivers well on certain aspects of deliberative accountability: in the unelected EAC, deliberation as an ideal is more in evidence, in that arguments are well-informed, discourse is respectful and polarization (from partisanship) is minimal; in the TSC, where MPs are to some extent beholden to electoral pressures, the 'bite for accountability' is strong, and so along with that comes more grandstanding, more partisan rhetoric and more adversarial discourse. The system across the UK Parliament appears to enable a specialization of deliberative accountability by legislative chamber.

4.3.5.2 UK vs US

As noted in Chapter 1, in previous research, I have analysed monetary policy deliberations in the US (Schonhardt-Bailey, 2013), and particularly have sought to compare deliberation in monetary policy oversight hearings in both the US and the UK (Schonhardt-Bailey, Dann et al., 2021). It thus made sense to utilize the interviews for this work to further explore differences in deliberative accountability in the US and the UK. Donald Kohn, former Vice Chairman of the US Federal Reserve *and* member of the UK Financial Policy Committee, is perhaps the best person to question on the differences in the forms and quality of deliberation across the two national systems. Interestingly, drawing in part on his experience in having testified before the TSC (on top of extensive experience before the two US congressional committees), Kohn suggested to the Fed ways to improve its accountably (Kohn and Wessel, 2016). In his interview with the author, Kohn identified a number of factors which, in his view, lessened the quality of deliberation in the US congressional committees. First, he noted the intense partisanship, which lent itself to hostility in committee hearings. Second was the rigid adherence to time-keeping in the US committees, and third was the 'revolving door' effect in the US, where members arrive and leave throughout the hearing. Fourth, he noted the nonverbal message sent to Fed officials by the nature of the seating arrangement. And, finally, overall, he thought that the dialogue was more 'honest' in the UK TSC:

Partisanship

In the US Congress, in the House side in particular, it's so obvious, I mean there is just this hostility, at least these days, since the late 90s, the mid-to-late 90s maybe, there's this huge hostility and growing gap between the Republicans and Democrats and it comes out in these hearings quite substantially. [Kohn]

Time-Keeping

So, [having had] my experience with the Treasury Committee, I actually wrote my letter to Andrew Tyrie, wrote an email to Andrew after he left, saying that I thought the hearings were well-organised, that it was clear to me that they kind of divvied up the topics ahead of time, that the questions were informed, and could respond to the answers they were getting. There wasn't a clock. In the US Congress, there is a series of lights sitting in front of you, green, yellow, red: green for four minutes, yellow for one minute, and then at five minutes it's red and things get cut off. In the Parliament, the chairman was kind of keeping track and he knew how much time he had … but every once in a while he would have to intervene and say 'You know, we need to get on with this thing. We are going to run out of time here' but there was a lot more back-and-forth, that the members of Parliament were much better informed about what they were doing, what the Financial Policy Committee had been doing, than the members of Congress, particularly in the House. [Kohn]

Revolving Door
I don't know what the average count is but [the House Financial Services Committee] is a huge committee and there are lots of people and they drift in and out. That is also one thing that doesn't tend to happen, it happens a little bit at the TSC but not to the degree that it happens particularly in the House [Financial Services Committee] where members come in, do their questioning, and leave, and they are not even there to hear the previous questions and the line of questioning. That is rare in the TSC. [Kohn]

Seating
My experience in the US Congress, it is completely different feel, and I think an important symbol of this is the seating arrangement. So in the Parliament, everybody's on the same level, and you are sitting around a rectangle … Then, [in] the Congress of course, they are up, they are elevated, and you are down, and … I think that is reflected in the attitudes, so you're there in Congress, and they are kind of looking down, and trying to catch you, and score points. [Kohn]

Honesty
It seems to me that Carney and King were more willing to argue with the committee, to tell [them] that 'you're wrong, here's why'. The FOMC in the US was more 'how can I find some way to agree with you even if I don't really agree with you' and not telling a lie, not saying something you don't believe in, but trying to find a positive angle into this…. whereas it seems to be that the dialogue [in the UK] actually is sharper than it is in the US … I think in the UK it is a more honest dialogue actually, yes. [Kohn]

Other respondents added to these remarks a number of other factors which detracted from deliberation in the congressional committees—namely, the reading out of statements in the US committees (which one Bank official viewed as 'not particularly interactive'), the overly large committee sizes in the US (which O'Donnell remarked detracted from having a 'proper dialogue'), the primary objective of congressional committees being to draft legislation and so 'regular hearings of oversight are less important to your political base back home [and] less important to your prestige' [Bank of England official]. This same interviewee also added that, importantly, the UK hearings reflected a strong consensus in support of independent central banking, while this consensus was not necessarily as broadly endorsed in the US:

> I think quite an important pre-condition for this relatively joined-up approach to the hearings of the Bank of England is that up to now at least there has been a relatively strong bipartisan consensus that monetary independence is a good-ish thing and should continue. When Yellen and Bernanke are appearing in front of the Senate committee and particularly the House committee there will be people with an agenda to reform the Fed, or even in some extreme cases to abolish it. That isn't something that the Bank of England has faced … to date. [Bank of England official]

4.3.6 Personalities

Question 6 from Table 4.2 sought to explore the extent to which members of the select committee who might be seen (or perceive themselves as) mavericks might affect the quality of deliberation during hearings. In discussions with interviewees, this broadened into assessments of key personalities in the hearings, including so-called mavericks, the committee chair, and the governor of the Bank of England. This section addresses the first of these two, leaving interviewees' views of the personality of the governor for the next section, as it pertains directly to the topic of nonverbal communication.

Using the term 'independent-minded' rather than 'maverick', TSC Chairman Tyrie noted that (in his capacity as chairman) they could be problematic but should nonetheless be divided into three categories—rational, irrational, and wreckers. In chairing the committee with independent-minded members of any sort, he stressed the importance of maintaining collegiality on the committee and most importantly, a nonpartisan ethos. In a subsequent communication,[7] Tyrie maintains that 'for the most part, unanimous reports are the only ones that have the capacity to be influential (and notably, under my chairmanship, all reports were unanimous, even those on Brexit)'.

While one Treasury official remarked that mavericks tend to make witnesses 'more cautious', and therefore are a negative influence on the deliberative process, others were more positive in their appraisals of the role of mavericks on accountability hearings. One TSC member argued that mavericks can be both useful *and* potentially disruptive:

[Referring to one such individual—John Mann[8]] It can be useful because sometimes he'll bring out something that isn't in what we are going to talk about. It can sometimes be very amusing. It can sometimes be very irritating, and sometimes just because he always does it, it weakens his position because he is a very bright, and very able man but people always expect him to do the off-the-wall question or the 'when was the last time you bought a pasty' so I think you can do that occasionally but to do it all the time weakens your position but it does bring levity into the [committee] but it also means … that] when it gets to those questions, everybody just switches off and thinks 'here we go' so it can be both: it can be useful and it can be disruptive. [TSC member]

Again, in reference to TSC member John Mann, another committee member remarked that his influence on the committee could be quite positive:

I think it is very, very useful having someone like John Mann who will score the points that you can't otherwise score in the Chamber … Here, you have 5 or 10 minutes to really exercise a point and then grill the chancellor, and John Mann was probably the one who started the omnishambles budget fiasco, with his questions about a pasty tax: 'When, Chancellor, did you last go into Greggs pasty shop?' And so it is that kind of questioning which is quite theatrical but nonetheless highlights the point. So, having a maverick is very, very important. [TSC member]

Similarly, about John Mann,

I always remember his question I think it was to Bob Diamond[9] about a camel going through the eye of a needle and he completely blind-sided Osborne on the pasty debacle, the pasty tax. I mean, mind you, the Treasury had been trying to tax VAT on things like pasties for twenty years, and intelligent politically-savvy politicians have been quietly telling them to get lost and George [Osborne] fell for it as did Danny Alexander … Anyway, they duly stuck it out there and John Mann looked at it and looked at one or two other things and single-handedly wrecked the budget. A brilliant achievement but he wasn't collegiate. [TSC member]

Interestingly, all three respondents remarked on Mann's questioning of Chancellor George Osborne on the so-called 'pasty tax' (Mason, 2012), which received widespread news headlines and certainly raised the media profile of

John Mann. While a maverick such as Mann can be disruptive and occasionally amusing, his style of questioning was for the most part accepted as integral to the deliberative process.

Turning to the role of the chair of the TSC, it was apparent that personal relationships between the committee chair and key witnesses—such as the governor of the Bank of England—are critical to the deliberative process. However, an intriguing insight was offered by Governor King in his assessment of the TSC chairmanships of both John McFall (2001–2010) and Andrew Tyrie (2010–2017). King notes that he found McFall's approach to his chairmanship more inclusive of the views of the Bank of England, and Tyrie's less so:

> [McFall's] personal focus was to try and keep the committee looking at potential reforms and to get the views of people from the Bank about the merits of these potential reforms. That was less true under Andrew Tyrie because he felt he knew what the reforms he wanted to see were already, and therefore was using the appearances with the Bank not in order to get the Bank to explain what they thought had gone wrong, and what could be done in future but actually to say things which would support or, not support, positions that he had already decided were the right ones. One of the reasons why I think the committee was particularly successful under John McFall after Northern Rock was because they asked us, what did we think needed to happen? We said 'Well, we have to have a resolution regime. We need a reform of regulation, we need to re-capitalise the banks', and the Treasury Select Committee pushed that very hard, and because it was their recommendation rather than just that of the Bank, actually I think we were quite successful in getting major legislative reforms, and from that perspective I think the McFall Treasury Committee had a bigger impact on policy. [King]

Importantly, however, King attributes the inclusive nature of the McFall chairmanship not only to personality, but also to fundamental changes in the role of the TSC before and after 2010. As noted earlier, 2010 saw the strengthening of the select committees with the introduction of the election of committee chairs by the whole of the House of Commons. This, in King's view, gave Tyrie a stronger and more independent mandate than his predecessor, as Tyrie enjoyed support across all parties and 'did not feel that he was in any way the government's person there' [King]. A second change was that the thinking of politicians and policymakers on the nature of financial reform in the wake of the financial crisis had evolved by 2010, so that there was greater certainty as to the shape of the major reforms by the time that Tyrie assumed the chairmanship:

> The other key factor was that after Northern Rock and the financial crisis in 2008 it was clear that there needed to be big changes so the case for change as such didn't need to be made very forcefully. The question was: what change? And that meant that the Treasury Select Committee under John McFall were looking for ideas. By the time we got to 2010 people had thought so long and hard about the financial crisis that the major reforms were already in train. [King]

4.3.7 Nonverbal Communication, Gender

This final section surveys the views of respondents on the role of nonverbal communication (or 'body language') during the parliamentary committee hearings, as well as the extent to which gender plays a role in the deliberative process.

4.3.7.1 Nonverbal Communication

While nonverbal communication was universally accepted as playing a significant role in the deliberations, respondents offered a wide variety of perspectives on *how* they perceived its effects. A commonly noted feature was that nonverbal communication served as a *signal* of underlying intentions or emotions. One member of the EAC remarked that he paid close attention to the signals of fellow committee members, such as headshaking, smiling, looking at one another—as these potentially indicated the disbelief, enthusiasm, and so on, of the committee members to the testimony of the witness. Another EAC member described the nonverbal communication in the Lords as highly interactional between questioner and witness:

> So [as for] the nonverbal from the members of the committee in the Lords, if you start saying something that they don't agree with, there will be a nonverbal, which is a sort of quizzical look which indicates 'I'm not quite convinced of that yet' whereas a nonverbal from [some EAC members would be] a kind of 'he's trying to hide something' and actually you should look at that. Or it looks as if the guy is about to explode with fury. There is a sort of [growling noises] going on in the corner and what is interesting there is how people respond to it. [EAC member]

With respect to signals from witnesses, interviewees commented that nonverbal behaviour often revealed the extent to which witnesses might be bluffing in their responses, or instead might be conveying authenticity and openness:

We recently had two ministers in ... [and] one of them was, how shall I put this diplomatically, one was very careful and precise and answered the questions and when he didn't know the answer, didn't answer the question and made it clear that he was going to write to us. The other was more of a bluffer, if I can put it that way, and it was quite evident and of course when you are bluffing or blustering you tend to move your body in a different way. You don't sit calmly, you say 'well of course, that's the situation' and gesticulate energetically. Bluffers are easy to spot. [EAC member]

If you see people looking slightly shifty, slightly nervous and slightly flushed in the cheeks and that kind of thing then you know you are probably hitting a rich vein. [TSC member]

Yes, I think these issues are very relevant to how committee hearings go. Committees are a bit like hunting packs. They can tell if someone is nervous, shifty, evasive, uncomfortable, and they will exploit these issues. If you are a committee member, part of your objective is I think to sort of chip away at an individual's potential weaknesses in the hope that this may reveal, if it doesn't reveal something about policy, then it might at least reveal something about the person ... My advice to anyone appearing before a committee is 'Look, you are not going to change who you are, you are not suddenly going to become very articulate but you have just got to find a way of being authentic, making these people think you're not being shifty' and I think nonverbal communication is very important in that ... Often I see people who just are so clearly uncomfortable and are never prepared to really quite explain what actually went on and people just really dislike that. So, openness matters; it doesn't even have to be real openness but appearing to be open seems to me to be a good thing. [Macpherson]

One TSC member further links this perception of honesty and openness to the overall persuasiveness of the witness. When pushed on whether the member thought that nonverbal communication had a bearing on changing the member's mind on a particular issue, the individual replied:

I think it does because I think one of the things that can happen is you'll ask a question and you genuinely want to know the answer and what is quite powerful is when the person, rather than just looking down their list of what the answer is, they actually reflect. And the witnesses who do that, who actually sit, and you can see them considering the question, even if that's pretend, it makes you feel that it was worth asking so when a witness … They are not actually saying anything but they are just thinking and considering and they are really thinking carefully about the answer: it makes the whole thing better because you think 'yes, these are important questions and they are considering' and the answer is going to be truthful and not just what somebody has written down for them. I'm not saying that that is not truthful but … because they've done that 'reflect, consider, look like they are concentrating' you feel like it is their answer rather than a prepared answer … because if you are just going to get prepared questions and prepared answers you might as well write a letter. [TSC member]

One interviewee[10] mentioned a number of witnesses who, each in their own way, conveyed ineffective or 'poor body language':

His performance in terms of his body language was abysmal. He was hesitant, he looked uncomfortable, he looked shifty … [and this affected the outcome].

[He] used to suffer a bit because he would lean back and then … your voice goes away from the microphone and it's not a great [testimony].

He tried to be too chatty, too friendly, choice of language … You have to be respectful even though they are being completely rude to you and treating you with no respect whatsoever.

Some interviewees described how they had consciously adapted their use of nonverbal behaviour in the committee hearings. For one TSC member, this was to elicit a fuller response from a witness by deliberately creating a pause:

I did an elementary course in Interview Techniques for hiring people. I remember the guy said 'use the pause' and explained that human beings abhor a vacuum. Therefore, if you simply stop talking, if you tough it out, the other guy will jump in and very often, if they are giving an answer, they answer your question and you just sit and smile and nod, they will get more and more uncomfortable and they will start adding to their answer …. [TSC member]

For some MPC members, nonverbal behaviour served as a way to cope with attending a hearing when the vast majority of the time was spent staying silent, while the governor answered the bulk of the questions. For both an MPC member and a Bank official, nonverbal 'tricks' offered a means to remain focused on the questioning (even as a passive observer) but also ways to signal to the committee an intent to join the dialogue:

The first thing I would say about nonverbal communication is that I once watched a hearing that I'd been at and you think 'Oh, s**t when the governor is talking, I just look like I've died'. And so, after that during the hearings I would try really hard to gaze, to look at Mervyn as if he was completely fascinating, so I'd try and fix this 'Mervyn you are so interesting' expression on my face and then I'd think about my shopping list. You had to listen actually: the worst thing about these hearings was that you weren't asked much initially but you had to listen because I wouldn't have been unhappy about contradicting the governor but I wouldn't want to do it by accident if you see what I mean? I wanted it to be something serious not a kind of trivial thing so you had to pay a reasonable amount of attention. I used to pay [attention] … it is pretty dull when it is somebody else talking, you know, so I tried very hard, I don't know whether this would come across if you watch me, to look as if I was engaged even when I wasn't speaking but it is a myth. It doesn't mean I'm engaged at all; it means I think it is important to look engaged … I did try and say to myself 'how am I looking?' if I am on the wide shots? If they pull back, what is it going to look like? What is this group of people going to look like? If you are all fiddling about, it doesn't make the right impression. So, I used to think 'how do we look to the outside world watching this?' and I also used to watch the MPs very carefully to see what tweaked them. You know, who is looking happy about this? Where are they likely to go? Is there something they are going to come back to? … One of the things you could do if … you really wanted to say something, the way you got to say something was by making terrible faces so that it was apparent that you really wanted to jump in … I deliberately tried to catch the chairman's eye if I wanted to say something—I really did try to do that, particularly latterly when I got more confident. [MPC member]

I wasn't very comfortable with [governor-centric hearings because in part] I was actually more nervous. I mean, I was nervous before every single hearing … and actually I was more nervous the longer it went before I broke my duck so I … I was worried that my mind … [*Cheryl Schonhardt-Bailey: Would wander?*] Yeah; and then you've let down your institution, and your colleagues and yourself and, you know, all of that ... [And so] I decided that occasionally if there was a question addressed to Mervyn which I had something to say, that I would intervene after his answer, and I started doing that ... [Bank of England official]

In discussions with interviewees on nonverbal communication, comparisons were invariably made between the key witnesses—namely Chancellor George Osborne, Governor Mervyn King, and Governor Mark Carney. Chapter 3 examined these three witnesses systematically, but here the impressions were more informal and anecdotal. For Osborne, one committee clerk remarked on his humor and his 'smirk', while a Treasury official noted Osborne's frequent use of his arms as a tool of persuasion:

The chancellor is an incredibly effective performer...and he is very robust in his answers but also knows how to employ humor to defuse situations but also without undermining his own authority.... The chancellor has this sort of wry smirk, that he delivers quite funny lines in a dead-pan way that I think are a very, very effective way of dealing with the committee. [Committee clerk]

George is a politician. George wants to persuade you: he's going to do this; he is going to be using his arms more.... George Osborne is used to talking to the Salisbury Conservative Club who are a wide mix, and he wants to entertain them so he will have to tell jokes. That requires you to get the body language right as well as the [words] ... If you are a politician, you are giving a lot of speeches ... You are looking to become popular, you are looking to win over the audience so you are trying to drag them in so that is why you need a lot more nonverbal, you need to kind of look around, you need to make them feel included, if they are over there, the ones at the back ... Whereas if you are an official [from the Bank or Treasury] and you are thinking about 'I need to get the answer right and I need to not mention the "recession" word and actually I don't particularly want this to be on television', you know, being boring is absolutely fine. [O'Donnell]

Comparisons between the two governors could be summarized as Carney conveying the charismatic nonverbal behaviour of a politician, and King conveying the more intellectual mannerisms of a professor:

When Carney comes in, it is like he is enjoying the performance and it makes it very different, it makes it less dull, it also makes it that you are aware that he is not intimidated. Not that Mervyn was ever intimidated, but the energy was lower, with this [governor] the energy is higher because Mark Carney is very aware that the cameras are there, the people are there, and he is enjoying being Mark Carney. I think he actually winked at me once. … I don't know if he does it to the men as well but it is off-putting because … you think … he winking in a flirtatious way or is it [something else]? [Pearce]

The thing about Mervyn is that he is a successful academic with a very analytical mind. Both his way of answering and his style were professorial, and his answers were very organized. He never ceased to amaze me. Most of us when we are talking are comprehensible but there are a lot of half-words, half-sentences and the like. Mervyn presented perfectly-formed sentences and paragraphs with great precision. It is almost unreal. His spoken English reflects the fact that he has a very organized mind, and knows exactly what he wants to say, and often the answer he would give, he would already have in mind that 'here is a point I want to get across' and he will channel the answer in a direction to make the point he wants to. Mark's style is a bit more natural if you like. He is a charismatic individual, someone who is very good in one-to-one and small group situations but partly because of that style he doesn't have the same sort of organization to his answers that Mervyn often had. So Mark would start with 'there are a couple of things I want to say here' and he would then add a third thing during the course of his answer. It is a sort of more natural journey but it doesn't come across as organized or as professional as Mervyn does but these differences reflect the differences in the individual personalities and their respective backgrounds … The committee has certainly related well to Mark as an individual. He has natural warmth that comes across whereas the professorial air is perhaps a little daunting to them. They know it is always going to be very difficult to get one past Mervyn because of his intellectual ability. [Bank of England official]

Both an MPC member and an FPC member remarked on the cultural differences between the two governors (Carney, originally a Canadian,[11] and King, a Briton):

Carney, although he is very persuasive, you always feel that you are being sold something. It is charm, and in Britain we distrust charm I think. There is some evidence that we really distrust charm in Britain. [MPC member]

So when Mark started he completely unnerved the politicians because of his informal style because this is actually pretty formal you know from an American perspective, and when Mark started he was very informal and it was driving the British politicians crazy. You could see it in their faces, you could see it in their body language and they hammered and hammered and hammered and got Mark down so that now Mark is much more scripted so everybody is happy but it is not as good as it was ... [When] Mark first came ... I think somebody forgot to say 'You know Mark, you must never use their first name, ever, ever, ever', you know, first rule ... [FPC member]

Perhaps one of the most intriguing responses on nonverbal communication came from Mervyn King's own assessment of his verbal strengths and visual weaknesses, and his ability to manage his governorship in a way that recognized these:

I consciously decided to go on television only very sparingly. I went on television to talk about why we'd started quantitative easing. I did an interview about banking and so on, but I did it very, very sparingly, partly because all the Treasury Committee appearances were televised, partly because the speeches I gave were televised live on BBC World and often on Channel 4 and others so that there was always television footage and I worked out that in that sense I was doing a television appearance, on average every three weeks and I thought this is too much. I didn't do television for two reasons. One is, I thought that it wasn't my natural habitat. Radio was much more suited to me than television. Partly because with television what matters is what you look like not what you say, and I felt my skill was in using words, ideas, explaining things simply to people. I've always felt that my greatest ability was to stand up in front of an audience that wasn't qualified to know about economics or finance and make them understand what we were doing and what the issues were ... I thought 'this is my comparative advantage—that's what I should be doing'. Going on television, which is very much part of the impression image you make, I just knew this was not my comparative advantage, and I also knew, and was very conscious of the fact, that television is a very exhausting medium, in the sense that people get bored with you quite quickly and, you know, a central bank governor has got to be in it for the long-haul. [King]

4.3.7.2 Gender

While gender has not been the focus of this research project, a final question sought to gain some impression from the interviewees as to their perceptions of both women committee members and women witnesses (recognizing, of course, the relative scarcity of these during the period under investigation). While it may be that, as a woman interviewer, the responses may have been skewed to favour the attributes of women, nonetheless it is worth noting these responses, which in some ways were surprisingly positive, although one less so:

> Female witnesses generally give us as full an answer as possible. They want to be helpful and are usually well-briefed and well-prepared. In contrast with an occasional tendency among male witnesses to show how smart they are. [EAC member]

For TSC member Teresa Pearce, her gender and her social class were intertwined:

> It is not nice at all, as a class thing ... but I've got a working-class London accent and there was this sort of attack I got from people in banking who thought 'well, you've got a working-class accent, you must be ignorant' and 'How dare you question somebody like this?' I got loads of abuse about that and that's horrible, it is really horrible. I think for quite a long time I was the only woman on the committee ... The first three years I was elected, [people] always asked me who I worked for because they assumed I was a secretary ...[*Cheryl Schonhardt-Bailey: Does gender shape the hearings?*] I think it just does; when you are outnumbered you are outnumbered and even though people might not be making an issue of your gender you do feel isolated ... I mean I remember once the chair saying 'We are all honourable gentlemen here' and I said 'Excuse me?' and it is that sort of thing. So I think you feel it puts more pressure on you because you've got to be better because you are the only torch-carrying person. And so you've put more pressure on yourself and you feel you have to be better. Occasionally there was one witness once who just patronized me so much. You know, I asked a question and he went [sigh] as if you know 'silly girl' sort of thing and it was horrible because it made me feel about that big and I just thought 'no, you are not going to do this' and I had to give myself quite a lot of talkings-to, to say 'actually you deserve to be here.' [*Cheryl Schonhardt-Bailey: is this a social or a gender thing?*] It is both but it is a social thing, you know, it is a class thing. There are jobs that are up there and they are not for the likes of us. [Pearce]

4.4 Discussion and Conclusion

This chapter has sought to complement the earlier chapters by adding more substance to the reasons and the thinking behind the words and actions of participants in the select committee hearings on monetary policy, fiscal policy, and financial stability. This discussion and conclusion will serve to highlight some of the more important or fundamental findings from the interviews with key participants. As such, it will address each of the seven thematic categories in turn.

(1) **The role that select committees have come to play in holding government agencies to account, as it has developed from their modern creation in 1979**

As the overview of the history of modern select committees in the UK Parliament suggested, their importance in holding government to account has grown significantly, particularly since the reforms of 2010. The interviewees recognized this growing importance, characterizing the TSC as having become 'more powerful' and 'more self-confident'. The EAC was also noted as having become more influential, but perhaps more targeted at topics of interest to its members and with an appreciation for the weight and significance of the reports it produces. Broadly speaking, select committees were perceived as having (in the words of one Bank official) 'shifted a bit of power back to Parliament away from the executive'.

(2) **Assessments of the interviewees as to the quality of deliberation and accountability in select committee hearings**

While interviewees generally agreed that accountability meant questioning the decisions or the judgments of policymakers, there was an underlying tension on the part of Bank of England officials as to the scope of the accountability role of the TSC. One described a mismatch of expectations, with the Bank expecting to be held accountable for technical decisions and MPs expecting to hold the Bank to account for 'the political consequences of the technical decisions' made by the Bank. Moreover, Governor King maintained that accountability of the Bank should constitute an assessment of its policy decisions, but not extend to the internal organization of the Bank. The focus of TSC Chairman Tyrie on reforming the internal governance of the Bank is well-known (not least because Tyrie himself explains his efforts (Tyrie, 2015)) and is clearly evident as a distinct thematic class in the quantitative text analysis of committee hearings. The response by Governor King allows us a measured view of why the Bank (under his governorship) resisted the TSC on this front.

A second intriguing finding is the perception of some witnesses of the growing assertiveness and self-confidence of the TSC in the deliberative process. In the words of one respondent, the committee 'can make inaccurate assertions, they can lead people to say or imply something they didn't mean, and there is no come-back because it is all under parliamentary privilege.' In short, the committee can be 'rude' and aggressive, but witnesses must be 'polite' and try to answer the questions asked. This assessment (which is a view of the TSC shared by some EAC members) is reflected quite clearly in the chapter on nonverbal communication, where the TSC exhibits an emotive stance of 'anger' while the response of Bank officials is one of 'appeasement'.

With respect to the scope for witnesses to *persuade* committee members, there was general agreement that the Bank had been effective in persuading the TSC on certain key issues, particularly, as King notes, on the resolution regime. And, it was seen that the obligation to explain itself before Parliament created something of a 'brake' on the decision making of the Bank, but this was accepted and endorsed as essential to proper accountability.

(3) **Motivations and intentions of the parliamentarians who serve on these committees**

Perhaps not surprisingly, the motivations of members of select committees included both public spirited ones ('public service is the highest call a person can have'; 'the thirst for knowledge'; 'demystify the language' of financial services for the public) but also ones of self-promotion (building one's ego, making headlines, gaining recognition in hopes of a ministerial position). Nonetheless, virtually all the interviewees recognized that a strong motivation for serving on either the TSC or the EAC rested in a keen interest in the subject matter (for example, from one TSC member: 'It is like going to university. I can learn so much about how the country is run in terms of the fiscal and monetary policy stuff.').

(4) **The extent to which partisanship and political incentives vary across policy type (fiscal, monetary, financial stability)**

The findings of the textual analysis were strongly confirmed in terms of the inherent partisanship (and lack of deliberative reciprocity) in fiscal policy hearings, particularly relative to monetary policy hearings.

However, perhaps the most insightful remarks stemmed from the responses on financial stability, where the unique and serious challenges to accountability included its inherent technical complexity (along with the lack of an established academic literature to inform committee members), the absence of clear, definable metrics to gauge success in financial stability, the necessity for some lack of transparency, the inherent fragility of financial stability—and, ultimately, politicians knowing that should 'things go wrong' the blame from the public would invariably fall on the politicians, not the Bank's Financial Policy Committee.

(5) **Variations in deliberation across chambers (Commons, Lords), and between the UK and the US**

The interviewees' responses clearly supported the findings from the nonverbal communication chapter, where the Lords committee was seen as 'happier' (more relaxed, congenial) than the more 'angry' Commons committee. Notably, the expertise and knowledge of the members of the EAC enabled a dialogue within those hearings which resembled an academic seminar, whereas the TSC deliberations reflected less knowledge, more grandstanding, and more rudeness towards witnesses. Yet, accountability in the TSC also offers a more direct link to voters and constituents (and, as we saw in Chapter 2, it also exhibited clear deliberative reciprocity in monetary policy hearings).

In the case of the UK–US comparison, the assessments of Donald Kohn were particularly insightful, given his lengthy experience in testifying in both settings. While the TSC may be seen as less deliberative and less relaxed than the EAC, when compared to the two US congressional committees, the TSC is favorably seen as less partisan, more expert, more focused on oversight (rather than drafting legislation), and more 'honest'.

(6) **The role that individual personalities play in the conduct of oversight**

With respect to the role of individuals on the committee who might be described as mavericks, the general agreement was that they served an important purpose in asking questions that others may not have asked, although their questioning could nonetheless be disruptive to the committee's deliberations.

(7) **The role of nonverbal communication and gender in the oversight hearings**

While individual interviewees differed in their perceptions of the role of nonverbal communication, some key themes were that: (1)

nonverbal communication served a useful role in signalling both the thinking and assessments of fellow committee members, but also the credibility or openness of the witness (for example, for one TSC member: 'If you see people looking slightly shifty, slightly nervous and slightly flushed in cheeks ... then you know you are probably hitting a rich vein.'); (2) truthfulness—or at least the appearance of it—factored highly in assessments of witnesses; and (3) in hearings with a group of witnesses and a tendency of the committee to focus its questioning on one witness (for example, the Governor), some witnesses were particularly conscious of their nonverbal behaviour as they sat in relative silence.

Finally, as noted earlier, this study has not focused on gender, but the responses of interviewees suggest that this may well offer a fruitful line of future research. Whether or not women are better prepared, less partisan, more helpful, less likely to want to show of how smart they are, and more critical of other women—all raise intriguing questions for another day.

Notes

1. The Interim FPC came into existence with the new Coalition Government after 2010, while the permanent FPC awaited final legislation in 2013 (Kohn, 2011).
2. One clerk noted that if whole sections of a briefing document were ignored by committee members, the staff may then send written questions to the witnesses, requesting written replies.
3. For this quote, the respondent requested greater anonymity and so institutional association is not given.
4. The FPC differs from the MPC in that its decision involves multiple levers and is formulated mostly in words, rather than a vote centred around, for example, a decision to change the interest rate. Moreover, unlike the MPC which takes decisions by voting, the FPC seeks to take decisions by consensus, but if this is not possible it will vote (Kohn, 2014).
5. One Bank of England official estimates that under Chairman McFall, 'the Governor probably did 80 per cent of the answering' whereas well into the chairmanship of Tyrie, this percentage had fallen to 'probably about 60 per cent'.
6. In a subsequent email communication (10 June 2021) King notes that 'I am now a member of the EAC, and since we spoke I can see that there are far more follow up question at EAC appearances than was the case before 2013 when I would give evidence. Some things do change.'
7. Phone conversation between Tyrie and author on 4 June 2021.
8. Mann is a former Labour MP, who served on the TSC. He was well-known for his aggressive style of questioning, but also his willingness to independently challenge

witnesses on a wide variety of topics. He has subsequently become Baron Mann, a non-affiliated member of the House of Lords.

9. Diamond was a former CEO of Barclays bank, who in the wake of the LIBOR interest rate scandal, resigned his position.
10. For this quote, the respondent requested greater anonymity and so institutional association is not given.
11. Carney acquired British citizenship during his tenure as governor of the Bank of England, and in the late 1980s, he also acquired Irish citizenship.

Reference

Gaskell, G. and M. W. Bauer (2000). Towards Public Accountability: beyond Sampling, Reliability and Validity. *Qualitative Researching with Text, Image and Sound—A Practical Handbook.* G. a. M. W. B. Gaskell. London, Sage: 336–350.

Kohn, D. (2011). "The Financial Policy Committee at the Bank of England." *Brookings On the Record* (https://www.brookings.edu/on-the-record/the-financial-policy-committee-at-the-bank-of-england/). Retrieved 15 August 2019.

Kohn, D. (2014). Financial Policy Committee at the Bank of England: Presentation at the Federal Reserve Board of Governors. Washington, DC, Brookings (accessed 23 March 2018: https://www.brookings.edu/wp-content/uploads/2016/06/financial_policy_committee_kohn.pdf).

Kohn, D. L. and D. Wessel (2016). Eight Ways to Improve the Fed's Accountability, Bloomberg (https://www.bloomberg.com/view/articles/2016-02-09/eight-ways-to-improve-the-fed-s-accountability).

Mason, R. (2012). George Osborne 'can't remember' eating in Greggs amid ridicule over pasty tax. *The Telegraph (accessed 28/3/2018:* https://www.telegraph.co.uk/news/politics/9169900/George-Osborne-cant-remember-eating-in-Greggs-amid-ridicule-over-pasty-tax.html).

Schonhardt-Bailey, C. (2013). *Deliberating American Monetary Policy: A Textual Analysis.* Cambridge, MA, MIT Press.

Schonhardt-Bailey, C., et al. (2021). "The Accountability Gap: Deliberation on Monetary Policy in Britain and America During the Financial Crisis," London School of Economics Working Paper.

Tyrie, A. (2015). *The Poodle Bites Back: Select Committee and the Revival of Parliament.* Surrey, Centre for Policy Studies.

5

Conclusion

5.1 The Adversarial Context in Deliberative Accountability

When policymakers are held to account for their decisions by parliamentary select committees, one might have hoped for discourse to exhibit reasoned argumentation, equality of participation, and high levels of civility and respect— that is, one might hope for something resembling a deliberative ideal. And yet, in these select committee hearings, we find that deliberation is far from ideal—for example, the hierarchical nature of accountability and the adversarial context mean that there is an imbalance of authority among participants, and civility can give way to rudeness, anger and contempt. Deliberation in parliamentary accountability hearings is, as I have argued, an inherently political exercise.

A parallel expectation is that a common understanding as to what constitutes high-quality accountability might have accompanied the trend towards more accountability demanded from public officials. As we saw from the graphs in Chapter 1, accountability and reason-giving have become core concepts in parliamentary discourse, thus mirroring the larger accountability explosion in public life (which ironically has not fostered more trust in politicians and governments). This demand for accountability spreads well beyond the UK, as evidenced by the current global pandemic. Throughout COVID-19, governments worldwide have been challenged as never before in living memory, and their policies have intruded into nearly every aspect of our personal lives. These policies have quite literally translated into life and death for millions. Government policies are also shaping our economic well-being and entire national economies both in the short-term and the long-term. As of summer 2021, it may be too early to properly assess the success or failure of the policies adopted by governments as they cope with COVID-19. Nonetheless difficult questions are already being asked of politicians and policymakers. The aftermath of COVID-19 will be largely one of government accountability. Were government policies the right ones, and made at the right

Deliberative Accountability in Parliamentary Committees. Cheryl Schonhardt-Bailey, Oxford University Press.
© Cheryl Schonhardt-Bailey (2022). DOI: 10.1093/oso/9780192847874.003.0005

time? What were the successes and what were the failures? Why did policies fail? What were the consequences of these failures? The bottom line is that questions will be asked of national leaders and answers will be demanded by their publics. Most certainly, policymakers will be held accountable for their decisions.

And yet, although we might expect a clear public understanding for what constitutes high-quality accountability as it pertains to the reasons given by policymakers for their policy actions, this work has argued that a lacuna of understanding exists for what can be described as deliberative accountability. The inherent adversarial nature of the grilling of policymakers by parliamentarians means that the context for this deliberative heart of accountability is hardly one in which we might expect to find ideal deliberation. Both the public and politicians appear to want more accountability for public policy decisions, as this would presumably bolster democratic legitimacy. And yet, with no clear standards or understanding for what constitutes quality in deliberative accountability, and thus no identifiable threshold for having met a given standard, trust in politicians and in government suffers.

This work has sought to unpack deliberative accountability, both theoretically and empirically, to better understand the reason-giving process that underpins government accountability, and thereby shed light on the question of how to better judge its quality. The distinctive adversarial nature of deliberative accountability challenges us to examine both the specific contexts (for example, type of policy and policymakers being held to account, and the characteristics and institutional norms of the parliamentarians who are conducting the accountability) but also the potential for trade-offs and counterbalancing effects across the system of accountability.

This latter point gives rise to two key insights of this work. First, not all policy types are suited to high-quality deliberative accountability. As will be seen in the summary of findings in the next section, fiscal policy appears to be poorly suited to deliberative accountability, for the simple reason that neither the questioners nor the witness is motivated to engage in reason-giving which is evidenced by respect, non-partisanship and reciprocity. In contrast, both monetary policy and financial stability appear to be well-suited to deliberative accountability. One might conclude that this constitutes a failing of fiscal policy, but it need not be, since those who make fiscal policy are subject to a separate (and blunter, to be sure) form of accountability—namely political accountability. In the UK, the chancellor of the Exchequer and his government can be electorally removed from office, should voters wish to reject their fiscal policy decisions. In contrast, independent central bankers are not subject to the ballot box, and so it is not unreasonable to expect high-quality deliberative accountability as a substitute for political accountability.

Second, as will be summarized in the next section, deliberative accountability varies across the Commons and the Lords committees, and this is closely linked to the proximity of MPs and peers to electoral representation. While the merits of the unelected nature of the UK House of Lords in terms of democratic legitimacy and democratic representation extend well beyond this work (see, for example, (Farrington, 2015, Kippin and Campion, 2018)), the evidence appears to suggest that hearings in the Lords Economic Affairs Committee (EAC) are closer to the deliberative ideal than are hearings in the Commons Treasury Select Committee (TSC). At the same time, the evidence also suggests that hearings in the TSC have greater 'bite for accountability' as MPs are motivated by electoral, partisan and career ambitions. This may, at times, result in angry, rude questioning by MPs but along with these questions comes the awareness by witnesses that their policy decisions will be showcased and scrutinized, and so this expectation by policymakers forces careful consideration of policy choices, in anticipation of having to publicly defend these. By focusing on deliberative accountability as a process which occurs across both the Commons and Lords committees, we can observe that while each chamber may exhibit a specialism towards either deliberation or accountability, together, whether intentionally or not, they appear to counter-balance each other.

5.2 What have we found?

We began this work with the assumption that accountability and deliberation are both desirable in the process of governing. As we saw in the previous chapter, the people who participate in parliamentary hearings that seek to hold policymakers and politicians to account are clearly of the view that these hearings are essential. For one MPC member, parliamentary hearings are the only venue where decisions which affect the whole of the British population can be questioned: 'if it weren't for those sessions, nobody is questioning the decisions.' In the view a TSC member, accountability hearings and the reports of select committees are 'where you get in-depth scrutiny, it is where you can change things, [and] you can actually have a massive effect on policy.' The member also remarks that one purpose of these hearings is to get policy experts to explain themselves, but in language that is comprehensible to politicians and the public. Moreover, knowledge that policymakers ultimately will be required to explain their decisions before a committee of parliamentarians causes these policymakers to think carefully about the reasons for their decisions, and whether these reasons would be publicly acceptable, and therefore about the decisions themselves when they are taken. If policymakers know that their decision cannot be publicly defended, this casts doubt on whether that policy decision is indeed the correct one, or, as one Bank of England official puts it: 'If I can't actually explain to anyone why I've made that decision, is it the right decision?'

In part to unravel the apparent paradox of more accountability with less trust in government, this work has explored one distinct aspect of accountability, namely the process of *reason-giving*. Even with ample scholarly literature on accountability, relatively little attention has been given to the metrics of the reason-giving deliberative process that lies at the heart of accountability. Surely if we accept that this process is central to accountability, we should seek to understand it better? What exactly constitutes quality in this process of reason-giving and how would we begin to measure it? As noted above, the public values the explanations and reasons that accountability promises to deliver—but it is not certain that they actually know what they are looking for when they seek these explanations, or whether they would recognise quality in deliberative accountability, should it be delivered to them.

This work has set out a framework for better understanding the reason-giving process of decision makers and has focused on three critical areas of economic policy—monetary policy, financial stability, and fiscal policy. The primary focus has been on hearings in both the House of Commons and House of Lords, where democratic legitimacy is sought through deliberative accountability. Deliberation in these hearings is contingent not only on reason-giving but may also be shaped by nonverbal communication.

Three metrics were set out to gauge systematically the quality of deliberative accountability as it varies across policy type and parliamentary chamber, as well as across different types of legislative settings. These are, *respect towards others*, the *degree of partisanship* (or electoral pandering), and *reciprocity*. Table 5.1 provides a high-level summary of the findings from the analysis in the three preceding chapters. Whereas the end of Chapter 2 summarized the findings for the quantitative text analysis, Table 5.1 adds to that summary the metric of respect which the analysis of nonverbal communication sought to deliver, together with interpretations offered from the participants, as discussed in in Chapter 4.

Table 5.1 Summary Findings for Verbal and Nonverbal Deliberative Accountability in Parliamentary Hearings.

Contextual Setting	(Verbal) Reciprocity between Parliamentarians and Witnesses, across Themes	(Verbal) Non-Partisanship exhibited in Discourse of Parliamentarians	(Nonverbal) Respect Shown by Witnesses towards Parliamentarians	Linking Empirical Findings to Interpretative Evidence: What are the contextual factors which give rise to these findings?
Economic Policy Type				**Contributing factors**
Monetary Policy	**High**	**High**	**High**	Clarity of statutory objective; common understanding of monetary theory; motivation of (some) MPs to learn/become experts; nonpartisan ethos of select committee members; deference of central bankers to parliamentary committees (especially in face of 'rudeness' by committee members)
Financial Stability	**Medium**	**High**	**High**	Ambiguous/unclear metrics for success in policy; little understanding of theory of financial stability; attraction of MPs to politicizing financial scandals; potential for lobbying from disproportionate effect of financial policy on different groups/businesses
Fiscal Policy	**Low**	**Medium**	**Low**	Redistributive consequences exacerbate political conflict; tendency toward deliberation as ritual (posturing, point-scoring, grandstanding); potential dispute over the hierarchical status in hearings; covers public spending across large array of policy areas, allowing both committee members and witness to focus on separate themes/topics

Continued

Table 5.1 *Continued*

Contextual Setting	(Verbal) Reciprocity between Parliamentarians and Witnesses, across Themes	(Verbal) Non-Partisanship exhibited in Discourse of Parliamentarians	(Nonverbal) Respect Shown by Witnesses towards Parliamentarians	Linking Empirical Findings to Interpretive Evidence: What are the contextual factors which give rise to these findings?
Chamber (Monetary Policy and Fiscal Policy)				
Lords	**Low** (Fiscal) **Medium** (Monetary)	**Medium**	**Low** (Fiscal) **High** (Monetary) [*Peers more respectful of witnesses]	For differences between policies, see above. Broadly, the Lords committee is seen as better for deliberation, owing to stronger nonpartisan ethos, more subject area expertise by committee members, and a tendency to be more 'polite' to witnesses
Commons	**Low** (Fiscal) **High** (Monetary)	**Low** (Fiscal) **High** (Monetary)	**Low** (Fiscal) **High** (Monetary) [*MPs less respectful of witnesses]	For differences between policies, see above. Broadly, the Commons committee is seen as better for accountability, owing to electoral link to constituents (explicit representative link), stronger 'bite for accountability' (possibly lending to more scope for 'rudeness', however), greater agility/willingness to cover more themes (in content)

5.2.1 Respect

In Chapter 1, *respect towards others* during the accountability hearings was set out as a first measure of quality in deliberative accountability. After all, if legislators and witnesses fail to respect one another, the entire legitimacy of the hearings is undermined, as one would quite rightly question the seriousness of the process and that of its key participants.

Parliamentarians see their role on either the TSC or EAC as a vitally important one. For one MP, serving on the Treasury Select Committee was, 'like going to university', since he found that he could learn about fiscal and monetary policy from the experts themselves. And yet, the adversarial nature of the hearings can also compromise exchanges between parliamentarians and witnesses, thereby pitting them against each other. One Bank of England official characterized the adversarial context as a mismatch of intentions, where Bank 'officials are there trying to give technical answers to what they would see as technical questions, and the other side are busy trying to make political points out of asking political questions.' Others characterized MPs on the Commons committee as 'aggressive' and 'rude' in their behaviour and thereby leaving witnesses severely disadvantaged. Particularly when the witness is either the chancellor or an official from the Treasury, Nicholas Macpherson describes the hearing as a 'political knock-about'.

These assessments from the interviews provide interpretations for the clear evidence of variations in levels of respectful behaviour as assessed by nonverbal communication. In Chapter 3 we found a prevailing emotion of anger among members of the TSC, which does seem to support the informal assessments of rude and aggressive questioning by MPs. In response to this questioning, the nonverbal behaviour by Bank officials is broadly one of appeasement and deference. And, as seen in their verbal responses, Bank officials tend to respond directly to the topics raised by MPs, which might be seen as a reciprocal form of respect in that these officials seek not to skirt questions or obfuscate, but rather appear to respond directly to the questioning.

The story in UK fiscal policy hearings is quite different. Here we found animosity and a struggle for dominance between backbench and frontbench MPs, with members of the TSC exhibiting a stance of anger, and the chancellor responding with one of contempt. These findings were linked back to the textual analysis of the hearings, revealing an apparent correlation between deliberative encounters in which the actors talk past one another and where there are also nonverbal cues of anger and contempt. This raises the puzzle of whether talking past one another in hearings leads to angry body language or whether

latent feelings of anger/contempt lead to an unwillingness to engage in reciprocal dialogue (and on this question, the present research design cannot discern
the direction of causality). A particularly intriguing finding from the experimental evidence is that observers assess the witness as least persuasive and
least competent when the exchange between the questioner and the witness is
highly aggressive and confrontational. Deliberative accountability is judged to
be of poor quality when the nonverbal behaviour on both sides is heated. This
finding potentially offers a key insight to help understand why more accountability can contribute to less trust in politicians and government. If both the
questioner and witness exhibit nonverbal behaviour that is confrontational,
the quality of accountability as perceived by observers would appear to suffer.

Across parliamentary chambers, the relaxed, less confrontational nonverbal expressions of peers on the EAC, together with 'happier' nonverbal cues
from Bank officials suggest a more congenial interaction between parliamentarians and witnesses in the Lords committee. This more discursive, more
thematically focused (at the level of the individual) dialogue in the Lords committee, contrasts with the angrier, more confrontational atmosphere in the
Commons committee. Whether it stems from peers' greater respect for expertise, the more nonpartisan nature of deliberation in the House of Lords, or
less attention paid to outside audiences, the overall level of respect in hearings
in the Economic Affairs Committee is simply higher than that in the Treasury
Select Committee.

In short, for hearings with central bankers, respect towards others may be
somewhat greater in the Lords committee than in the Commons, but as noted,
all the Bank officials interviewed expressed respect for the scrutiny work that
the Treasury Select Committee performs. In fiscal policy, the contemptuous
nonverbal cues of the chancellor strongly suggest that little respect is given
to these hearings in the TSC. Remarks from interviewees support this, with
one TSC member remarking that the chancellor sees the hearings 'as a set-
piece speech' so that regardless of the questions of MPs, the chancellor 'will go
back to his themes', concluding that his success depends on the absence of any
embarrassing 'soundbites' that might appear in the news and that in the end,
little scrutiny or understanding results.

Again, we can discern within these observations that the failure to respond
directly to the questions posed by MPs seems to contribute to low levels of
respect. Thus, it is apparent that while respect has been set out as a distinct
metric, it is closely related to our third metric—lack of reciprocal dialogue.
We will turn to this in Section 5.2.3.

5.2.2 Partisanship/Electoral Incentives

Our expectation from Chapter 1 was that the role for partisanship in deliberative accountability would be more complicated than for our other two metrics. Because of the more technical nature of monetary policy and financial stability, we expected less scope for partisanship (and electoral pandering) in these areas than in fiscal policy.

Even though UK select committees aspire to be nonpartisan, some partisanship was nonetheless expected. Specifically, partisanship was expected to feature more prominently in fiscal policy hearings than in either monetary policy or financial stability hearings. As noted in Chapter 1, because fiscal policy decides tax and spending decisions, there are invariably assumed to be winners and losers from any given fiscal policy decision. In monetary policy, the long-run rate of growth of the economy is not influenced by policy decisions, although it is a necessary condition to allow other economic policies (like fiscal policy) to affect the long-run growth rate. And, in financial stability, while there is some distance from party politics, because decisions by these policymakers can affect the fortunes of lenders and borrowers (institutional and individual), scope for lobbying potentially brings politics into the fray. The very question of who benefits from policy decisions and how closely aligned are they with party political cleavages invariably allows partisanship to leak into what are (purportedly) nonpartisan hearings.

Partisanship in fiscal policy hearings is exactly what we find, along with some degree of anger and contempt in nonverbal behaviour. While we may contend that partisanship in fiscal policy hearings lessens the quality of deliberative accountability by exacerbating and contributing to lack of reciprocity, we may recognize that partisan allegiances can also promote accountability, by challenging the opposing party in government. Moreover, because it is elected politicians who are being held to account in fiscal policy, in a democratic society, voters also have recourse to political accountability (the ballot box) to directly hold these politicians to account—something that is absent in holding central bankers to account. So, we might argue that partisan rhetoric in accountability hearings is acceptable, since it challenges the opposing party politicians to explain themselves. But what if they fail to explain themselves, by essentially failing to directly answer the challenges (that is, reciprocity is lacking)? One fallback alternative then becomes the mechanism of political accountability.

If it is unrealistic to impose the same (nonpartisan) standard of deliberative accountability on fiscal policy as we do on monetary policy or financial stability, why do parliamentarians even go to the trouble of conducting fiscal policy hearings? Although parliamentarians might value the ritual aspect of fiscal policy deliberative accountability (for example, the opportunity to grandstand, and to pander to constituents or partisan allegiances), it may well be that for democratic legitimacy, political accountability is preferable to deliberative accountability. After all, given the comments of interviewees who remarked that fiscal policy hearings were merely a venue for 'government bashing', an opportunity for the opposition to 'beat up' the chancellor and the ruling party to allow him 'to explain how brilliant everything is', it is possible that this sort of hearing is accountability in name only. It is also possible that this is precisely the sort of accountability that contributes to the paradox of more accountability yet less trust in politicians and government. If we find (as is summarized in the following section), little in the way of reciprocal dialogue in fiscal policy hearings, what indeed is the point of the process except to undermine the very reason-giving that the public expects from deliberative accountability?

From Chapter 1, we recognized that value-based discourse may not be ideal for deliberation, and so, in fiscal policy, where decisions determine who wins and who loses, 'opportunities for deliberation are likely to turn anti-deliberative', and the wiser course would be to abandon deliberation and instead pursue alternative methods (Mendelberg, 2002, 160–61). One alternative to deliberative accountability in fiscal policy is political accountability, but others might include a written format for challenges to be addressed and responses to be given. Without the potential for negative nonverbal behaviour (anger, contempt), this written approach might lessen the attraction for partisan rhetoric and thereby improve at least the reason-giving aspect of accountability. On the other hand, it may be easier to obfuscate in written replies and of course, there is no scope for direct follow-up, as with live questioning.

Other alternatives for fiscal policy include deliberation behind closed doors, where the absence of cameras diminishes concerns about soundbites and lessens the potential to pander to outside audiences. But, the trade-offs between accountability and transparency are significant and the tension between the two pursuits has been recognized by scholars (Hood, 2010, Warsh, 2014, Ferry, Eckersley et al., 2015, Williams, 2015). At its core, the problem with deliberative accountability in UK fiscal policy is the inverted hierarchical relationship noted in earlier chapters, where backbench MPs hold front-bench ministers to account. In monetary policy and financial stability, the hierarchical relationship aligns with the statutory arrangement whereby independent agencies are delegated policymaking authority but are ultimately responsible to legislators. This alignment avoids the sort of partisan conflict that we observe in fiscal policy.

5.2.3 Reciprocity

The third metric for quality in deliberative accountability refers to the justifications that are owed to citizens for the laws and public policies made on their behalf. In a deliberative setting, reciprocity requires participants to engage with one another, to give reasons and to listen and take up the reasons offered by others. In deliberative accountability, reciprocity requires questioners to pose relevant and public-regarding questions (that is, questions which relate to the statutory requirements of the policymaker being held to account, as well as ones that are not meant to enhance one's own electoral position), and for witnesses to answer these questions directly, competently and credibly. As such, reciprocity is interactive and dynamic—it is inherently a give-and-take exchange between questioner and witness, with each listening and responding to one another.

In Chapter 2, we found clear evidence of reciprocal dialogue in monetary policy and very little in fiscal policy. In monetary policy, both MPs and peers tended to converge with MPC members on most themes, whereas in fiscal policy, the chancellor tended to speak to one theme and committee members focused on other themes. In financial stability, reciprocity appears to be constrained by the technical expertise of the subject matter, where MPs were less comfortable engaging with BoE experts.

While the content analysis in Chapter 2 provided a visually compelling depiction of poor reciprocity in fiscal policy, it did not tell us why this is the case. From our interviews, the answers become clearer. Several interviewees likened the chancellor's appearances before the TSC to a media appearance, where he for all intents and purposes sticks to a pre-determined script. As such, the chancellor seeks to avoid answering the questions asked and instead, responds according to his own agenda. Interestingly, his ability to do so is, as noted by one interviewee, protected by parliamentary privilege. Parliamentary privilege is officially defined as granting: 'certain legal immunities for Members of both Houses to allow them to perform their duties without interference from outside of the House. Parliamentary privilege includes freedom of speech and the right of both Houses to regulate their own affairs, which is supposed to better enable parliamentarians to fulfill their obligations.'[1] While parliamentary privilege has a history dating to 1689, there have been a number of issues recognized with how it currently functions in Parliament (Gay, 2013). The feature of interest here is that unlike central bankers, the chancellor is afforded far greater license to respond as he wishes in these hearings:

[The chancellor] is just going to say what he is going to say and disregard the questions. It is very hard for the committee to get after him because he is the chancellor and he is as much protected by parliamentary privilege as they are. They can't get him. They can do all sorts of things with [un]elected officials for contempt of Parliament or anything else if we don't appear or we don't answer questions, or we try to plead silence on something. You can't do that with members of Parliament. [Former Bank of England official]

Thus, while parliamentary privilege may serve an important purpose, it does not appear to enhance the quality of deliberative accountability in fiscal policy hearings.

And, finally, it is not realistic to expect the same sort of reciprocity in fiscal policy as we find in monetary policy, for the simple reason that the former encompasses a broad array of topics while the latter is an inherently narrow subject matter. As Cabinet Secretary, Gus O'Donnell, explains, whereas monetary policy is a 'very narrow subject', fiscal policy covers public spending across a whole array of policy areas (health, education, defense, and so on). As a result, 'you would expect there to be much more mismatch' between parliamentarians and the chancellor, since he is 'talking about the whole of Government' and 'will want to concentrate on the bits where he thinks it is going well and they will want to concentrate on the bits where they think it is going badly' [O'Donnell]. Simply put, there is more scope for picking and choosing areas of interest in fiscal policy than there is in monetary policy. Importantly, however, one institutional feature created in the 2010–15 Parliament sought to lessen this mismatch in the oversight of fiscal policy. In 2011 the Office for Budget Responsibility was formally established to provide independent economic analysis and assessment of public finances. Nonetheless, as an example of an official fiscal 'watchdog' which is intended to be nonpartisan, it is not a policymaker nor is it part of any parliamentary select committee, and so it offers only a partial solution. Importantly, it provides an example of seeking to carve out those areas of fiscal policy that can be best handled by an operationally independent agency.

5.3 Weighting Accountability and Deliberation between the Commons and Lords

Just as we recognized in Chapter 1 that deliberation, democracy and real-istic dialogue may, to some extent, conflict with one another, one thread of our analysis suggests that our two core concepts—accountability and deliberation—may not always sit well together. Indeed, at times, there may be something of a trade-off between the two. In comparisons between the two parliamentary chambers, interviewees often remarked on distinct styles of dis-course. Whereas in the TSC, MPs were more confrontational (often 'rude' and nonverbally, 'angry'), in the EAC, peers tended to be more relaxed. Peers were also noted for having greater expertise than MPs and so the nature of scrutiny tended to be deeper and informed more by a broader knowledge base. And yet, instead of greater expertise, a Bank of England official remarked that the TSC 'has more of a feel that the policymakers are responding to the represen-tatives of the people' and that 'what you don't get in the Lords is the same sort of bite for accountability.' One peer also described the difference in mind-set between the two committees; '[in the Lords] you are unelected, your mind-set is a scrutiny mind-set but you are not there to upset the applecart to the same extent as you are in the House of Commons.' This 'bite for accountability' and a willingness 'to upset the applecart' may enhance accountability by provid-ing a closer link back to the voting public, but perhaps at the expense of more in-depth and enhanced reason-giving deliberation.

It is worth repeating Governor King's depiction of the style of each committee:

> The problem was that although they were good questions, and they were more thoughtful and more substantive than the House of Commons questions, in the House of Lords there was no follow-up. ... It was just the norm. They didn't follow up their question with a second or third question, partly because of time so what you would do in the House of Lords, you would get a question that could be quite profound and you'd give a little five-minute lecture and then the next person would ask their question, a different question, so in a sense it wasn't teasing things out and pressing. There was no pressing. People were very polite and they [were] good questions so it was an opportunity to say something thoughtful so the things that we volunteered in the House of Lords committee were often I think more interesting and more substantive than things that came out in the Treasury committee.
>
> (King)

By King's reckoning, the Lords committee in the 2010-2015 Parliament lacked the ability or inclination to 'press' for answers or to tease out issues, although at the same time, witnesses found that the opportunity to be more thoughtful in the Lords committee allowed 'more interesting and more substantive' material to emerge. So, there is something of a trade-off between greater scope for democratic accountability in the TSC, and more in-depth reason-giving deliberation in the EAC. When viewed across the whole of Parliament, it may not matter that accountability may have greater weight in the TSC and deliberation more in the EAC, but rather what matters is that each has a comparative advantage, which is appropriate to the context and purpose of each chamber.

5.4 The Contribution of Nonverbal

The focus on the what, the how and the why in Chapters 2, 3 and 4 has revealed that institutional arrangements surrounding the process for making different policies (including an agreed recognition of who sits where in the hierarchical framework for accountability, a well-developed understanding of the policy area, and so on) as well as the rules and norms in legislative settings all help to determine the quality of deliberative accountability. We have come to better recognize the pillars for quality in deliberative accountability (namely, respect, nonpartisanship and reciprocity) and have acquired ways to measure these empirically. We know from Chapter 3 that subtleties like the perception of competence and credibility can matter in the deliberative process, and we also know from the comments of participants themselves (Chapter 4) that appearances of truthfulness (apart even from truthfulness itself) can shape the degree to which a witness is persuasive. One aspect of the nonverbal experiment in Chapter 3 which bears emphasizing is the finding that observers of accountability hearings are clearly less persuaded by the reasons given from witnesses when the exchange between a questioner and witness is acrimonious. While some degree of combativeness is rated highly in perceptions of witness competence, this appears to be only when this combativeness is on the part of the witness, but not the questioner.

As has been noted, this finding may help us to better understand the paradox of more accountability alongside less trust in government. That is, when the public perceives both parties in an accountability hearing as simply 'going at each other' the findings here suggest that these observers are less likely to judge the policymaker who is being held to account as persuasive or competent.

Where conflict is all that is observed in an exchange between a parliamentarian and a witness, this may reduce rather than enhance the public's trust in government. And, where the questioner is conciliatory (perhaps is more respectful) and the witness is combative, the perception of observers is that the witness is most persuasive and most competent. There may be a lesson here in the value given to respectful questioning on the part of parliamentarians. A portion of respect in the process of accountability may go some way to enhancing the public's trust in government.

5.5 Takeaways for Deliberative Democrats, Accountability and Central Bank Communication Scholars

What have we learned that we did not already know (or at least suspect)? From Chapter 1, we noted that empirical studies have established several findings for deliberation in legislatures. One finding of relevance here is that deliberation is of higher quality in second chambers than in first chambers. So, it should come as no surprise that we should find the deliberation in the Lords Economic Affairs Committee to be of higher quality than that in the Commons Treasury Select Committee. And yet, what these studies have not previously considered is that, at least with respect to deliberative accountability, this apparent 'win' for the committee in the Lords is less a win and more a counter-balance in a system which delivers one chamber specializing more in deliberation and the other more in accountability. In other words, while deliberative scholars may emphasize the desirability of high-quality deliberation as a means for enhancing political legitimacy, what may have been overlooked is the parallel desirability for public policy accountability, which has acquired a high level of saliency over the past 40 years. With its more direct link back to voters (to whom, ultimately, policymakers and politicians are accountable in a representative democracy), accountability can be at odds with deliberative ideals. With greater expertise and less partisanship, peers are closer to the deliberative ideal, whereas with greater responsiveness to electoral and partisan pressures, MPs are more adept in delivering aggressive accountability.

A second finding from empirical studies of deliberation is that polarization (for example, in partisan ideology) makes quality deliberation more challenging. This work has helped to develop this analysis further, by juxtaposing different types of economic policy accountability hearings. In monetary policy, where the redistributive effects are less than in fiscal policy, and where the analytical toolkit is more focused and where there is a more unified theoretical understanding, we find higher quality deliberation. The summary results from Table 5.1 suggest that across the three metrics, quality of deliberative accountability in fiscal policy is low, as the underlying polarization is greater. Hence, this work has pushed us to consider more fully the effect of low-quality deliberative accountability in fiscal policy. In nonverbal behaviour, we see anger and contempt in these hearings—suggesting low levels of respect—and from the interpretations of interviewees, we observe little acceptance that fiscal policy hearings actually deliver quality in either deliberation or accountability. If the goal of the chancellor is to deliver a set-piece speech and then leave the hearings unscathed, and the goals of the committee members are shaped by their political allegiances, then we are left to consider whether valuing these hearings as delivering 'ritual deliberation' is sufficient, if this means that trust in politicians and government erodes as a product of this ritual. As has been argued, the challenge to deliberative scholars is to consider when deliberation in certain contexts is better reconceived entirely.

Overall, this work has offered to deliberative scholars a methodologically diverse analysis of deliberation (*what* is said, *how* it is said and *why* it is said) in a politicized, adversarial context. By focusing on deliberative accountability, it has sought to examine a particularly challenging context for deliberation and has, at the same time, offered suggestions for how one might reconceive the role for deliberation in this context.

For accountability scholars, this work has similarly provided a mixed-method approach to understanding and gauging quality in accountability. It has sought to address the paradox of greater expectations of, and greater quantities of accountability alongside less trust in politicians and governments. By focusing on the core of accountability—namely the reason-giving by policymakers for the decisions taken—and identifying three metrics for quality in deliberative accountability, this work has sought to empirically unpack the notion of quality in deliberative accountability. Key insights from the findings reveal that accountability varies across policy types and across parliamentary chambers. In fiscal policy, where respect is compromised by anger by the parliamentarians and contempt by the chancellor, and where there is little reciprocity in the process of questioning, more accountability but of a poor quality may be contributing to lower levels of trust among the public. Additionally, from the experiment in Chapter 3, we found that the process of accountability is shaped by the nonverbal behaviour of those holding policymakers to account—the more aggressive their behaviour, the more attention of the audience is drawn to the responding nonverbal behaviour of the policymaker (for example, when the questioner appears to be riling the witness, does the witness remain calm or does the witness become riled?). Importantly, observers were especially dissatisfied with the persuasiveness and competence of the witness when the exchange between questioner and witness was acrimonious. This helps to target more specifically for accountability scholars the conditions under which accountability becomes counterproductive for democratic legitimacy.

And finally, for the literature on central bank communication, where communication has been examined largely in the form of quantitative text analysis, this work challenges scholars to focus more on both the deliberative aspects of communication, but also where personal interactions, in the form of non-verbal communication, shape assessments of competence and persuasiveness. The awareness of the importance of facial expressions, vocal cues and gestures will no doubt make some central bank officials more wary in their appearances before parliamentary committees. But intriguingly, one practical lesson for central bank policymakers is that, if faced with a confrontational questioner, the preferred response is appeasement over combativeness, since the latter response yields negative assessments of the competence and persuasiveness of the witness.

Aside from contributions to these literatures, the final insight might be that as voters demand more answers and explanations from policymakers who shape their lives and livelihoods, it is hoped that this work has provided more clarity on where and how deliberative accountability can enhance political legitimacy—and where it cannot.

Note

1. From the UK Parliament website: https://www.parliament.uk/site-information/glossary/parliamentary-privilege/ (accessed 7 August 2019).

Reference

Farrington, C. (2015). "Lords Reform: Some Inconvenient Truths." *Political Quarterly* **86**(2): 297–306.

Ferry, L., et al. (2015). "Accountability and Transparency in English Local Government: Moving from 'Matching Parts' to 'Awkward Couple'?" *Financial Accountability and Management in Governments, Public Services and Charities* **31**(3): 345–361.

Gay, O. (2013). "Parliamentary privilege: current issues (Standard Note: SN/PC/06390)" House of Commons Library.

Hood, C. (2010). "Accountability and Transparency: Siamese Twins, Matching Parts, Awkward Couple?." *West European Politics* **33**(5): 989–1009.

Mendelberg, T. (2002). The Deliberative Citizen: Theory and Evidence. *Political Decision Making, Deliberation and Participation, vol. 6.* M. X. D. Carpini, L. Huddy and R. Y. Shapiro. Greenwhich, CT, JAI Press: 151–193.

S. Campion and S. Kippin (2018). How undemocratic is the House of Lords? *The UK's Changing Democracy: The 2018 Democratic Audit.* P. Dunleavy, A. Park and R. Taylor. London LSE Press: https://www.democraticaudit.com/2018/10/02/audit2018-how-undemocratic-is-the-house-of-lords/.

Warsh, K. M. (2014). Transparency and the Bank of England's Monetary Policy Committee (https://www.hoover.org/sites/default/files/transparency_and_the_bank_of_englands_monetary_policy_committee.pdf). London.

Williams, A. (2015). "A global index of information transparency and accountability." *Journal of Comparative Economics* **43**(3): 804–824.

Appendices

APPENDIX 1: LIST OF 37 HEARINGS OVER 2010–2015 PARLIAMENT
(12 SELECTED FOR NONVERBAL CODING IN ITALICS)

House of Commons Treasury Select Committee

Monetary Policy Hearings

28 July 2010, Inflation Report
10 November 2010, Inflation Report
1 March 2011, Inflation Report
28 June 2011, Inflation Report
25 October 2011, Quantitative Easing
28 November 2011, Inflation Report
29 February 2012, Inflation Report
26 June 2012, Inflation Report
27 November 2012, Inflation Report
25 June 2013, Inflation Report
12 September 2013, Inflation Report
26 November 2013, Inflation Report
24 June 2014, Inflation Report
10 September 2014, Inflation Report
25 November 2014, Inflation Report
24 February 2015, Inflation Report

Fiscal Policy Hearings

15 July 2010, Budget
4 November 2010, Spending Round
29 March 2011, Budget
27 March 2012, Budget
26 March 2013, Budget
11 July 2013, Spending Round
17 December 2014, Autumn Statement

House of Lords Economic Affairs Committee

Monetary Policy

16 November 2010, Meeting with the Governor
27 March 2012, Economic Outlook, Meeting with the Governor and MPC members

17 December 2013, Meeting with the Governor of the Bank of England
10 March 2015, Meeting with the Governor of the Bank of England

Fiscal Policy

30 November 2010, Economic Outlook, Meeting with the Chancellor and Treasury Staff
8 December 2011, Economic Outlook, Meeting with the Chancellor and Treasury Staff
4 February 2014, Meeting with the Chancellor of the Exchequer

Financial Stability Reports and Hearings 2011–2015 (All in TSC)

17 January 2012, December 2011 FSR
17 July 2012, June 2012 FSR
15 January 2013, November 2012 FSR
2 July 2013, June 2013 FSR
15 January 2014, November 2013 FSR
15 July 2014, June 2014 FSR
14 January 2015, December 2014 FSR

APPENDIX 2: DETAILS OF COMMITTEE MEMBERS

Committee members and party affiliations

House of Commons Treasury Select Committee, 2010–2015

2010

    Chairman: Andrew Tyrie (*Conservative*)
    John Cryer (*Labour*)
    Michael Fallon (*Conservative*)
    Mark Garnier (*Conservative*)
    Stewart Hosie (*Scottish National Party*)
    Andrea Leadsom (*Conservative*)
    Andy Love (*Labour*)
    John Mann (*Labour*)
    George Mudie (*Labour*)
    Jesse Norman (*Conservative*)
    David Rutley (*Conservative*)
    John Thurso (*Liberal Democrat*)
    Chuka Umunna (*Labour*)

2011

    Chairman: Andrew Tyrie (*Conservative*)
    John Cryer (*Labour*)
    Michael Fallon (*Conservative*)
    Mark Garnier (*Conservative*)
    Stewart Hosie (*Scottish National Party*)
    Andrea Leadsom (*Conservative*)

Andy Love (*Labour*)
John Mann (*Labour*)
George Mudie (*Labour*)
Jesse Norman (*Conservative*)
David Ruffley (*Conservative*)
John Thurso (*Liberal Democrat*)
Chuka Umunna (*Labour*)

2012

Chairman: Andrew Tyrie (*Conservative*)
Michael Fallon (*Conservative*)
Mark Garnier (*Conservative*)
Stewart Hosie (*Scottish National Party*)
Andrea Leadsom (*Conservative*)
Andy Love (*Labour*)
John Mann (*Labour*)
Pat McFadden (*Labour*)
George Mudie (*Labour*)
Jesse Norman (*Conservative*)
Teresa Pearce (*Labour*)
David Ruffley (*Conservative*)
John Thurso (*Liberal Democrat*)

2013

Chairman: Andrew Tyrie (*Conservative*)
Mark Garnier (*Conservative*)
Stewart Hosie (*Scottish National Party*)
Andrea Leadsom (*Conservative*)
Andy Love (*Labour*)
Pat McFadden (*Labour*)
John Mann (*Labour*)
George Mudie (*Labour*)
Brooks Newmark (*Conservative*)
Jesse Norman (*Conservative*)
Teresa Pearce (*Labour*)
David Ruffley (*Conservative*)
John Thurso (*Liberal Democrat*)

2014

Chairman: Andrew Tyrie (*Conservative*)
Steve Baker (*Conservative*)
Mark Garnier (*Conservative*)
Stewart Hosie (*Scottish National Party*)
Andy Love (*Labour*)
Pat McFadden (*Labour*)
John Mann (*Labour*)
George Mudie (*Labour*)
*Brooks Newmark (*Conservative*)

Jesse Norman (*Conservative*)
Teresa Pearce (*Labour*)
David Ruffley (*Conservative*)
John Thurso (*Liberal Democrat*)
Alok Sharma (*Conservative*)
**Rushanara Ali (*Labour*)
**Mike Kane (*Labour*)

* Appointed Minister for Civil Society on 15 July 2014 and attended no Committee meetings after this date
** Elected by the Labour Party to replace Pat McFadden who was promoted to the Shadow Front Bench in October 2014 and George Mudie who resigned in November 2014.

2015

Chairman: Andrew Tyrie (*Conservative*)
Rushanara Ali (*Labour*)
Steve Baker (*Conservative*)
Mark Garnier (*Conservative*)
Stewart Hosie (*Scottish National Party*)
Mike Kane (*Labour*)
Andy Love (*Labour*)
John Mann (*Labour*)
Jesse Norman (*Conservative*)
Teresa Pearce (*Labour*)
David Ruffley (*Conservative*)
Alok Sharma (*Conservative*)
John Thurso (*Liberal Democrat*)

House of Lords Economic Affairs Committee, 2010-2015

2010

Chairman: Lord MacGregor of Pulham Market (*Conservative*)
Lord Best (*Crossbencher*)
Lord Currie of Marylebone (*Crossbencher*)
Lord Forsyth of Drumlean (*Conservative*)
Lord Hollick (Labour)
Baroness Kingsmill (Labour)
Lord Lawson of Blaby (Conservative)
Lord Levene of Portsoken (Crossbencher)
Lord Lipsey (Labour)
Lord Maclennan of Rogart (Liberal Democrat)
Lord Moonie (Labour)
Lord Shipley (*Liberal Democrat*) [*appointed by Committee Members, rather than the House]
Lord Smith of Clifton (*Liberal Democrat*)
Lord Tugendhat (*Conservative*)

2012

Chairman: Lord MacGregor of Pulham Market (*Conservative*)

Lord Best (*Crossbencher*)
Lord Currie of Marylebone (*Crossbencher*)
Lord Forsyth of Drumlean (*Conservative*)
Lord Hollick (*Labour*)
Baroness Kingsmill (Labour)
Lord Lawson of Blaby (*Conservative*)
Lord Levene of Portsoken (Crossbencher)
Lord Lipsey (*Labour*)
Lord McFall of Alcluith (*Labour*)
Lord Moonie (Labour)
Lord Rowe-Beddoe (*Crossbencher*)
Lord Shipley (*Liberal Democrat*)

2013

Members of the Committee appointed, 16 May 2013
Chairman: Lord MacGregor of Pulham Market (*Conservative*)
Baroness Blackstone (*Labour*)
Lord Griffiths of Fforestfach (*Conservative*)
Lord Hollick (*Labour*)
Lord Lawson of Blaby (*Conservative*)
Lord Lipsey (*Labour*)
Lord May of Oxford (*Crossbencher*)
Lord McFall of Alcluith (*Labour*)
Baroness Noakes (*Conservative*)
Lord Rowe-Beddoe (*Crossbencher*)
Lord Shipley (*Liberal Democrat*)
Lord Skidelsky (*Crossbencher*)
Lord Smith of Clifton (*Liberal Democrat*)

2014–2015

Members of the Committee appointed, 12 June 2014
Chairman: Lord Hollick (*Labour*)
Baroness Blackstone (*Labour*)
Lord Carrington of Fulham (*Conservative*)
Lord Griffiths of Fforestfach (*Conservative*)
Lord Lawson of Blaby (*Conservative*)
Lord May of Oxford (*Crossbench*)
Lord McFall of Alcluith (*Labour*)
Lord Monks (*Labour*)
Lord Rowe-Beddoe (*Crossbench*)
Lord Shipley (*Liberal Democrat*)
Lord Skidelsky (*Crossbench*)
Lord Smith of Clifton (*Liberal Democrat*)
Baroness Wheatcroft (*Conservative*)

APPENDIX 3: MEMBERS AND WITNESSES ATTENDING HEARINGS

Monetary Policy Hearings

Treasury Select Committee, 28 July 2010

Members present:

    Chairman: Andrew Tyrie (*Conservative*)
    Michael Fallon (*Conservative*)
    Mark Garnier (*Conservative*)
    Andrea Leadsom (*Conservative*)
    Brooks Newmark (*Conservative*)
    Jesse Norman (*Conservative*)
    David Ruffley (*Conservative*)
    David Rutley (*Conservative*)
    John Cryer (*Labour*)
    Andy Love (*Labour*)
    John Mann (*Labour*)
    Pat McFadden (*Labour*)
    George Mudie (*Labour*)
    Teresa Pearce (*Labour*)
    Chuka Umunna (*Labour*)
    John Thurso (*Liberal Democrat*)
    Stewart Hosie (*Scottish National Party*)

Witnesses

    Mervyn King, Governor, Bank of England
    Charlie Bean, Deputy Governor, Bank of England
    Paul Fisher, Executive Director, Markets, Bank of England
    David Miles, External Member of the Monetary Policy Committee
    Mr Andrew Sentance, External Member of the Monetary Policy Committee.

Lords Economic Affairs Committee Meeting with Governor of the Bank of England, 16 November 2010

Declaration of Interests

    Members declared the following relevant interests: Lord Levene of Portsoken: Chairman, Lloyd's

Members present:

    Chairman: Lord MacGregor of Pulham Market (*Conservative*)
    Lord Forsyth of Drumlean (*Conservative*)
    Lord Lawson of Blaby (*Conservative*)
    Lord Tugendhat (*Conservative*)
    Lord Hollick (*Labour*)
    Baroness Kingsmill (*Labour*)
    Lord Lipsey (*Labour*)

Lord Smith of Clifton (*Liberal Democrat*)
Lord Best (*Crossbencher*)
Lord Currie of Marylebone (*Crossbencher*)
Lord Levene of Portsoken (*Crossbencher*)

Witnesses

Mervyn King, Governor, Bank of England
Paul Tucker, Deputy Governor, Financial Stability, Bank of England
Spencer Dale, Executive Director and Chief Economist, Bank of England

Treasury Select Committee, 25 November 2010

Members present:

Chairman: Andrew Tyrie (*Conservative*)
Michael Fallon (*Conservative*)
Mark Garnier (*Conservative*)
Andrea Leadsom (*Conservative*)
Jesse Norman (*Conservative*)
David Rutley (*Conservative*)
John Cryer (*Labour*)
Andy Love (*Labour*)
John Mann (*Labour*)
George Mudie (*Labour*)
Chuka Umunna (*Labour*)
John Thurso (*Liberal Democrat*)
Stewart Hosie (*Scottish National Party*)

Witnesses

Mervyn King, Governor, Bank of England
Paul Tucker, Deputy Governor, Financial Stability, Bank of England
Spencer Dale, Executive Director and Chief Economist, Bank of England
Dr Adam Posen, External member of the Monetary Policy Committee
Dr Andrew Sentance, External member of the Monetary Policy Committee

Treasury Select Committee, 1 March 2011

Members present:

Chairman: Andrew Tyrie (*Conservative*)
Michael Fallon (*Conservative*)
Mark Garnier (*Conservative*)
Andrea Leadsom (*Conservative*)
Jesse Norman (*Conservative*)
David Ruffley (*Conservative*)
Andy Love (*Labour*)
John Mann (*Labour*)
George Mudie (*Labour*)
Chuka Umunna (*Labour*)
John Thurso (*Liberal Democrat*)
Stewart Hosie (*Scottish National Party*)

Witnesses

Mervyn King, Governor
Charlie Bean, Deputy Governor, Monetary Policy
Paul Fisher, Executive Director, Markets
Professor David Miles, External Member of the Monetary Policy Committee
Dr Martin Weale, External Member of the Monetary Policy Committee

Treasury Select Committtee, 28 June 2011

Members present:

Chairman: Andrew Tyrie (*Conservative*)
Michael Fallon (*Conservative*)
Mark Garnier (*Conservative*)
Andrea Leadsom (*Conservative*)
Jesse Norman (*Conservative*)
David Ruffley (*Conservative*)
John Mann (*Labour*)
George Mudie (*Labour*)
John Thurso (*Liberal Democrat*)

Witnesses

Sir Mervyn King, Governor, Bank of England
Paul Tucker, Deputy Governor, Financial Stability, Bank of England
Spencer Dale, Chief Economist, Bank of England
Professor David Miles, External Member, Monetary Policy Committee
Dr Adam Posen, External Member, Monetary Policy Committee

Treasury Select Committee, 25 October 2011 (Quantitative Easing)

Members present:

Chairman: Andrew Tyrie (*Conservative*)
Michael Fallon (*Conservative*)
Mark Garnier (*Conservative*)
Andrea Leadsom (*Conservative*)
Jesse Norman (*Conservative*)
David Ruffley (*Conservative*)
Andy Love (*Labour*)
John Mann (*Labour*)
George Mudie (*Labour*)
John Thurso (*Liberal Democrat*)
Stewart Hosie (*Scottish National Party*)

Witnesses

Sir Mervyn King, Governor of the Bank of England
Charles Bean, Deputy Governor Monetary Policy, Bank of England

Treasury Select Committee, 28 November 2011

Members present:

Chairman: Andrew Tyrie (*Conservative*)
Michael Fallon (*Conservative*)
Mark Garnier (*Conservative*)
Andrea Leadsom (*Conservative*)
Jesse Norman (*Conservative*)
David Ruffley (*Conservative*)
Andy Love (*Labour*)
Mr Pat McFadden (*Labour*)
George Mudie (*Labour*)
Teresa Pearce (*Labour*)
John Thurso (*Liberal Democrat*)
Stewart Hosie (*Scottish National Party*)

Witnesses

Sir Mervyn King, Governor, Bank of England
Paul Fisher, Executive Director, Markets, Bank of England
Dr Ben Broadbent, External member of the Monetary Policy Committee
Dr Martin Weale CBE, External member of the Monetary Policy Committee

Treasury Select Committee, 29 February 2012

Members present:

Chairman: Mr Andrew Tyrie MP (*Conservative*)
Michael Fallon MP (*Conservative*)
Andrea Leadsom MP (*Conservative*)
Jesse Norman MP (*Conservative*)
David Ruffley MP (*Conservative*)
Mr Andy Love MP (*Labour*)
John Mann MP (*Labour*)
Rt Hon Pat McFadden MP (*Labour*)
Mr George Mudie MP (*Labour*)
John Thurso MP (*Liberal Democrat*)
Stewart Hosie MP (*Scottish National Party*)

Witnesses

Sir Mervyn King, Governor of the Bank of England
Charlie Bean, Deputy Governor of the Bank of England (Monetary Policy)
Paul Tucker, Deputy Governor of the Bank of England (Financial Stability)
Dr Adam Posen, External Member of the Monetary Policy Committee

Lords Economic Affairs Committee, 27 March 2012 (Economic Outlook)

Chairman: Lord MacGregor of Pulham Market (*Conservative*)
Lord Forsyth of Drumlean (*Conservative*)
Lord Hollick (*Labour*)
Baroness Kingsmill (*Labour*)

Lord Lipsey (*Labour*)
Lord Moonie (*Labour*)
Lord Shipley (*Liberal Democrat*)
Lord Smith of Clifton (*Liberal Democrat*)
Lord Currie of Marylebone (*Crossbencher*)
Lord Levene of Portsoken (*Crossbencher*)
Lord Tugendhat (*Crossbencher*)

Witnesses

Sir Mervyn King, Governor, Bank of England
Paul Fisher, Executive Director, Markets, Bank of England
Dr Ben Broadbent, External member of the Monetary Policy Committee

Treasury Select Committee, 26 June 2012

Members present:

Chairman: Mr Andrew Tyrie MP (*Conservative*)
Michael Fallon MP (*Conservative*)
Andrea Leadsom MP (*Conservative*)
Jesse Norman MP (*Conservative*)
David Ruffley MP (*Conservative*)
Mr Andy Love MP (*Labour*)
Rt Hon Pat McFadden MP (*Labour*)
Mr George Mudie MP (*Labour*)
John Thurso MP (*Liberal Democrat*)
Stewart Hosie MP (*Scottish National Party*)

Witnesses

Sir Mervyn King, Governor of the Bank of England
Spencer Dale, Chief Economist, Bank of England
Dr Ben Broadbent, External Member, Monetary Policy Committee
Professor David Miles, External Member, Monetary Policy Committee

Treasury Select Committee, 27 November 2012

Members present:

Chairman: Mr Andrew Tyrie MP (*Conservative*)
Mark Garnier (*Conservative*)
Andrea Leadsom MP (*Conservative*)
Mr Brooks Newmark (*Conservative*)
Jesse Norman MP (*Conservative*)
David Ruffley MP (*Conservative*)
Mr Andy Love MP (*Labour*)
Rt Hon Pat McFadden MP (*Labour*)
Mr George Mudie MP (*Labour*)
John Thurso MP (*Liberal Democrat*)

Witnesses

Sir Mervyn King, Governor of the Bank of England
Paul Fisher, Executive Director, Markets, Bank of England
Dr Ben Broadbent, External Member of the Monetary Policy Committee
Dr Martin Weale CBE, External Member of the Monetary Policy Committee

Treasury Select Committee, 25 June 2013

Members present:

Chairman: Mr Andrew Tyrie MP (*Conservative*)
Mark Garnier (*Conservative*)
Andrea Leadsom MP (*Conservative*)
Mr Brooks Newmark (*Conservative*)
Jesse Norman MP (*Conservative*)
Mr David Ruffley (*Conservative*)
John Mann (*Labour*)
Rt Hon Pat McFadden MP (*Labour*)
John Thurso MP (*Liberal Democrat*)
Stewart Hosie (*Scottish National Party*)

Witnesses

Sir Mervyn King, Governor, Bank of England
Spencer Dale, Executive Director and Chief Economist, Bank of England
Dr Ben Broadbent, External member, Monetary Policy Committee
Dr Martin Weale CBE, External member, Monetary Policy Committee

Treasury Select Committee: Bank of England November 2013 Inflation Report, Tuesday 12 September 2013

Members present:

Chairman: Andrew Tyrie (*Conservative*)
Mark Garnier (*Conservative*)
Andrea Leadsom (*Conservative*)
Mr Brooks Newmark (*Conservative*)
Jesse Norman (*Conservative*)
David Ruffley (*Conservative*)
Mr Pat McFadden (*Labour*)
John Thurso (*Liberal Democrat*)
Stewart Hosie (*Scottish National Party*)

Witnesses

Dr Mark Carney, Governor of the Bank of England
Paul Fisher, Executive Director, Markets, Bank of England
Ian McCafferty, External Member of the Monetary Policy Committee
Professor David Miles, External Member of the Monetary Policy Committee

Treasury Select Committee: Bank of England November 2013 Inflation Report, Tuesday 26 November 2013

Members present:

Chairman: Andrew Tyrie (*Conservative*)
Mark Garnier (*Conservative*)
Andrea Leadsom (*Conservative*)
Mr Brooks Newmark (*Conservative*)
Jesse Norman (*Conservative*)
David Ruffley (*Conservative*)
Andy Love (*Labour*)
John Mann (*Labour*)
Mr Pat McFadden (*Labour*)
Mr George Mudie (*Labour*)
Teresa Pearce (*Labour*)
John Thurso (*Liberal Democrat*)
Stewart Hosie (*Scottish National Party*)

Witnesses

Dr Mark Carney, Governor, Bank of England
Charles Bean, Deputy Governor, Monetary Policy, Bank of England
Spencer Dale, Executive Director and Chief Economist
Dr Ben Broadbent, External Member, Monetary Policy Committee

House of Lords Select Committee on Economic Affairs: Meeting with the Governor of the Bank of England, Dr Mark Carney, Tuesday, 17 December 2013

Members present:

Chairman: Lord MacGregor of Pulham Market (*Conservative*)
Lord Griffiths of Fforestfach (*Conservative*)
Lord Lawson of Blaby (*Conservative*)
Baroness Noakes (*Conservative*)
Baroness Blackstone (*Labour*)
Lord Lipsey (*Labour*)
Lord McFall of Alcluith (*Labour*)
Lord Shipley (*Liberal Democrat*)
Lord May of Oxford (*Crossbench*)
Lord Rowe-Beddoe (*Crossbench*)
Lord Skidelsky (*Crossbench*)

Treasury Select Committee: Bank of England May 2014 Inflation Report, Tuesday 24 June 2014

Members present:

Chairman: Andrew Tyrie (*Conservative*)
Steve Baker (*Conservative*)
Mark Garnier (*Conservative*)
Mr Brooks Newmark (*Conservative*)
Jesse Norman (*Conservative*)

David Ruffley (*Conservative*)
Andy Love (*Labour*)
John Mann (*Labour*)
Mr Pat McFadden (*Labour*)
Mr George Mudie (*Labour*)
Teresa Pearce (*Labour*)
John Thurso (*Liberal Democrat*)
Stewart Hosie (*Scottish National Party*)

Witnesses

Dr Mark Carney, Governor of the Bank of England
Sir Charles Bean, Deputy Governor of the Bank of England
Ian McCafferty, Monetary Policy Committee Member
Professor David Miles, Monetary Policy Committee Member

Treasury Select Committee: Bank of England August 2014 Inflation Report, Wednesday 10 September 2014

Members present:

Chairman: Andrew Tyrie (*Conservative*)
Steve Baker (*Conservative*)
Mark Garnier (*Conservative*)
Jesse Norman (*Conservative*)
David Ruffley (*Conservative*)
Andy Love (*Labour*)
John Mann (*Labour*)
Mr George Mudie (*Labour*)
Stewart Hosie (*Scottish National Party*)

Witnesses

Dr Mark Carney, Governor, Bank of England
Dr Nemat Shafik, Deputy Governor, Markets and Banking, Bank of England
Professor David Miles, External Monetary Policy Committee member
Dr Martin Weale, External Monetary Policy Committee member

Treasury Select Committee: Bank of England August 2014 Inflation Report, Tuesday, 25 November 2014

Members present:

Chairman: Mr Andrew Tyrie (*Conservative*)
Steve Baker (*Conservative*)
Mark Garnier (*Conservative*)
David Ruffley (*Conservative*)
Alok Sharma (*Conservative*)
Rushanara Ali (*Labour*)
Mike Kane (*Labour*)
Andrew Love (*Labour*)
John Mann (*Labour*)

John Thurso (*Liberal Democrat*)
Stewart Hosie (*Scottish National Party*)

Witnesses

Dr Mark Carney, Governor of the Bank of England
Sir Jon Cunliffe, Deputy Governor, Financial Stability, Bank of England
Ian McCafferty, External Monetary Policy Committee Member
Kristin Forbes, External Monetary Policy Committee Member

Treasury Select Committee: Bank of England, February 2015 Inflation Report, 24 February 2015

Members present:

Chairman: Andrew Tyrie (*Conservative*)
Steve Baker (*Conservative*)
Mark Garnier (*Conservative*)
Jesse Norman (*Conservative*)
David Ruffley (*Conservative*)
Alok Sharma (*Conservative*)
Rushanara Ali (*Labour*)
Mike Kane (*Labour)*
Andy Love (*Labour*)
John Mann (*Labour*)
John Thurso (*Liberal Democrat*)
Stewart Hosie (*Scottish National Party*)

Witnesses

Dr Mark Carney, Governor, Bank of England
Dr Ben Broadbent, Deputy Governor, Monetary Policy Committee
Professor David Miles, External Monetary Policy Committee member
Dr Martin Weale, External Monetary Policy Committee member

House of Lords Select Committee on Economic Affairs: Meeting with the Governor of the Bank of England, Dr Mark Carney, Tuesday, 10 March 2015

Chairman: Lord Hollick (Labour)
Lord Griffiths of Fforestfach (*Conservative*)
Lord Carrington of Fulham (*Conservative)*
Lord Lawson of Blaby (*Conservative*)
Baroness Wheatcroft (*Conservative)*
Baroness Blackstone (*Labour*)
Lord McFall of Alcluith (*Labour)*
Lord Monks (*Labour)*
Lord Shipley (*Liberal Democrat*)
Lord Smith of Clifton (*Liberal Democrat*)
Lord May of Oxford (*Crossbencher*)
Lord Rowe-Beddoe (*Crossbencher*)

Financial Stability Hearings

December 2011 FSR

(Oral evidence, 17 January 2012)

Members present:

Chairman: Mr Andrew Tyrie MP *(Conservative)*
Michael Fallon MP *(Conservative)*
Mark Garnier MP *(Conservative)*
Andrea Leadsom MP *(Conservative)*
Jesse Norman MP *(Conservative)*
David Ruffley MP *(Conservative)*
Mr Andy Love MP *(Labour)*
John Mann MP *(Labour)*
Mr Pat McFadden *(Labour)*
Mr George Mudie MP *(Labour)*
Teresa Pearce MP *(Labour)*
John Thurso MP *(Liberal Democrat)*
Stewart Hosie MP *(Scottish National Party)*

Witnesses

Sir Mervyn King, Governor of the Bank of England
Andrew Haldane, Executive Director for Financial Stability, Bank of England
Michael Cohrs, External member of the interim Financial Policy Committee
Robert Jenkins, External member of the interim Financial Policy Committee

June 2012 FSR

(Oral evidence, 17 July 2012)

Members present:

Chairman: Mr Andrew Tyrie MP *(Conservative)*
Michael Fallon MP *(Conservative)*
Mark Garnier MP *(Conservative)*
Andrea Leadsom MP *(Conservative)*
Jesse Norman MP *(Conservative)*
David Ruffley MP *(Conservative)*
Mr Andy Love MP *(Labour)*
John Mann MP *(Labour)*
Mr Pat McFadden *(Labour)*
John Thurso MP *(Liberal Democrat)*
Stewart Hosie MP *(Scottish National Party)*

Witnesses

Sir Mervyn King, Governor of the Bank of England
Lord Turner of Ecchinswell, Chairman of the Financial Services Authority

Paul Tucker, Deputy Governor, Financial Stability, Bank of England
Paul Fisher, Executive Director Markets, Bank of England
Donald Kohn, External member of the interim Financial Policy Committee

November 2012 FSR

(Oral evidence, 15 January 2013)

Members present:

Chairman: Mr Andrew Tyrie MP *(Conservative)*
Mark Garnier MP *(Conservative)*
Andrea Leadsom MP *(Conservative)*
Mr Brooks Newmark *(Conservative)*
David Ruffley MP *(Conservative)*
Mr Andy Love MP *(Labour)*
John Mann MP *(Labour)*
Mr George Mudie MP *(Labour)*
Teresa Pearce MP *(Labour)*
John Thurso MP *(Liberal Democrat)*
Stewart Hosie MP *(Scottish National Party)*

Witnesses

Sir Mervyn King, Governor of the Bank of England
Andrew Bailey, Executive Director and Managing Director of the Prudential Business
    Unit, Bank of England
Andy Haldane, Executive Director, Financial Stability, Bank of England
Robert Jenkins, External Member, Financial Policy Committee
Michael Cohrs, External Member, Financial Policy Committee

June 2013 FSR

(Oral evidence, 2 July 2013)

Members present:

Chairman: Mr Andrew Tyrie MP *(Conservative)*
Mark Garnier MP *(Conservative)*
Andrea Leadsom MP *(Conservative)*
Mr Brooks Newmark *(Conservative)*
Jesse Norman MP *(Conservative)*
David Ruffley MP *(Conservative)*
Mr Andy Love MP *(Labour)*
Mr George Mudie MP *(Labour)*
Teresa Pearce MP *(Labour)*
John Thurso MP *(Liberal Democrat)*
Stewart Hosie MP *(Scottish National Party)*

Witnesses

Paul Tucker, Deputy Governor, Financial Stability, Bank of England

Andrew Bailey, Deputy Governor, Prudential Regulation, Bank of England
Dr Donald Kohn, External Member, Financial Policy Committee
Martin Taylor, External Member, Financial Policy Committee

November 2013 FSR

(Oral evidence, 15 January 2014)

Members present:

Chairman: Mr Andrew Tyrie MP *(Conservative)*
Mr Brooks Newmark *(Conservative)*
Jesse Norman MP *(Conservative)*
David Ruffley MP *(Conservative)*
Mr Pat McFadden *(Labour)*
Teresa Pearce MP *(Labour)*
John Thurso MP *(Liberal Democrat)*
Stewart Hosie MP *(Scottish National Party)*

Witnesses

Dr Mark Carney, Governor, Bank of England
Sir Jon Cunliffe, Deputy Governor, Bank of England
Dame Clara Furse DBE, External Member, Financial Policy Committee
Mr Richard Sharp, External Member, Financial Policy Committee

June 2014 FSR

(Oral evidence, 15 July 2014)

Members present:

Chairman: Mr Andrew Tyrie MP *(Conservative)*
Steve Baker *(Conservative)*
Mark Garnier MP *(Conservative)*
Jesse Norman MP *(Conservative)*
John Mann MP *(Labour)*
Mr Pat McFadden *(Labour)*
Mr George Mudie MP *(Labour)*
Teresa Pearce MP *(Labour)*
John Thurso MP *(Liberal Democrat)*

Witnesses

Dr Mark Carney, Governor of the Bank of England
Andrew Bailey, Deputy Governor, Prudential Regulation & Chief Executive of the
   Prudential Regulation Authority
Donald Kohn, External Member of the Financial Policy Committee
Martin Taylor, External Member of the Financial Policy Committee

December 2014 FSR

(Oral evidence, 14 January 2015)

Members present:

Chairman: Mr Andrew Tyrie MP *(Conservative)*
Steve Baker MP *(Conservative)*
Jesse Norman MP *(Conservative)*
Rushanara Ali MP *(Labour)*
Mike Kane MP *(Labour)*
Mr Andy Love MP *(Labour)*
John Thurso MP *(Liberal Democrat)*

Witnesses

Dr Mark Carney, Governor, Bank of England
Sir Jon Cunliffe, Deputy Governor, Financial Stability, Bank of England
Dame Clara Furse, External member, Financial Policy Committee
Martin Taylor, External Member, Financial Policy Committee

Fiscal Policy Hearings

House of Commons Treasury Select Committee: Budget: 15 July 2010

Thursday 15 July 2010

Members present:

Chairman: Mr Andrew Tyrie *(Conservative)*
Michael Fallon *(Conservative)*
Mark Garnier *(Conservative)*
Andrea Leadsom *(Conservative)*
Jesse Norman *(Conservative)*
David Rutley *(Conservative)*
Andrew Love *(Labour)*
John Mann *(Labour)*
Mr Chuka Umunna *(Labour)*
John Thurso *(Liberal Democrat)*
Stewart Hosie *(Scottish National Party)*

Witnesses

Rt Hon George Osborne MP, Chancellor of the Exchequer
Sir Nicholas Macpherson, Permanent Secretary
Mr Mark Bowman, Director, Budget and Tax, HM Treasury

House of Commons Treasury Select Committee: Spending Round: 3-4 November 2010

Members present:

Chairman: Mr Andrew Tyrie *(Conservative)*
Michael Fallon *(Conservative)*
Mark Garnier *(Conservative)*
Andrea Leadsom *(Conservative)*

Jesse Norman (*Conservative*)
David Rutley (*Conservative*)
John Cryer (*Labour*)
Mr Andrew Love (*Labour*)
John Mann (*Labour*)
Mr George Mudie (*Labour*)
Mr Chuka Umunna (*Labour*)
John Thurso (*Liberal Democrat*)
Stewart Hosie (*Scottish National Party*)

Witnesses

Wednesday 3 November 2010

Rt Hon Danny Alexander MP, Chief Secretary to the Treasury
James Richardson, Director, Public Services
Indra Morris, Director, Personal tax and Welfare Reform, HM Treasury

Thursday 4 November 2010

Rt Hon George Osborne MP, Chancellor of the Exchequer
Sir Nicholas Macpherson, Permanent Secretary
Mr James Richardson, Director, Public Services, HM Treasury

Lords Economic Affairs Committee, 30 November 2010 (Economic Outlook)

Chairman: Lord MacGregor of Pulham Market (*Conservative*)
Lord Forsyth of Drumlean (*Conservative*)
Lord Lawson of Blaby (*Conservative*)
Lord Tugendhat (*Conservative*)
Lord Hollick (*Labour*)
Baroness Kingsmill (*Labour*)
Lord Shipley (*Liberal Democrat*)
Lord Smith of Clifton (*Liberal Democrat*)
Lord Best (*Crossbencher*)

Witnesses

The Rt Hon George Osborne MP, Chancellor of the Exchequer
Mr Dave Ramsden, Managing Director, Macroeconomic and Fiscal Policy
Mr James Richardson, Director, Public Spending, HM Treasury

House of Commons Treasury Select Committee: Budget: 29 March 2011

Members present:

Chairman: Mr Andrew Tyrie (*Conservative*)
Michael Fallon (*Conservative*)
Mark Garnier (*Conservative*)
Andrea Leadsom (*Conservative*)
Jesse Norman (*Conservative*)
Mr David Ruffley (*Conservative*)
John Cryer (*Labour*)

Mr Andrew Love (*Labour*)
John Mann (*Labour*)
Mr George Mudie (*Labour*)
Mr Chuka Umunna (*Labour*)
John Thurso (*Liberal Democrat*)
Stewart Hosie (*Scottish National Party*)

Witnesses

Rt Hon George Osborne MP, Chancellor of the Exchequer
Sir Nicholas Macpherson, Permanent Secretary
Mark Bowman, Director, Budget and Tax, HM Treasury

Lords Economic Affairs Committee, 8 December 2011 (Economic Outlook)

Chairman: Lord MacGregor of Pulham Market (*Conservative*)
Lord Forsyth of Drumlean (*Conservative*)
Lord Lawson of Blaby (*Conservative*)
Lord Tugendhat (*Conservative*)
Lord Lipsey (*Labour*)
Lord Smith of Clifton (*Liberal Democrat*)
Lord Levene of Portsoken (*Crossbencher*)

Witnesses

The Rt Hon George Osborne MP, Chancellor of the Exchequer
Mark Bowman, Director for Strategy, Planning and Budget, Treasury

House of Commons Treasury Select Committee: Budget: 27 March 2012

Members present:

Chairman: Mr Andrew Tyrie (*Conservative*)
Michael Fallon (*Conservative*)
Mark Garnier (*Conservative*)
Mr David Ruffley (*Conservative*)
Mr Andrew Love (*Labour*)
John Mann (*Labour*)
Mr Pat McFadden (*Labour*)
Mr George Mudie (*Labour*)
Teresa Pearce (*Labour*)
John Thurso (*Liberal Democrat*)
Stewart Hosie (*Scottish National Party*)

Witnesses

Rt Hon. George Osborne MP, Chancellor of the Exchequer
Sir Nicholas Macpherson KCB, Permanent Secretary to the Treasury
James Bowler, Director, Strategy, Planning and Budget, HM Treasury

House of Commons Treasury Select Committee: Budget: 26 March 2013

Members present:

   Chairman: Mr Andrew Tyrie (*Conservative*)
   Mark Garnier (*Conservative*)
   Andrea Leadsom (*Conservative*)
   Mr Brooks Newmark (*Conservative*)
   Jesse Norman (*Conservative*)
   Mr David Ruffley (*Conservative*)
   Mr Andrew Love (*Labour*)
   John Mann (*Labour*)
   Mr Pat McFadden (*Labour*)
   Mr George Mudie (*Labour*)
   Teresa Pearce (*Labour*)
   John Thurso (*Liberal Democrat*)

Witnesses

   Rt Hon George Osborne MP, Chancellor of the Exchequer
   Sir Nicholas Macpherson KCB, Permanent Secretary
   James Bowler, Director, Strategy, Planning and Budget

House of Commons Treasury Select Committee: Spending Round: 9-11 July 2013

Members present:

   Chairman: Mr Andrew Tyrie MP (*Conservative*)
   Mark Garnier MP (*Conservative*)
   Andrea Leadsom MP (*Conservative*)
   Mr Brooks Newmark MP (*Conservative*)
   Jesse Norman MP (*Conservative*)
   David Ruffley MP (*Conservative*)
   Mr Andy Love MP (*Labour*)
   John Mann MP (*Labour*)
   Mr Pat McFadden MP (*Labour*)
   Mr George Mudie MP (*Labour*)
   Teresa Pearce MP (*Labour*)
   John Thurso MP (*Liberal Democrat*)
   Stewart Hosie MP (*Scottish National Party*)

Witnesses

Tuesday 9 July 2013

   Rt Hon Danny Alexander MP, Chief Secretary, HM Treasury
   Sharon White, Director General for Public Spending, HM Treasury.

Thursday 11 July 2013

   Rt Hon George Osborne MP, Chancellor of the Exchequer, HM Treasury
   Sharon White, Director General for Public Spending, HM Treasury

House of Lords Select Committee on Economic Affairs: Meeting with the Chancellor of the Exchequer: 4 February 2014

Chairman: Lord MacGregor of Pulham Market (*Conservative*)
Lord Lawson of Blaby (*Conservative*)
Lord Griffiths of Fforestfach (*Conservative*)
Baroness Noakes (*Conservative*)
Baroness Blackstone (*Labour*)
Lord Lipsey (*Labour*)
Lord McFall of Alcluith (*Labour*)
Lord Shipley (*Liberal Democrat*)
Lord May of Oxford (*Crossbench*)
Lord Rowe-Beddoe (*Crossbench*)
Lord Skidelsky (*Crossbench*)

House of Commons Treasury Select Committee: Autumn Statement, 17 December 2014

Members present:

Chairman: Mr Andrew Tyrie (*Conservative*)
Steve Baker (*Conservative*)
Mark Garnier (*Conservative*)
Jesse Norman (*Conservative*)
Alok Sharma (*Conservative*)
Mr David Ruffley (*Conservative*)
Rushanara Ali (*Labour*)
Mike Kane (*Labour*)
Andrew Love (*Labour*)
John Mann (*Labour*)
Teresa Pearce (*Labour*)
John Thurso (*Liberal Democrat*)
Stewart Hosie (*Scottish National Party*)

Witnesses

Rt. Hon. George Osborne MP, Chancellor of the Exchequer, HM Treasury
James Bowler, Director, Strategy, Planning, and Budget, HM Treasury

APPENDIX 4: KEY WORDS AND PHRASES JOINED FOR LEMMATIZATION

Lemmatization for Quantitative Text Analysis (UK Parliamentary Committees, 2010–2015)

The lemmatization process was supervised, in order to avoid distortions and errors. For instance, without correction, a hyphen is not recognized as a liaison link by the software.
   The following edits were thus part of the pre-processing of the transcripts:

- All names were joined with hyphens ('Andrew_Tyrie').

- Countries, regions, states were similarly joined, as needed (Southeast_Asia, United_Kingdom, United_States).
- Key institutions and phrases were changed as follows:

<u>Keywords</u> (e.g., inflation target→inflation_target)

Asset purchase
Asset sales
Bank of England
Bank rate
Banking Commission
Banking crisis
Banking system
Board of Banking Supervision
Budget deficit
Capital investment
Capital spending
Consumer Price Index
Consumer Protection and Markets Authority
Credit crunch
Economic growth
European Central Bank
European Systemic Risk Board
European Union
Eurozone
Federal Open Market Committee: FOMC
Federal Reserve: Fed
Financial crisis
Financial markets
Financial Policy Committee
Financial Services Authority
Financial stability
Fiscal policy
Forward Guidance
Greek default
Gross Domestic Product: GDP
Gross National Product: GNP
Inflation rate
Inflation Report
Inflation target
Interest rates
International Monetary Fund: IMF
LIBOR
Monetary policy
Monetary Policy Committee: MPC
Northern Rock
Office for Budget Responsibility
Oil prices

Organisation for Economic Co-operation and Development: OECD
Prudential Regulation Authority
Quantitative Easing
Spending Review
Spending Round
Unemployment rate
Value Added Tax: VAT
Welfare cap

APPENDIX 5: CODING SCHEME

Questioner		Witness		Witness (2)	
Facial	*Number of Instances*	**Facial**	*Number of Instances*	**Facial**	*Number of Instances*
Fear		Fear		Fear	
Anger		Anger		Anger	
Disgust		Disgust		Disgust	
Contempt		Contempt		Contempt	
Happy		Happy		Happy	
Sad		Sad		Sad	
Surprise		Surprise		Surprise	
[Other expression]		[Other expression]		[Other expression]	
Eye Movement (wink, closed eyes)		Eye Movement (wink, closed eyes)		Eye Movement (wink, closed eyes)	
Twitch		Twitch		Twitch	
Summary Score-Facial		*Summary Score-Facial*		*Summary Score-Facial*	
Vocal		**Vocal**		**Vocal**	
Volume		Volume		Volume	
Variation		Variation		Variation	
Accent (e.g., non-British)		Accent (e.g., non-British)		Accent (e.g., non-British)	
Vocal Response ('uh huh')		Vocal Response ('uh huh')		Vocal Response ('uh huh')	
Pauses		Pauses		Pauses	
Stress on Words		Stress on Words		Stress on Words	
Speed Variation		Speed Variation		Speed Variation	

Questioner	Witness	Witness (2)
Interruptions	Interruptions	Interruptions
Summary	*Summary*	*Summary*
Score-	*Score-*	*Score-*
Vocal	*Vocal*	*Vocal*
Gestures/	**Gestures/**	**Gestures/**
Posture	**Posture**	**Posture**
Head	Head	Head
Movement	Movement	Movement
(nod,	(nod,	(nod,
shake)	shake)	shake)
Hands	Hands	Hands
(waving,	(waving,	(waving,
open and	open and	open and
extended	extended	extended
in move-	in move-	in move-
ment,	ment,	ment,
etc.)	etc.)	etc.)
Posture	Posture	Posture
(higher	(higher	(higher
score for	score for	score for
leaning	leaning	leaning
forward,	forward,	forward,
upright	upright	upright
and alert)	and alert)	and alert)
Summary	*Summary*	*Summary*
Score-	*Score-*	*Score-*
Gestures	*Gestures*	*Gestures*

APPENDIX 6: DETAILED CODES

Appendix Table 6A Aggregate Scores (Counts) for Nonverbal Communication (Including Facial, Vocal, and Gestures)

Group	Witness (Bank/Her Majesty's Treasury, HMT) Mean Score		
	G	J	R
All Bank of England	**11.71**	**7.17**	**148.26**
All Financial Policy Committee	8.62	7.18	172.53
All Monetary Policy Committee	12.74	7.17	140.16
All Her Majesty's Treasury	**17.35** *[1.5x]*	**12.21** *[1.7x]*	**364.78** *[2.5x]*

Appendix Table 6B   Mean Scores for Nonverbal Communication, by Type

Group	Facial: Committee			Facial: Witness			Vocal: Witness			Gesture: Witness		
	G	J	R	G	J	R	G	J	R	G	J	R
All Bank of England	**2.19** [1.5x]	**1.19**	**2.75**	**1.89**	**1.42**	**7.94**	3.68	0.77	31.79	**6.14**	**4.98**	**110.71**
All Financial Policy Committee	2.12	1.29	5.00	1.45	1.79	11.07	2.51	1.06	30.06	4.66	4.33	131.41
All Monetary Policy Committee	2.22	1.15	2.00	2.04	1.30	6.90	4.07	0.67	32.37	6.63	5.19	103.81
All Her Majesty's Treasury	**3.23** [1.5x]	**1.03 ≈ tie**	**5.85** [2.1x]	**2.98** [1.6x]	**2.01** [1.4x]	**38.27** [4.8x]	5.65	0.44	92.78	**8.73** [1.4x]	**7.55** [1.5x]	**233.73** [2.1x]
All Lords Economic Affairs Committee	2.24	0.78	10.14	3.10	1.31	66.50	4.33 ≈ tie	1.05 [1.5x]	135.50 [3.2x]	6.84	9.06	312.34
All Treasury Select Committee	2.60	1.12	2.71	2.08	1.51	11.71	4.34	0.69	42.76	7.03	5.14	137.37

Appendix Table 6C Mean Scores for Nonverbal Communication: Facial Scores, by Emotion

Group	All Anger Scores: Committee			All Anger Scores: Witness		
	G	J	R	G	J	R
All Bank of England	**0.89**	**0.06**	**0.32**	**0.41**	**0.00**	**0.43**
All Financial Policy Committee	1.06	0.00	0.09	0.15	0.01	0.50
All Monetary Policy Committee	0.83	0.08	0.4	0.50	0.00	0.41
All Her Majesty's Treasury	**0.97** *[1.1x]*	**0.13** *[2.2x]*	**0.87** *[2.7x]*	**0.78** *[1.9x]*	**0.01** *≈ tie*	**3.08** *[7.2x]*

Appendix Table 6C *continued* Mean Scores for Nonverbal Communication: Facial Scores, by Emotion.

Group	All Contempt Scores: Committee			All Contempt Scores: Witness			All Happy Scores: Witness		
	G	**J**	**R**	**G**	**J**	**R**	**G**	**J**	**R**
All Bank of England	0.19	0.27	0.03	**0.22**	**0.14**	**0.29**	**0.21**	**0.80**	**4.44**
All Financial Policy Committee	0.10	0.31	0.00	0.08	0.18	0.63	0.16	0.69	5.42
All Monetary Policy Committee	0.22	0.75	0.03	0.27	0.13	0.17	0.22	0.83	4.12
All Her Majesty's Treasury	0.47 [1.6x]	0.26 ≈ tie	0.01 [94x]	0.76 [3.5x]	0.24 [1.7x]	0.94 [3.2x]	0.32 [1.5x]	1.05 [1.3x]	24.02 [5.4x]
All Lords Economic Affairs Committee	0.30	0.07	0.00	0.53	0.03	1.17	0.52 [1.6x]	0.99 [1.4x]	41.00 [5.7x]
All Treasury Select Committee	0.22	0.29	0.02	0.29	0.19	0.35	0.20	0.73	7.16

Appendix Table 6C *continued* Mean Scores for Nonverbal Communication: Facial Scores, by Emotion.

Group	All Sad Scores: Committee			All Sad Scores: Witness		
	G	J	R	G	J	R
All Bank of England	0.49	0.02	0.52	**0.48** *[2.2x]*	**0.04** *tie*	**0.31** *[5.2x]*
All Financial Policy Committee	0.40	0.00	1.52	0.57	0.09	0.45
All Monetary Policy Committee	0.53	0.02	0.19	0.46	0.03	0.26
All HMT	0.70	0.06	0.18	**0.22**	**0.04**	**0.06**
All Lords Economic Affairs Committee	0.46	0.00	0.05	0.36	0.00	0.00
All Treasury Select Committee	0.52 *[1.1x]*	0.02 *≈ tie*	0.47 *[9.4x]*	0.42 *[1.2x]*	0.03 *≈ tie*	0.26 *[26x]*

APPENDIX 7: EXAMPLE OF QUESTIONS FOR EXPERIMENT (PRE-GROUP DISCUSSION)

The above is a video clip of an exchange between the Treasury Select Committee Member Michael Fallon and George Osborne, the Chancellor of the Exchequer.
Please watch the entire video before answering the questions.
NB:

AME = Annually Managed Expenditure is money spent on programmes which are demand-led, such as welfare benefit provision, tax credits, or public sector pensions. AME is therefore spent on items that may be unpredictable or not easily controlled by departments, and are relatively large compared to other government departments.

DEL = Departmental Expenditure Limits is the government budget that is allocated to be spent by government departments. This amount, and how it is divided between government departments, is set at Spending Reviews.

Please select no more than TWO answers.

What were the concern(s) or area(s) of focus of Michael Fallon?

Public Expenditure cuts
Deficit reduction
The financial crisis
The previous Labour Government

Departmental spending
Spending Review
Welfare spending
Debt management

In my opinion, George Osborne addressed the issues and concerns of Michael Fallon very well.

Strongly disagree
Disagree
Agree
Strongly Agree

In my opinion, the arguments and rationale offered by George Osborne were persuasive.

Strongly disagree
Disagree
Agree
Strongly Agree

Based on this video excerpt, I would rate George Osborne's overall ability and competence as:

Poor
Below average
Average
Above average
Very good

Based only on the video clip you just viewed, explain why you think George Osborne was persuasive—or not—AND why you believe George Osborne was competent—or not. [Open-ended responses]

APPENDIX 8: VIDEO CONTENT FOR HEARINGS AND TOPICS COVERED (TIMES EXTRACTED FROM HEARINGS IN BRACKETS)

Treasury Fiscal Policy hearings

- Michael Fallon (Conservative) & George Osborne, 15 July 2010 [1:38:55-1:42:50]

  Topics: deficit, spending review, welfare spending, debt management

- John Mann (Labour) & George Osborne, 27 March 2012 [49:15-54:56]

  Topics: petrol prices, pensions, misc topics (interest rates, QE, asset prices, gilts)

- Andrew Tyrie (Conservative) & George Osborne, 17 December 2014 [2:45-4:55]

  Topics: inflation, energy costs

Treasury Select Committee Monetary Policy and Financial Policy Committee

- Jesse Norman (Conservative) & Mervyn King, 25 October 2011 [9:15-15:58]

  Topics: asset purchases, QE, corporate debt, credit easing, reputation of Bank of England

- George Mudie (Labour) & Mervyn King, 27 November 2012 [56:24-59:35]

  Topics: MPC, asset purchases, independence of Bank of England (indirectly, political intervention)

- Andrew Tyrie (Conservative) & Mark Carney, 14 January 2015 [FPC] [10:04-17:36]

  Topics: business cycle, expertise of Bank of England, stress tests, financial regulation

Lords Economic Affairs Committee

- Lord Lawson (Conservative) & George Osborne, 8 December 2011 [1:13:16-1:19:08]

  Topics: environmental policy, fuel poverty, energy costs, climate change, government subsidies, industrial development, EU

- Lord MacGregor (Conservative) & Mervyn King, 27 March 2012 [0:30-6:15]

  Topics: QE, gilt yields, pensions, asset purchases & asset prices, economic growth

- Lord Hollick (Labour) & Mervyn King, 27 March 2012 [18:12-23:05]

  Topics: QE, SMEs, lending, UK banking system, economic growth

Rationale for selection of video clips

The excerpts were chosen to include (a) fiscal policy hearings before the Treasury Select Committee, (b) monetary policy and financial policy committee hearings before the Treasury Select Committee, and (c) hearings both on fiscal policy and monetary policy before the Lords Economic Affairs Committee. For the TSC, only excerpts that included Labour and Conservative MPs were included. For all three hearing types, one Deliberative Exchange involved the Committee Chairman. Only men were included, and the file content was intended to be broadly representative of the hearings in their totality over the Parliament with the samples representing the different levels of engagement (as judged from the manual codings) apparent in the various exchanges. The number of hearings (nine) was balanced against the length of time allowable within the experiment, along with capturing meaningful dialogue content.

Complete Running Time for Videos: 45 minutes, 25 seconds

Lords EAC, 16:29
TSC Fiscal: 11:27
TSC Monetary: 17:29

The sequence of hearings was varied within each of the twelve groups of experiment participants as follows:

1A	TSC Fiscal (7, 8, 9)	TSC Monetary (1, 2, 3)	Lords EAC (4, 6, 5)
1B	TSC Fiscal (7, 8, 9)	TSC Monetary (1, 2, 3)	Lords EAC (4, 6, 5)
2A	Lords EAC (5, 4, 6)	TSC Fiscal (9, 7, 8)	TSC Monetary (3, 1, 2)
2B	TSC Monetary (3, 1, 2)	TSC Fiscal (8, 9, 7)	Lords EAC (5, 4, 6)
3A	TSC Fiscal (8, 9, 7)	Lords EAC (6, 5, 4)	TSC Monetary (1, 3, 2)
3B	Lords EAC (6, 5, 4)	TSC Monetary (1, 3, 2)	TSC Fiscal (8, 9, 7)
4A	TSC Fiscal (7, 8, 9)	TSC Monetary (1, 2, 3)	Lords EAC (4, 6, 5)
4B	TSC Monetary (1, 2, 3)	Lords EAC (4, 6, 5)	TSC Fiscal (7, 8, 9)
5A	Lords EAC (5, 4, 6)	TSC Fiscal (9, 7, 8)	TSC Monetary (3, 1, 2)
5B	TSC Monetary (3, 1, 2)	TSC Fiscal (9, 7, 8)	Lords EAC (5, 4, 6)
6A	TSC Monetary (3, 1, 2)	Lords EAC (5, 4, 6)	TSC Fiscal (9, 7, 8)
6B	Lords EAC (5, 4, 6)	TSC Fiscal (9, 7, 8)	TSC Monetary (3, 1, 2)

APPENDIX 9:   GROUP DISCUSSION RESULTS FROM NONVERBAL EXPERIMENT

(STAGE 3: GAUGING EFFECT OF NONVERBAL CUES ON WHETHER RESPONDENTS CHANGED ATTITUDES, AFTER DISCUSSION WITH OTHERS)

As noted in Chapter 3, the nonverbal communication experiment included a group discussion component. That is, following completion of the nine videos (and the set of questions after each video), subjects met in focus groups of five to discuss their individual impressions of the witnesses. Each subject was asked by a research assistant (who remained in the meeting room) to evaluate Osborne, King and Carney according to his (1) likeability; (2) competence; and (3) persuasiveness. Following these discussions, participants returned to their computer stations, and were asked whether the group discussion changed their initial impressions of each witness (Osborne, King, Carney), and if so, why or why not. This post-group element sought to gauge the extent to which social persuasion may have prompted participants to alter their initial assessments of the witnesses. In particular, I sought to evaluate whether any nonverbal effect might be observed from some subjects remarking on facial expressions, gestures or vocal cues, and then other subjects picking up on these as 'reasons' for any change in their views. From this potential social persuasion effect, I hypothesize that from the group discussion:

H5: Nonverbal cues may exhibit an indirect effect on subjects' assessments of witnesses, with one (or more) subjects mentioning such cues, and others picking up on these and using them as justifications for their own assessments.

Following the group discussions, the experiment asked each subject whether—after hearing the views of fellow students—his/her assessment of the witnesses had changed. This final open-ended question prompted both a judgement and an explanation: 'After participating in your group discussion, did your assessment of the persuasiveness and/or competency of [George Osborne / Mervyn King / Mark Carney] change? Why or why not?'

For this third stage of the analysis, the outcome variable (attitude change) was coded dichotomously (after the focus group discussion was there either some or a significant change in the assessment of the witness?) while the open-ended reasons given for the possible change of attitude were coded in the same way as the 'why' variables in stage two. In addition to the control variables used in stage two, the predictor variables of interest in stage three were mentions of four different (not mutually exclusive) reasons for change or continuity of attitude; (1) *competence*; (2) *views of others in the group* (typically as confirmation of one's own); (3) *verbal reasoning*; and (4) *nonverbal cues*. We added the 'views of others' variable, since many of the responses seemed to find affirmation in the views of others. For instance, as justification for no change of attitude, a typical response was: 'Others expressed similar views and observations, which only reaffirmed my assessment of his persuasiveness and competency.' Another participant who also did not change his attitude remarked, 'Based on the videos, I was under the impression that George Osborne was not a very likeable character and the group seemed to have similar opinions about him. I believe he is not very competent in his job and some of his views about climate change seemed very wrong. Some members of the group did not think so, but their reasons weren't persuasive enough to convince me.'

STAGE 3 VARIABLES

Dichotomous outcome (% changed view):
Attitude change towards Osborne [35.8%]
Attitude change towards King [25%]
Attitude change towards Carney [25%]

Open-ended reasons given for attitude change, coded dichotomously:
From competence [Osborne: 40.8%; King: 58.3%; Carney: 43.3%]
From agreement with others in discussion [Osborne: 45.0%; King: 45.8%; Carney: 36.7%]
From verbal reasoning [Osborne: 41.7%; King: 31.7%; Carney: 25.8%]
From nonverbal cues [Osborne: 5.8%; King: 11.7%; Carney: 14.2%]
(+Control variables)

As can be seen from above a larger percentage of subjects changed their attitudes on Osborne (35.8%) than for King or Carney (for both, 25%). As for the reasons given for an attitude change (or no change) where verbal reasoning was referenced, a larger share (41.7%) noted this for Osborne than for either King (31.7%) or Carney (25.8%). Where nonverbal cues were mentioned, a larger share (14.2%) noted this in reference to Carney, and far fewer for Osborne (5.8%), with King in the middle (11.7%).

Appendix Table 9a Cross tabulation of *Attitude Change Towards Osborne* with same for *King*, and with *Carney* as Layer Variable (in counts by subjects)

Attitude Changed Towards Carney		Attitude Changed Towards King		Total
		No change (King)	Changed (King)	
No change (Carney)	Attitude Changed Towards Osborne — No change (Osborne)	41	17	58
	Changed (Osborne)	24	8	32
	Total	65	25	90
Changed (Carney)	Attitude Changed Towards Osborne — No change (Osborne)	17	2	19
	Changed (Osborne)	8	3	11
	Total	25	5	30
Total	Attitude Changed Towards Osborne — No change (Osborne)	58	19	77
	Changed (Osborne)	32	11	43
	Total	90	30	120

Appendix Table 9a gives the three-way cross-tabulation for the dichotomous *Changed attitude* variable for each of the witnesses. Notably the data for stage three retain the original format of 120 subjects (i.e., there are no repeated measures, as in stages one and two), and so the table counts are given at the subject level. This table clearly shows that 41 subjects (34%) remained firm in their original assessments—i.e., their attitudes did not change on *any* of the three witnesses. On the other hand, three subjects (2.5%) actually changed their attitudes on all three witnesses.

The predictor variables code the reasons for why the respondent did or did not change her views of each of the three witnesses: *competence*, the *agreement or views of others* in the group discussion, *verbal reasoning*, and/or *nonverbal behaviour*. This part of the experiment sought to gauge the effect that social persuasion might have as an indirect factor in shaping subjects' assessments of witnesses. I hypothesized that nonverbal cues may have an indirect effect on these assessments, with some individuals mentioning nonverbal cues in the focus group discussion, thereby leading others to reference these same cues as justification for their change/lack of change in attitude.

As contextual background, I also asked the research assistants who led the discussions to provide their own summaries of these discussions. While only anecdotal, these summaries were informative in highlighting a number of findings. One remark of the RAs was that the first subject to speak in each focus group tended to 'set the tone' of the discussion in that the phrases or key observations of the first subject were then often repeated by others. Second, the RAs noted that in some of the focus groups, subjects explicitly distinguished between Osborne as a politician, and both King and Carney as independent central bankers, with one subject then advancing the idea that for a politician like Osborne, 'competence' would mean something different—i.e., 'something relating to his political role'—than for independent central bankers. As the instructions in the experiment provided no criteria for the definition of 'competence', this observation raises implications for the potential conclusions to be drawn from findings pertaining to competence. With respect to nonverbal behaviour, some RAs also remarked that the audio-only focus groups were typically 'more attentive to the details' of the hearings, as they would 'often use direct quotes during group discussions, or fix themselves upon some detail' in a particular hearing. On the other hand, the viewing groups often tended to 'organically' gravitate to discussing body language (particularly with respect to Osborne), as subjects found nonverbal cues to be a sign of competence and persuasiveness.

It is also useful to note how the subjects perceived the effect of the group discussion. For instance, one participant whose view of Carney changed, remarked that: 'It didn't change because of the group. It changed because I had to put it into perspective and compare it with the other characters.' Another participant who also changed assessment of Carney commented: 'My assessment of Mark Carney was slightly worsened, but not by much. This was because everyone else concurred that his answers were rather vague and he tended to repeat his points. However, this was already evident from the videos. Perhaps the discussion just made it more evident that he was unable to articulate his views and hence seemed less competent in comparison to King especially.'

Appendix Table 9b Logistic Regression Analysis of Views Changed (1=changed; 0=no change), Post-group Discussion, Osborne

	OSBORNE			
Predictor: Reason Given for Change or Continuity of View (1=mentioned, 0=no mention)	B	S.E.	Wald	df
From COMPETENCE	0.38	0.45	0.73	1
From AGREEMENT WITH OTHERS IN GROUP	−1.63	0.47**	12.10	1
From VERBAL REASONING	0.55	0.46	1.43	1
From NONVERBAL CUES	0.53	0.91	0.34	1
Student Status	1.12	0.47*	5.60	1
Gender	−0.84	0.46	3.29	1
English Speaking	−0.51	0.60	0.71	1
Partisanship	0.37	0.36	1.04	1
Intercept	−0.77	0.96	0.65	1
Model summary (N=120)	−2 Log likelihood	Cox & Snell R Square	Nagelkerke R Square	
	131.13	.191	.262	

$^*p < .05.$ ** $p < .01.$ *** $p < .001.$

OBSERVED	PREDICTED		
	No change	Change	Percentage Correct
No change (77)	65	12	84.4
Change (43)	19	24	55.8
Overall			74.2

Interestingly, the responses of subjects suggest that occasionally some members of the group noticed nonverbal cues, remarked upon these in the discussion, which seemed to jog an awareness among others. In several cases, participants commented on the age of the witness as a nonverbal cue (King being considerably older than Carney and Osborne), but age was judged both positively and negatively—for example:

'My assessment did not change because we agreed on King's competency and persuasiveness regarding his experience, age and knowledge of dealing with situations like this. The committee member could not be as dominant with him as he was with Osborne.'

Appendix Table 9c Logistic Regression Analysis of Views Changed (1=changed; 0=no change), Post-group Discussion, King

Predictor: Reason Given for Change or Continuity of View (1=mentioned, 0=no mention)	B	S.E.	Wald	df
	KING			
From COMPETENCE	0.06	0.48	0.02	1
From AGREEMENT WITH OTHERS IN GROUP	−1.44	0.52**	7.75	1
From VERBAL REASONING	−0.00	0.51	0.00	1
From NONVERBAL CUES	−0.22	0.78	0.08	1
Student Status	−0.65	0.50	1.68	1
Gender	0.95	0.51	3.53	1
English Speaking	0.57	0.61	0.87	1
Partisanship	0.44	0.41	1.16	1
Intercept	−1.17	1.15	1.03	1

Model summary (N=120)	−2 Log likelihood	Cox & Snell R Square	Nagelkerke R Square
	116.63	0.14	0.21

$^{*}p < .05.$ $^{**}p < .01.$ $^{***}p < .001.$

OBSERVED	PREDICTED		Percentage Correct
	No change	Change	
No change (90)	86	4	95.6
Change (30)	21	9	30.0
Overall			79.2

Versus,

'Yes [my view changed]. I had a dislike for old men and judged partly by his appearance and look. But after the discussion, I realised that he is actually quite experienced and persuasive, even though he is not always correct.'

Appendix Table 9d: Logistic Regression Analysis of Views Changed (1=changed; 0=no change), Post-group Discussion, Carney

Predictor: Reason Given for Change or Continuity of View (1=mentioned, 0=no mention)	CARNEY			
	B	S.E.	Wald	df
From COMPETENCE	−0.55	0.56	0.98	1
From AGREEMENT WITH OTHERS IN GROUP	−1.57	0.71*	4.93	1
From VERBAL REASONING	1.67	0.55**	9.21	1
From NONVERBAL CUES	0.97	0.63	2.37	1
Student Status	−0.16	0.53	0.09	1
Gender	−0.50	0.51	0.96	1
English Speaking	−0.66	0.76	0.73	1
Partisanship	−0.09	0.40	0.05	1
Intercept	−0.17	1.08	0.02	1
Model summary (N=120)	−2 Log likelihood	Cox & Snell R Square	Nagelkerke R Square	
	104.28	0.23	0.33	

$^*p < .05.$ ** $p < .01.$ *** $p < .001.$

OBSERVED	PREDICTED		
	No change	Change	Percentage Correct
No change (90)	84	6	93.3
Change (30)	14	16	53.3
			83.3

Even if occasional nonverbal behaviour is noted in the open-ended comments, this does not appear to have been a significant factor in accounting for why participants did or did not change their initial assessments. Using the dataset in a non-repeated measures format (N=120) and instead performing separate analyses for each witness, the results from logistic regression reveal a somewhat unexpected finding—the effect of confirmation bias (Nickerson, 1998)—on the post-group assessments of the witnesses. Appendix Tables 9b, 9c and 9d present the results of the binary logistic regressions of the various reasons given for why participants either changed their assessment of Osborne, King and Carney after the group discussion, or retained their pre-group assessment of each of these witnesses. The one variable that is consistently highly significant (at 1% for Osborne and King, and 5% for Carney) and negatively signed is the agreement of fellow group members. That is, participants who retained their pre-focus group assessment (i.e., did not change their view) tended to justify this stance by reference to the agreement of the other members of the group. In the simple words of one participant: 'My assessment has been affirmed by the group's consensus.' For evaluations of Carney (but not for Osborne or King), verbal reasoning is positively associated with a change of attitudes.

In short, participants consistently justified their assessments of Osborne, King, and Carney by recourse to the agreement of others in their group, a type of confirmation bias which was not anticipated in this experiment. The social persuasive effect that was anticipated by Hypothesis 5—i.e., that nonverbal cues might have an indirect effect via the focus group discussion—is not supported by these findings.

APPENDIX 10: ANALYSIS OF EXCHANGE DYNAMIC DICHOTOMOUS VARIABLE FOR QUESTIONER (CONCILIATORY OR CONTENTIOUS) BY NONVERBAL BEHAVIOR RESPONSE VARIABLE (YES OR NO), USING QUANTITATIVE TEXT ANALYSIS[a] OF SELECTED OPEN-ENDED RESPONSES OF EXPERIMENT PARTICIPANTS

Appendix Table 10a Analysis of Open-ended Responses to Video Clips Where the Questioner Category is *Conciliatory* and *Nonverbal Behaviour* is <u>not</u> mentioned.

Over-used words, relative to whole corpus	Frequency of word in subset	Frequency of word in whole corpus	Chi squared significance	P value
STRESS	63	65	11.30	0.000
TARGET	38	39	7.18	0.007
SMALL	36	37	6.70	0.009
MARK CARNEY	27	28	4.55	0.032
CHANGE	40	43	4.34	0.037
LORD	52	57	4.23	0.039
PROBLEM	39	42	4.12	0.042
SOLUTION	32	34	4.05	0.044
Top representative elementary context units	Mark Carney definitely sounded like he knew what he was doing, had considered the questions Andrew Tyrie might ask, and his responses appeared reasonably persuasive. Even though they might not be strong enough reassurance to the concerns Andrew Tyrie might have, they were sensible approaches, e. g. to stress tests.			
	From the change of attitude of Michael Fallon. At last, it seems that Michael Fallon agreed. George Osborne was persuasive as he managed to explain the situation he was in, and what he is doing to improve on that.			

Continued

Appendix Table 10a *Continued*

Mr Carney aptly answers, and shows competency by relating the rationale of policies of the Bank. On the question that the Bank only carried out one stress test, he well answered that to run a good stress test, it should be coherent. The stress test the Bank had carried out had included more than one type of test, and they would be carrying out another stress test later.
He used the statistic that the net lending to small companies increase from −5 to + 5, so as to convince that the problem of small and medium-sized enterprise is actually an over narrowly addressed problem. In the long run there can be other ways to increase lending to the small and medium-sized enterprise.
He brings out the environmental policies sensibly and has rationally answered most of the questions brought up. He brought up the current problems arising in the banking system with respect to the SMEs and talked about the solutions through the introduction of economic schemes. He described the problem on climate change and then explained how he planned to tackle this problem.

[a] This analysis uses the 'Specificity Analysis' feature in the *T-Lab Plus* software.

Appendix Table 10b Analysis[a] of Open-ended Responses to Video Clips Where the Questioner Category is *Contentious* and *Nonverbal Behaviour* <u>is</u> mentioned.

Over-used words, relative to whole corpus	Frequency of word in subset	Frequency of word in whole corpus	Chi squared significance	P value
DEFENSIVE	10	12	31.17	0.000
LOOK	16	27	27.27	0.000
KING	16	30	21.95	0.000
PRICE	14	26	19.59	0.000
MANNER	13	24	18.41	0.000
MERVYN KING	23	58	15.12	0.000
CONFIDENT	13	27	14.15	0.000
LANGUAGE	7	11	13.66	0.000

Top representative elementary context units	Mervyn King remained calm, polite and composed throughout the video, even though the accusations of George Mudie (= the lack of independence of the Bank of England) were strong and compelling. His argument was not very well formulated and constructed. At the end of the video, I am not sure what was his overall defence argument. As such, he did not appear as fully competent.
	I believe King is competent at his job—- he seems confident in his recommendations and corrects what Norman is trying to get at. His demeanour is calm and quiet (too quiet?), and he gets noticeably defensive (in body language and voice) when pushed, which hurts a little of his persuasion.
	King seemed persuasive as he was very confident—he corrected Mudie when Mudie was wrong or misinformed. King seemed competent as he was able to explain thoroughly and in depth the role of the bank and the purpose of policies, and the fact that he had a response for every question just demonstrates his wide range of knowledge.
	John Mann seems very disappointed with George Osborne's answers, because it cannot hit John Mann's point. John Mann looks a bit angry and he can't agree with George Osborne.
	King answered EVERY question he was asked directly. When pressed or questioned, he remained calm and again answered directly.
	Mervyn King addressed the concerns raised by Lord MacGregor in a structural manner by breaking down his arguments accordingly so as to pinpoint the possible outcomes and issues which are associated with the agenda highlighted. His confident delivery in speech and calm manner in portraying his argument also served to cement his persuasiveness in arguments.

[a] This analysis uses the 'Specificity Analysis' feature in the *T-Lab Plus* software.

Name Index

General Index